Please renew/return items by last date shown. Please call the number below:

Renewals and enquiries: 0300 123 4049

Textphone for hearing or speech impaired users: 0300 123 4041

www.hertsdirect.org/librarycatalogue
L32

Hertfordshire

Dominica

WORLD BIBLIOGRAPHICAL SERIES

General Editors:
Robert L. Collison (Editor-in-chief)
Sheila R. Herstein
Louis J. Reith
Hans H. Wellisch

VOLUMES IN THE SERIES

VOLUME 82

Dominica

Robert A. Myers

Compiler

CLIO PRESS

OXFORD, ENGLAND · SANTA BARBARA, CALIFORNIA
DENVER, COLORADO

© Copyright 1987 by Clio Press Ltd.

British Library Cataloguing in Publication Data

Myers, Robert A.
Dominica.——(World bibliographical
series; 82)
1. Dominica——Bibliography
I. Title   II. Series
016.97298'41   Z1536

ISBN 1-85109-031-2

Clio Press Ltd.,
55 St. Thomas' Street,
Oxford OX1 1JG, England.

ABC-Clio Information Services,
Riviera Campus, 2040 Alameda Padre Serra,
Santa Barbara, Ca. 93103, USA.

Designed by Bernard Crossland
Typeset by Columns Design and Production Services, Reading, England
Printed and bound in Great Britain by
Billing and Sons Ltd., Worcester

THE WORLD BIBLIOGRAPHICAL SERIES

This series will eventually cover every country in the world, each in a separate volume comprising annotated entries on works dealing with its history, geography, economy and politics: and with its people, their culture, customs, religion and social organization. Attention will also be paid to current living conditions – housing, education, newspapers, clothing, etc. – that are all too often ignored in standard bibliographies; and to those particular aspects relevant to individual countries. Each volume seeks to achieve, by use of careful selectivity and critical assessment of the literature, an expression of the country and an appreciation of its nature and national aspirations, to guide the reader towards an understanding of its importance. The keynote of the series is to provide, in a uniform format, an interpretation of each country that will express its culture, its place in the world, and the qualities and background that make it unique.

SERIES EDITORS

Robert L. Collison (Editor-in-chief) is Professor Emeritus, Library and Information Studies, University of California, Los Angeles, and is currently the President of the Society of Indexers. Following the war, he served as Reference Librarian for the City of Westminster and later became Librarian to the BBC. During his fifty years as a professional librarian in England and the USA, he has written more than twenty works on bibliography, librarianship, indexing and related subjects.

Sheila R. Herstein is Reference Librarian and Library Instruction Co-ordinator at the City College of the City University of New York. She has extensive bibliographic experience and has described her innovations in the field of bibliographic instruction in 'Team teaching and bibliographic instruction', *The Bookmark*, Autumn 1979. In addition, Doctor Herstein co-authored a basic annotated bibliography in history for Funk & Wagnalls *New encyclopedia*, and for several years reviewed books for *Library Journal*.

Louis J. Reith is librarian with the Franciscan Institute, St. Bonaventure University, New York. He received his PhD from Stanford University, California, and later studied at Eberhard-Karls-Universität, Tübingen. In addition to his activities as a librarian, Dr. Reith is a specialist on 16th-century German history and the Reformation and has published many articles and papers in both German and English. He was also editor of the *American Society for Reformation Research Newsletter*.

Hans H. Wellisch is a Professor at the College of Library and Information Services, University of Maryland, and a member of the American Society of Indexers and the International Federation for Documentation. He is the author of numerous articles and several books on indexing and abstracting, and has also published *Indexing and abstracting: an international bibliography*. He also contributes frequently to *Journal of the American Society for Information Science, Library Quarterly*, and *The Indexer*.

Contents

Contents

Contents

Preface

In keeping with the goals of the *World Bibliographical Series*, the aim of this bibliography is to provide an interpretation of Dominica expressing its 'culture, its place in the world, and the qualities and background that make it unique'. While it contains a wide selection of the available materials covering most aspects of the island, several areas receive special emphasis: the Island Caribs, geography, history, literature, travel and description, conservation and the national park, and flora and fauna. These particular facets of Dominica have absorbed the interests of most residents and visitors to the island. They best describe Dominica's distinct characteristics and contributions to the larger world.

The 493 selected references on this island nation of about 85,000 people provide far more thorough coverage than is possible for larger political or geographical units. For topics such as the Amerindians, flora, fauna and history, references were carefully chosen and represent only a small fraction of the available sources. Other topics commonly covered in the publications of larger countries are scarce or unavailable for Dominica. The topics public administration and local government have few existing publications; for banking, science and technology, and recreation, there are none at all.

The island's small size and location have influenced the nature of the references. Many are short periodical articles, reflecting the paucity of monographs and book-length studies on Dominica. Many are selections from larger works about this interconnected insular region. Studies of Caribbean islands often lead to information on the shared qualities of nearby islands and comparisons of their distinctive traits.

Publications by several individuals intimately associated with the island are an important part of this bibliography. Anthropologist Douglas Taylor's studies of Island Carib culture and language, and of the French-based Creole spoken throughout the

Dominican countryside are the product of his nearly five decades' residence on Dominica. They provide a scholarly effort unsurpassed in the Caribbean. In the field of literature, several residents and natives of the island have made notable contributions. Most famous is novelist Jean Rhys, who reveals in her writing the influence of her formative years spent on Dominica. Also important are politician Phyllis Allfrey, writer Elma Napier, poet and anthologist J. R. R. Casimir, and poet-physician Daniel Thaly. The work of author Lennox Honychurch, as well as historical articles by Joseph Boromé, research and recount the island's past.

While emphasis here is on contemporary and 20th-century items, materials from earlier periods are used when they are of enduring importance or shed light on events not illuminated by other studies. Therefore, works by 17th-century French missionary Raymond Breton on the Island Carib language are presented. Invaluable are the reports of several special commissions on island social conditions. The 19th-century publications of physicians John Imray and Sir Henry Nicholls, whose medical and agricultural work did much to make the island healthier and more productive, are included.

A few unauthored items and several government reports appear because they alone describe their topics. Most of the dissertations on Dominica are easily accessible and often provide a degree of information and analysis not available in other publications. I have selected several references to French-language sources because Dominica is situated between two French islands, and a strong French Creole stamp upon Dominican culture and language exists. In keeping with a goal of this series to enhance access to important resources, I have noted the addresses where several items can be obtained. Several Amerindian references can be found in the Human Relations Area Files (HRAF), an ethnographic resource in paper or microfiche available at many colleges and universities. HRAF Press's address is PO Box 2015, Yale Station, New Haven, CT 06520.

Entries within each section and subsection are arranged alphabetically by the name of the author. When there is no author or corporate author, items are listed by the first non-article word in the title. When an author has published several books or articles, they are arranged chronologically. Titles are spelled as they are in the original work.

Bibliographical work on Caribbean nations, particularly the

small islands, is notoriously difficult. People from an enormous range of professions, disciplines, and nationalities compile works which appear in publications throughout Europe and North America, many of limited circulation. Rarely are these materials collected or listed in a single source. Writings on Dominica appear in at least twelve languages, including Japanese, and are as scattered as those for any island anywhere. Many of the recent and more important references, however, can be located in good general collections. Most of the items described in this bibliography are available in larger university libraries or through inter-library loan arrangements.

I have examined all books and articles annotated here during several years of research on Dominica. Particularly useful collections include: the British Library and the Institute of Commonwealth Studies of the University of London; the libraries of the University of North Carolina at Chapel Hill; the libraries of Harvard University; the New York Public Library and the Schomberg Center for Research in Black Culture. The outstanding Caribbean collection of the Research Institute for the Study of Man, located in New York City, has been invaluable. I wish to thank its director, Lambros Comitas, and his staff, especially Judy Selakoff, for their assistance. Many items in this compilation were made available through the assistance of Jo Bianco of the inter-library loan staff of Long Island University.

Visitors to Dominica cannot expect to find all the books and periodicals mentioned here, but they may be pleasantly surprised with the general holdings and the West Indiana and Dominicana collections of the Roseau Public Library. The library opened in 1906 and was described until Hurricane David struck as 'the most attractive library building in the West Indies'. The library survived the storm with most of its collection, if not its once-graceful ambiance, intact. I wish to acknowledge the assistance and courtesy of its librarian, Cornelia Williams. Also on Dominica, I thank Lennox Honychurch and Sir Louis and Lady Eugene Cools-Lartigue for their help. John Dana Archbold, OBE, a deeply involved and generous supporter of projects on the island for more than half a century, deserves special appreciation for placing his collection and his considerable hospitality at my disposal. Finally, I thank my wife, Cathie Chester, for her assistance and support in this project.

Robert A. Myers

Introduction

The Commonwealth of Dominica, an eastern Caribbean island nation, is located centrally in the Lesser Antilles between the French islands of Guadeloupe and Martinique. Its geography, its size and its location have each played formative roles in the island's development and in the creation of a unique culture. Dominica's past is a microcosm of the history and general features of the West Indies, yet in many ways the island is a distinctive world unto itself.

Dominica is one of the volcanic Lesser Antilles and thus lacks the white-sand beaches characteristic of the tourist-oriented limestone islands. Instead, it offers a spine of forest-covered mountains rising dramatically from the sea and running the length of the island. Morne Diablotin at 4,747 feet is the second highest mountain in the Lesser Antilles and several peaks reach above 4,000 feet. Heavy clouds from the Atlantic meet the windward coast and drop their moisture as the elevation rises, causing daily rains as they cross the mountains. Interior rainfall of as much as 350 inches a year means that Dominica has the most bountiful supply of water of all the islands in the region, producing numerous rivers and a larger, less-disturbed tropical rainforest than those on other Caribbean islands. In contrast, the Caribbean leeward coast lies in the rain-shadow of the mountains and remains dry, hot and intensely sunny. Several black-sand beaches, volcanic steam vents, the world's second largest boiling lake and two small freshwater lakes can be found on the island.

Long a destination of naturalists, in the 1960s and 1970s botanists and zoologists on the Bredin-Archbold-Smithsonian Biological Survey of Dominica studied the tropical plant and animal life. Their work resulted in a better understanding of the complexities of the island ecosystem, the discovery of numerous new species of plants and insects, and the publication of dozens of scientific papers. Larger mammals on the island include the agouti, probably introduced by Amerindians, and the opossum or manicou, introduced by Europeans in the 1840s. Twelve species of bat, the most numerous mammal, occur. Bird life is extremely varied, with 162 species recorded. Two parrots, the Imperial or Sisserou Parrot and the Red-necked or Jacquot Parrot are endangered species. Boa constrictors are found on Dominica, but the poisonous Fer-de-lance, found on islands to the south, is absent. Insect species and floral varieties abound. Morne Trois Pitons National Park was established in 1975 to preserve the exotic flora and fauna of about 16,000 acres of the rainforest, or nine per cent of the island. In addition, much of the island interior is protected as a Forest Reserve. Plans have been laid to extend the national park system to the Cabrits Peninsula, a natural area surrounding the site of the 18th-century Ft. Shirley complex. As a result of these features, the Dominica Tourist Board promotes the island not as a beach island, but appropriately as the 'nature island of the Caribbean'.

When Columbus described the island to Queen Isabella he reportedly crumpled a piece of paper and placed it on a table to illustrate the island's mountainous nature. The high rainfall and the intense ruggedness produced a tropical paradise geographically, but also made settlement and agricultural development slower and less extensive than on most other islands. Until the 20th century, much travel from village to village was by sea. The road system was limited until the banana boom of the 1960s, making transportation and access to much of the island difficult. The cost of building roads or replacing those washed out by torrential rains was the highest in the islands. A relatively small population, located mainly in crowded villages around the coast, and a high rate of emigration have slowed the impact of humans on the environment. In the insular region, the island is usually considered to be the least developed. Consequently, Dominica remains the island most like the Antilles were when Columbus discovered them nearly five centuries ago.

One of the world's smallest nations, Dominica is about 29 miles long and at most 12 miles wide, resulting in a total area of 289.5 square miles (752.7 square kilometres). Among 178 countries Dominica ranks 155th in area and 166th in population-size (having a population of around 85,000). In area it is less than one-third the size of Luxembourg, and only slightly smaller than the city of New York. Its entire resident and emigrant population could fit easily into two seatings of a large sports stadium. Six

Caribbean nations are smaller in area, but in the region only St. Kitts-Nevis has fewer people. The population of Dominica is overwhelmingly descended from the African slaves of the small French and British planter and mercantile society. In the capital, Roseau, business interests are presently dominated by descendants of Syrian and Lebanese merchants who arrived after the First World War. Unlike many other Caribbean societies, Dominica has no Chinese minority and no descendants of 19th-century indentured workers from India. A small white Creole community engages in business and agricultural pursuits; a transient international community works in development and advisory governmental and private sector roles.

Dominica's population increased gradually in the 19th century, but actually dipped slightly between 1881 and 1891 when thousands left for Venezuela's gold fields. In the 20th century, population growth accelerated until large-scale emigration to Great Britain in the 1950s and 1960s took place. Since then, the United States, Canada and other islands have absorbed much of Dominica's population excess. Because of its proximity and similar French Creole culture, Guadeloupe has a large Dominican migrant group. Continued emigration, especially to Guadeloupe, has given a false impression of only slight population growth in recent official statistics.

On the only Amerindian reservation in the West Indies live about 2,000 Island Carib Indians, some of whom resemble their ancestors who once dominated the entire Lesser Antilles. After having lost virtually all distinctive customs and language, today they are initiating a cultural revival: renewing some traditions, creating others, asserting Carib interests over Afro-Dominican interests and petitioning for a national 'Carib Day'.

Dominica was the first land sighted on Columbus's second voyage on 3 November 1493. He named the island after its day of discovery, Sunday, or *dies Dominica*. The combination of winds, currents and Dominica's high mountains made the island the landfall sought by European voyagers for the next century. At discovery, the island was occupied by an unknown number of Carib Indians from South America who had displaced more sedentary Arawak Indians during relatively recent times. Archaeological investigations are incomplete to date and important Amerindian sites are often located under contemporary villages and towns. Much of the island's earliest human history remains to be uncovered.

For two centuries following its discovery. European ships stopped at Dominica to take on fresh water and wood after the ocean crossing. They frequently traded with the Indians and continued on to larger or more geographically accessible islands. During this time, island terrain afforded the Caribs a haven while they waged war against Spanish settlements as far away as Puerto Rico, and British settlements in St. Kitts, Antigua and Montserrat. Less often they raided the French on Guadeloupe or Marie Galante. The results were that while Europeans established themselves firmly on other islands, Dominica was to remain a 'Carib isle' or one of the 'neutral islands' by agreement between France and Britain. Although the Carib were nearly extinct by the 18th century due to disease and warfare, their early reputation for fierceness lingers in a mythology of cannibalism that became entrenched in regional lore.

During the 1630s, the French colonization of Dominica began with the establishment of farming settlements. French missionaries tried unsuccessfully to convert the Caribs. Although the island was claimed first by Britain, English settlers did not arrive until the very end of the century. Until the mid-18th century, the French and British repeatedly agreed on paper to abandon the island to its original inhabitants; French colonization continued, however. In 1761, Dominica was taken forcibly by the English and officially granted to Britain by the Treaty of Paris in 1763. At that time the island had only about 8,000 French planters and their slaves; the main exports were coffee and sugar.

Under the British, the population more than doubled as the island became a thriving colony producing cacao, coffee, sugar and cotton, and serving as a major regional slave entrepôt. Fortifications were built to protect Roseau, the capital, but the island was recaptured by the French in 1778. For five years trade was severed, development halted and the British islanders languished. In April 1782, Admiral Rodney defeated the French fleet at the Battle of the Saints off Dominica's north-western coast, thus re-establishing British maritime dominion. The Treaty of Versailles restored Dominica to British rule in 1783, after which trade and plantation life resumed their former vigour.

For the rest of the century and until the slave-trade was abolished in 1807, several thousand slaves were imported into Dominica and re-exported to other islands each year. Coffee grown on nearly 300 primarily French estates remained a major export crop. Often encouraged and armed by French planters, runaway slaves or Maroons hid in the mountains and waged periodic guerrilla warfare against the English planters. In British campaigns of 1785–86 and 1812–14, several hundred Maroons were killed or captured and surrendered. In 1795 the French threatened briefly to invade Dominica. In 1805 French General La Grange held Roseau for a week after the town was accidently razed to the ground by wadding from defending English cannon. The demoralized citizens bought their freedom with a £7,500 ransom and afterwards Dominica remained continuously in British hands until independence. However, the French influences of Roman Catholicism and French-based Creole remain strong to the present day. Despite periodically severe hurricanes, Maroon wars, fires, French-British hostilities, planter-slave tensions, and yellow fever epidemics, the colony managed a measure of economic prosperity.

Compared to other islands, Dominica had a larger number of 'free-coloured'. In 1831, these people were given certain political and social rights by the 'Brown Privilege Bill' and by 1838, non-whites were able to dominate the Legislative Assembly. In 1834, emancipation freed 14,175 slaves whose social and economic conditions changed little until the 20th century.

During the 1820s and early 1830s, Dominica reached its 19th-century zenith as it exported two and a half million pounds of coffee in one year and over six million pounds of sugar in another. Island fortunes changed radically when Dominica's worst hurricane killed 200 people and destroyed the sugar-cane crop, and a withering blight which had begun in 1830 ruined the coffee trees. The island never fully recovered economically as cane-sugar lost its value with the rise of beet-sugar in Europe.

The second half of the 19th century offered no relief. The island experienced a long period of social, political and economic stagnation. Many estates were abandoned and squatting became a problem. Labour was sometimes in short supply. Yaws spread in epidemic proportions among the rural population during the last quarter of the century. Cocoa was the dominant export by far as sugar and coffee cultivation virtually ceased. Periodic social unrest and continued lack of development were addressed by the Hamilton Commission of 1893 which recommended numerous changes. By century's end a small grant for road construction and the appointment of an energetic young administrator offered the islanders new hope.

H. Hesketh Bell's tenure (1899–1905) saw considerable improvement in the transport system, including a coastal steamer service, the arrival of the first automobiles, a telephone exchange in Roseau, development of the Botanic Gardens and the agricultural school, and the creation of the Carib Reserve. More importantly, he promoted the island in Britain and stimulated investment by a wave of new settlers to Dominica. An agricultural revival occurred, building upon the work done on lime cultivation and citric acid extraction by the island's Dr. John Imray in the 1860s and 1870s. An industrious agricultural department and tireless agricultural efforts by Imray's successor, Dr. Henry Nicholls, and the new planters resulted in Dominica becoming the world's leading producer of limes and lime products during the century's second decade. In addition, more than a million pounds of cocoa were exported one year. Dominica's contributions of both men and money to the British efforts in the First World War surpassed those of its island neighbours.

The successes were short-lived. West African cocoa production cut heavily into Dominica's market, a series of severe storms and withertip disease destroyed the lime trees, and a way to make citric acid artificially was discovered abroad. A food shortage was caused during the Second World War when several thousand Free French refugees fled to Dominica from Guadeloupe and Martinique, to escape the Vichy government and to take advantage of the Allies' guaranteed free-meal policy. The resulting protein shortage accentuated problems with malnutrition among rural Dominicans long after the war ended. Temporary prosperity occurred when Dominica became the largest producer of vanilla during the war while Madagascar was blockaded. However, when a Roseau fire destroyed a large vanilla harvest, unripe beans were shipped. When Madagascar's blockade was removed, local events and world economy had combined to cause the loss of a valuable market. The historic cycle of agricultural success and failure prompted writer Alec Waugh to describe the seemingly inevitable misfortune as 'typical Dominica'.

Since the early 1950s, banana production has dominated the economy, followed to different degrees by grapefruit, lime and lime oil, and coconut and coconut products exports. Thus far, bananas have proved to be Dominica's most reliable export crop.

British administration of the island reflected uncertainty as to how best to deal with the strategically-located possession. Separated from the drier, sugar-producing British Leeward Islands by Guadeloupe and from the more similar British Windwards by Martinique, the island was initially grouped with the Windward Islands and then in 1771 became a separate colony. In 1833 it was administered with the Leeward Islands; in 1871 it became a federal colony within the Leewards; by century's end, it had become a crown colony. In 1940 it was attached to the Windward Islands again. Dominican C. E. A. Rawle advocated federation in the 1930s, and while the West Indies Federation lasted (from 1958 to 1962) Dominicans played leading roles. In 1967, Dominica became entirely self-governing as an Associated State in the United Kingdom. This evolved to sovereign status on 3 November 1978, with the creation of the Commonwealth of Dominica.

Constitutional and political development on the island has followed a gradual and sometimes tumultuous course. Initial governance under the British was exclusively white and male. By 1838 legal and social changes resulted in black domination of the Legislative Assembly. Political assertions by the planters throughout the century caused elected representatives to be replaced by nominated and official members. In the 20th century elected members of the Legislative Council gradually gained in numbers. The new constitution of 1951 introduced universal adult suffrage and the election of a majority of the legislature. In the mid-1950s, trade unionist E. C. Loblack and Phyllis Allfrey formed the Dominica Labour Party. Mrs. Allfrey continued the strong role of women in island government begun by Elma Napier in the 1940s, carried on by Mable Moir James as first female government minister in 1966, and currently played by Prime Minister Eugenia Charles. The ministerial system of government was introduced in 1956, and in 1960 further constitutional changes increased domestic control and enlarged the Legislative Council.

Edward Oliver LeBlanc served as Chief Minister from the elections in 1961 until he resigned as Premier in 1974, allowing Patrick John to become Head of State. Throughout this period of increasing independence, social and political tensions grew as economic expectations were raised and opportunities for emigration declined. A group of politically radical and socially alienated youths called the Dreads became modern-day Maroons as they terrorized and murdered both visitors and residents between 1974 and 1981. Relations between unions and the government suffered, resulting in major strikes by the Civil Service Association in the 1970s. During John's five years in office, the discovery of various corrupt dealings on his part clouded Dominica's achievement of independence in November 1978.

Soon after independence John's schemes were revealed: plans

to turn a large northern part of the island into a semi-autonomous free port; the use of Dominica as a staging area for an invasion of Barbados; the sale of Dominican passports to international businessmen; and a plan to stockpile oil for South Africa. Disclosure of John's plots provoked widespread outrage. Violent confrontations between demonstrators and the Defence Force occurred during the House of Assembly sitting on 29 May. As a result, the opposition left the House and all trade unions and businesses joined with a planned Civil Service Association strike which paralysed the island until John's government could be ousted. By mid-1979 a 'constitutional coup' had replaced Patrick John with an interim government headed by Oliver Seraphin which stabilized the political situation. Despite the havoc wreaked by Hurricane David on 29 August and Hurricane Frederick on 4 September, the island recovered enough for elections to be held in July 1980. Opposition leader Eugenia Charles's Dominica Freedom Party won seventeen of the twenty-one seats, establishing her as the first female Prime Minister in the Caribbean.

During 1981 Dread activity intensified with the murder of a prominent planter. Links were discovered between some members of the Defence Force and the Dreads, and the Force was disbanded but not before a coup plot was revealed and a state of emergency was declared. In addition Dominica appeared prominently in the world press when the FBI arrested a group of Ku Klux Klan-backed mercenaries in New Orleans who planned to overthrow the Charles government. A third plot in December implicated the former head of the Defence Force in an effort to free Patrick John from jail. Despite this string of events, Prime Minister Charles actually kept the government working with constitutional principles in place, and island development gradually moved forward.

During her tenure in office, Prime Minister Charles has enjoyed widespread popularity and support, and has engaged in regional developments with characteristic personal vigour. Dominica was one of the countries instrumental in supporting the American invasion of Grenada in 1983, as Charles appeared on American television with President Reagan to explain the events. Re-elected by wide majorities in 1985, Charles and her Freedom Party continue to set the tone and pace of island developments into the late 1980s.

The Dominican economy has often experienced downturns but the worst in the 20th century occurred when hurricanes in 1979 and 1980 devastated the island. The entire banana industry was temporarily destroyed, and coconut and citrus crops were severely damaged. Three-quarters of the island's population was left homeless; thirty-seven people were killed and 5,000 were injured.

By the mid-1980s, the economy had recovered substantially with bananas, soaps and other coconut products, and citrus leading the exports, and with some growth of light industry. Because hydroelectric power supplies about three-quarters of the island's electricity, Dominica has been spared some of the burden of costly oil imports in recent years. Nevertheless, despite increased diversity, the economy remains weak as exports are only half the value of imports. Promotion of the Caribbean Basin Initiative by the United States government still has not resulted in significant investment in the island. With a per capita GDP of only about US$900, the country is one of the poorest in the Western Hemisphere; significantly better off than Haiti, but only marginally different from the second poorest nation, St. Vincent.

A modern visitor finds Dominica a water-bounded miniature of the developing world, a minor participant enmeshed in the international economy. Experts from international development agencies work on or visit the island lending their experience and preparing reports. United States Peace Corps workers contribute assistance. A new second airstrip accommodates businessmen pursuing their interests on the island. Local 'hucksters' island-hop to resell Dominican produce at nearby markets. A limited tourist traffic arrives mostly by air and at times on small cruise-ships. North American evangelical missionaries compete with the established island congregations for followers. Each week large Geest ships haul away tons of bananas to Britain in their refrigerated holds. International telephone and telex exchanges, and several radio and television stations link the island with the rest of the world. Through 24-hour cable television, at least in Roseau, Dominicans participate in the electronic global village, with music videos, sports, news and movies available day or night. Membership in an alphabet soup of organizations assures Dominica a voice in the international political and economic community: UN, OAS, UNESCO, WHO, FAO, ILO, IBRD, IMF, IDA, INTERPOL, GATT, CARICOM (Caribbean Common Market), ECCM (East Caribbean Common Market), CDB (Caribbean Development Bank), OECS (Organization of Eastern Caribbean States) and the Commonwealth.

Roseau's location on the leeward coast means warmer

temperatures, although less rainfall, than in the mountains or on the windward side of the island. Heavy clouds and sometimes the odour of sulphur from the distant Valley of Desolation drift towards the town. 'Roseau' means 'reeds' and the site for the capital was chosen at the mouth of the Roseau River, an abundant supply of fresh water on a malaria-free coast. Poor anchorage at Roseau discouraged large-scale shipping until a deep-water harbour was built in the mid-1970s. Architecture in Roseau consists of thick-walled 18th-century stone buildings, wooden town houses from the 19th century, and newer wood and concrete block constructions painted in the pastels favoured elsewhere in the Caribbean. Devastation from Hurricane David remains visible in the boarded-over ruins of local landmarks. Cars and trucks compete for space on narrow streets. Except on market day, business activity in the capital is paced and the town is quiet. Young women go about their business in cosmopolitan fashions. In play and sports areas basketball has been added to once-dominant cricket and football, and young people can occasionally be seen jogging or weightlifting. In numerous schools children now study their Caribbean heritage and their island's own history as written by a Dominican.

Away from Roseau, roads are alternately wide and recently laid around the coast, or narrow and deeply rutted in the interior. Peasants with the ubiquitous 'cutlass' carry 'ground provisions' or other produce from distant gardens to home, to market, or to boxing plants. The farmers' work takes place in gardens and orchards along the mountainsides, and in flatter banana and coconut estates along the coasts. Children learn their lessons in open-sided schoolrooms. Most of the daily life is lived outside, but at night homes are tightly shuttered against the dark. Reminders of the colonial past lie in tropical decay: crumbling estate buildings, sugar mills and factories with rusting machinery, and abandoned fortifications are hidden in the impenetrable greenness of rainforests and along rivers overhung with lianas. High coastal cliffs, frequent rainbows and spectacular vistas provide dramatic backdrops for daily activities.

Modern Dominica, a difficult paradise, has enjoyed several years of political stability since the turmoil accompanying independence. Vigorously conservative leadership, cautious economic policies, attempts to increase and diversify exports and create new markets, the strengthening of political ties with Western industrial powers and regional partners, and provision of basic social services to a growing population have characterized the leadership of Prime Minister Mary Eugenia Charles since taking office in 1980. The natural, economic and political challenges to this island nation will, if history is any guide, wax and wane with unpleasant frequency, but will never disappear. In all probability, Dominicans will be called on again to display the perseverance and resilience they have shown in the past. Dominica has experienced moderate prosperity briefly throughout its history; for most of its people life has meant a quiet struggle for a very modest level of living.

Dominica's French Creole motto *Apres Bondie C'Est La Ter* (After God, the Earth) perfectly embodies the people's relationship to their land. It is hoped that respect for this crucial relationship will guide Dominicans in their plans for their island. Dominica's future may resemble its past, but as the nation slowly finds its place in the modern world, foundations for a more secure living standard are being laid and a national identity is evolving.

The Country and Its People

General

1 The pocket guide to the West Indies.
Sir Algernon E[dward] Aspinall. New York: E. P. Dutton, 1911.
315p. 10 maps.
One of the earliest and longest-lived 20th-century guidebooks on the region.
Originally published in 1907, the 1911 edition contains a useful descriptive
chapter, with photographs, on Dominica, discussing its industry, history,
constitution and transport, as well as the principal sights (p. 226-39). The 10th
edition, revised by J. S. Dash (London, 1960) remains very useful and provides
practical information about Dominica (p. 193-205).

2 Stephen Haweis of Dominica.
E. C. Baker. *Caribbean Quarterly*, vol. 16, no. 3 (Sept. 1970),
p. 64-70. bibliog.
A biography of and tribute to Stephen Haweis, a long-term resident of Dominica,
written soon after his death. Haweis, born on 23 July 1878 in England, was
educated at Cambridge and studied art in Paris. He travelled in the South Seas
and East Africa before settling in Dominica. His paintings are found throughout
the West Indies as well as in Washington, DC, where he painted the backgrounds
for the insect house of the Zoological Gardens. He changed his name to Hawys in
1967. The author, a West Indian historian and archivist, proofread and amended
Haweis's book *Mount Joy* (London: Duckworth, 1968) and assisted in its
publication. He writes of Haweis, 'so few professional artists of his calibre have
lived in the West Indies that it would be ungrateful to forget him' (p. 64).

1

3 In old Roseau: reminiscences of life as I found it in the island of Dominica, and among the Carib Indians.
William S. Birge. New York: Isaac H. Blanchard, 1900. 105p.

A Massachusetts physician spent several weeks in and around Roseau, 'a quaint, sombre-looking place' (p. 15), and made a short visit to the Carib Reserve where he rejected the attentions of a young woman. His observations on health and obeah (sorcery) form the most interesting aspects of the book.

4 Far afield in the Caribbean: migratory flights of a naturalist's wife.
Mary Wickham Bond. Wynnewood, Pennsylvania: Livingston, 1971. 142p. map.

Essays by the wife of the region's famous ornithologist, James Bond, about her excursions with her husband over seventeen years. 'The little gnome of Dominica' (p. 87-95) recalls their visit with Stephen Haweis (who remains unnamed), an artist who studied at the Royal Academy and said he 'committed artistic suicide by coming to live in Dominica' (p. 92). She also describes their stay at the Cherry Lodge Hotel and the 'green flash'. Drawings by Elizabeth R. Leydon appear throughout the volume.

5 Caribbean island with a problem.
Basil E. Cracknell. *Geographical Magazine*, vol. 43, no. 7 (April 1971), p. 463-70. map.

Dominica's problem, according to the author, is that the island has reached a crossroads and must decide whether to continue its gradual agricultural development strategy or turn to tourism and industry, forsaking agriculture. He discusses three keys to this problem: the banana industry; improvements in communications; and a non-beach-based tourist industry. The article is illustrated by fourteen photographs.

6 Dominica.
Basil E. Cracknell. Newton Abbot, England: David & Charles; Harrisburg, Pennsylvania: Stackpole Books, 1973. 198p. 4 maps. bibliog. (The Island Series).

The first book-length account of modern Dominica is a wide-ranging, popular description of the island and its history. Ten chapters cover: 'Structure and scenery'; 'Natural history'; 'The Carib people: Dominica pre-1763'; 'War and slavery, 1763-1815'; 'The struggle for economic survival, 1815-1945'; 'Communications'; 'Agriculture today'; 'Tourism, timber and other industries'; 'Dominica society today'; and 'Dominica's role in the Caribbean'. Thirty black-and-white photographs supplement the text.

7 The West Indians: how they live and work.
Basil E. Cracknell. Kingston: Kingston Publishers; Newton Abbot, England: David & Charles, 1974. 168p. map. bibliog.

The standard chapters of this series delineate the book's subject matter well and integrate considerable information on Dominica: 'The region and the people'; 'How the countries are run'; 'How they live'; 'How they work'; and 'Hints for visitors'. The author has done an admirable job of giving an informed feel for the region's complexity. Sixteen photographs, three of Dominica, accompany the text.

8 Notes on the island of Dominica, West Indies.
George Cullen-Pearson. London: Blundell & Company, 1896. 35p.
Following a visit which lasted several months, the author enthusiastically promotes Dominica as, in the words of one official, 'one of the richest Islands in the possession of the Crown in the West Indies in the natural productiveness of its soil' (p. 4). Drawing on comments in published documents and reports, as well as on first-hand observations, Mr. Cullen-Pearson surveys Dominica's climate, water, population, land and produce, roads, and industrial development and cultivation. He advocates the construction of new roads and the establishment of a Land Bank enabling citizens and emigrants to more easily borrow money to buy land. Appendixes contain abstracts from Sir Robert Hamilton's 1894 *Report of the Royal Commission to inquire into the condition and affairs of the island of Dominica* (q.v.), and from J. A. Froude's *English in the West Indies* (q.v.) proclaiming Dominica 'a land fertile as Adam's paradise' (p. 33).

9 Dies Dominica: a publication commemorating Dominica Day 1967. (Statehood edition).
Compiled by the Public Relations Division, Premier's Office.
Hollywood, Florida: Dukane Press; Roseau: Government Printery, 1967. 49p. map.
The second wide-ranging compilation of fiction and non-fiction on Dominica, published on the occasion of Dominica achieving Associated Statehood status. In addition to facts on the island, the national song, French Creole proverbs, photographs of the House of Assembly and the Cabinet, there are articles on C. E. A. Rawle (1891-1938), a Dominican politician whose work resulted in constitutional reforms and progress in West Indian unity, 'Religion and Dominican festivals', and a selection of poems and short stories.

10 Dies Dominica: a publication commemorating Dominica Day 1972. (5th anniversary edition).
Compiled by the Public Relations Division, Premier's Office.
Lauderhill, Florida: Caribbean Creations, 1972. 71p.
To celebrate the 5th anniversary of the achievement of Associated Statehood status, the Premier's Office published the third compilation of brief articles on the island. Reports cover the constitutional developments, politics, forestry, industry, the Caribs, national costumes, music and songs, Creole proverbs and sports. Poems, short stories and numerous photographs fill out the volume.

11 A lovely island called Dominica.
Photographed by John Dominis. *Life*, vol. 59, no. 6 (6 Aug. 1965), p. 46-59.
A photographic essay with dramatic colour views of 'one of the last spots on earth largely undisturbed by man' and an attempt 'to portray that special essence of an island-beauty in isolation' (p. 47). He succeeds.

12 Ports of the sun: a guide to the Caribbean, Bermuda, Nassau, Havana and Panama.
Eleanor Early. Boston, Massachusetts: Houghton Mifflin, 1937. 316p. maps.

A travelogue including the author's visit to Dominica, 'the pleasantest place in the world' (p. 98-105), where for nine months she rented Wall House, the former residence of planter J. Cox Fillan. The author also published a travel account 'Dominica', in *The Atlantic Monthly*, vol. 182, no. 4 (Oct. 1948), p. 113-15.

13 Roaming through the West Indies.
Harry A. Franck. New York: Grosset & Dunlap, 1920. 486p.

The American author travelled overland through the southern United States and then toured the islands. He visited Dominica twice and describes his horseback trip through the rugged interior (p. 347-55).

14 The English in the West Indies: or, the bow of Ulysses.
James Anthony Froude, with illustrations by G. Pearson. New York: Charles Scribner's Sons; London: Longmans, Green, 1888. Reprinted, New York: Negro Universities Press, 1969. 373p. map.

Prejudiced and concerned with the 'preservation of the British Empire', Froude toured the West Indies in 1887, reporting his often perceptive observations in literate prose. 'Beyond all the West Indian islands I had been curious to see Dominica' (p. 129). He describes the Caribs as seen by Father Jean Baptiste Labat, a French historian and priest who visited Dominica briefly in 1700 (p. 129-32), and his own stay with Captain Churchill, the Administrator, and Dr. Henry Nicholls while he toured the island (p. 140-75), 'a land fertile as Adam's paradise'.

15 Commonwealth of Dominica.
Great Britain. Central Office of Information. London: HM Stationery Office, 1979. 20p. map. bibliog. (Reference Pamphlet 160).

An information-filled government booklet which provides a useful survey of 'The land and the people', 'History', 'Constitutional development', 'The economy', and 'Social services'. An excellent map and photographs form the centre pages.

16 Notes upon the island of Dominica (British West Indies) containing information for settlers, investors, tourists, naturalists, and others, with statistics from the official returns, also regulations regarding crown lands and import and export duties.
Symington Grieve. London: Adam & Charles Black, 1906. 126p. map. bibliog.

During his expedition to study flora and fauna in 1906, the author, an ex-president of the Edinburgh Field Naturalists' and Microscopical Society, gathered information 'regarding the island as a field for British settlers, and also as to its suitability for the safe investment of British capital' (Preface, p. 3). Despite its promotional flavour, the resulting work is the fullest general description of early 20th-century Dominica. The topics covered include the past and present states of the island, native villages, crown lands, export crops, flora and fauna, geography and geology, hints to settlers, the Caribs, and the whalers who visited Portsmouth. The author urges the construction of a better road system to open up the island's fertile interior lands. Seventeen well-chosen photographs by the author are interspersed with the text.

17 Mount Joy.
Stephen Hawys. London: Duckworth, 1968. 224p. map.

The author, who spelled his surname Haweis for most of his long life, moved from England to Dominica in 1929, after he 'burnt [his] fingers with wildcat investments upon the London Stock Exchange' (p. 13). Until his death in 1968, he lived on Mount Joy Estate, about seven miles from Roseau on the Imperial Road. In this book he offers a highly personal account of the estate, the island's flora and fauna, agriculture, and a variety of friends and historical figures. Twelve photographs and a detailed index enhance the book. The modest author reveals little of his distinguished and varied career before his move to Dominica. For that, one must read E. C. Baker's article, 'Stephen Haweis of Dominica' (q.v.).

18 Our island culture.
Lennox Honychurch. Roseau: Tropical Printers, [1982]. 55p. maps.

This perfect companion to the author's history of the island, *The Dominica story* (q.v.), surveys a diverse range of cultural aspects from housing types, fishing, herbs, religious festivals and story-telling, to literature, music, art, theatre and creative dance. The volume includes two articles by the late Mabel Caudeiron, 'Music and songs of Dominica' and 'From livré to douillette'. French patois terms, detailed sketches by the author, and numerous photographs make this an interesting and useful book for resident and tourist alike.

19 British West Indian interlude.
Anne Rainey Langley. *National Geographic*, vol. 79, no. 1 (Jan. 1941), p. 1-46. map.

The author travelled down the British Lesser Antilles by ship and recounts her impressions of St. Kitts, Antigua, Dominica (p. 17-19, 22-23), St. Lucia, Barbados, St. Vincent and Grenada. On Dominica she saw lime oil extracted by hand, copra preparation and the Carib Reserve. She gives a brief but informative description of the island sights in 1940. Colour and black-and-white photographs of Dominica and the other islands by Edwin L. Wisherd portray a wide selection of panoramic views and local residents.

20   **West Indian societies.**
David Lowenthal, foreword by Philip Mason.   New York, London,
Toronto: Oxford University Press for the Institute of Race
Relations, London, in collaboration with the American
Geographical Society, New York, 1972. 385p. map. bibliog.
(American Geographical Society Research Series, no. 26).

An admirable overview of the complex experiences of some eleven million West
Indians in fifty distinct societies analysed in chapters on 'History'; 'Social
structure'; 'East Indians and Creoles'; 'Ethnic minorities'; 'Emigration and neo-
colonialism'; and 'Racial and national identity'. Mention of Dominica occurs
throughout, reflecting the author's intimate familiarity with the island. The
author, both a geographer and historian, was a Research Associate at the
American Geographical Society and a Professor of Geography at University
College of the University of London.

21   **Caribbean circuit.**
Sir Harry Luke.   London: Nicholson & Watson, 1950. 262p.
7 maps.

The author's three-and-a-half-year tour of the islands included a visit to
Dominica, the 'loveliest, wildest, most rugged and least explored of all the
Antilles' (p. 123). His account (p. 123-32) mentions highlights of island history,
but emphasizes the Carib Indians, who are also discussed in chapters on Trinidad
and St. Vincent. Among numerous photographs are three of the Island Caribs
and two of the Dominica mace (p. 173), a staff used as a symbol of authority
during the colonial period.

22   **The West Indies illustrated, including the Isthmus of Panama and
Bermuda; historical and descriptive, commercial and industrial facts,
figures, & resources.**
Edited by Allister Macmillan.   London: W. H. & L. Collingridge,
1912. 562p.

One of the most informative of the early 20th-century guides, with information on
history, constitution, topography, products, finances, trade, towns and climate.
Best of all, however, are the twenty-two photographs of daily scenes in Dominica
(p. 384-404). The author later published another version of the guide as *The red
book of the West Indies* (London: W. H. & L. Collingridge, 1922) which also
contains twelve excellent photographs of the island (p. 337-43).

23   *Finisterre* **sails the Windward Islands.**
Carleton Mitchell.   *National Geographic*, vol. 128, no. 6 (Dec. 1965),
p. 755-801. maps.

The author describes the first half of his Lesser Antillean trip from Grenada to
Dominica in his 38-foot ocean cruiser-racer. His visit to Dominica focused on the
Carib Reserve. Numerous colour photographs by Winfield Parks capture varied
island life and views. Eighteen years earlier his similar voyage was described in

another *National Geographic* article, '*Carib* cruises the West Indies', vol. 93, no. 1 (Jan. 1948), p. 1-56. Then he described Dominica as his favourite isle, 'the most lush, most rugged, and most primitive of them all' (p. 14).

24 Isles of the Caribbees.
Carleton Mitchell, foreword by Melville Bell Grosvenor.
Washington, DC: Special Publications Division, National
Geographic Society, 1971. 214p. 2nd ed. maps. bibliog.
The author cruised from Grenada to St. Thomas in his 38-foot yawl *Finisterre* for the first edition of this book, published in 1966. For this edition, he visited the islands again and provides updated information. In chapter six, 'Dominica: the loneliest isle' (p. 86-99), he describes the gradual development of the island, expressing particular concern about the Dom-Can Timbers logging company which began cutting some of the largest forest trees in 1968. In addition, he recounts a visit to the Carib Reserve and Eric Lamb's Dominica Safaris, guided tours of remote island areas for tourists. Recalling changes since his 1947 visit, he writes, 'It is the loneliest and most savagely beautiful of the Caribbee Isles. But, for the first time, I wondered how long it would remain so' (p. 98). Dramatic colour photographs by John Dominis, Winfield Parks and Fred Ward portray the rugged island and its life.

25 The nest egg and I.
Mary Rogers Narodny. *Vassar Alumnae Magazine*, vol. 45, no. 5
(May 1960), p. 15-17.
A personal account of the author's experiences working in Dominica between 1943 and 1957, especially as manager of the Dominica Co-operative Bank guarding the nest-eggs of 4,300 people.

26 Isles of the Caribbean.
National Geographic Society, Special Publications Division, editor,
Robert L. Breeden, managing editor, Mary Ann Harrell.
Washington, DC: National Geographic Society, 1980. 215p. maps.
bibliog.
In seven chapters, five contributing authors give a considerable flavour of life in the Lesser Antilles, from Trinidad and Barbados to the Virgin Islands, examining 'the changes taking place as islands emerge into independence, with the rewards and the problems development brings'. 'North to the Leewards' by Charles McCarry and photographed by Jodi Cobb (p. 148-83) portrays aspects of Dominica at independence, following Hurricane David and on the Carib Reserve.

27 Our West Indian neighbors: the islands of the Caribbean Sea, 'America's Mediterranean' their picturesque features, fascinating history, and attractions for the traveler, nature lover, settler and pleasure seeker.
Frederick A[lbion] Ober. New York: James Pott, 1904. 433p.

The author, naturalist and traveller with a particular fondness for Dominica, gives the island special emphasis in his West Indian travel books. The chapters 'Dominica, an island of wonders' (p. 329-41) and 'The last of the West Indians' (p. 342-53), contain first-hand accounts by one who knows the island and its people well. The book is dedicated to Sir Henry Nicholls of Roseau and contains, among many photographs, the first ever taken of the Boiling Lake from the author's visit in 1877. Another travel book by Ober, *A guide to the West Indies, Bermuda and Panama* (New York: Dodd, Mead, 1908) also has a chapter on Dominica (p. 359-70).

28 West Indian odyssey: the complete guide to the islands of the Caribbean.
Charles B. Parmer. New York: Dodge, 1937. 285. map.

A tour of the islands in the 1930s. The author's chapter on Dominica, 'Island of rainbows' (p. 91-99), describes his visit to Roseau and the possible outings a tourist can take on the island.

29 Down the islands.
William Agnew Paton. New York: Charles Scribner's Sons, 1887. Reprinted, Westport, Connecticut: Negro Universities Press, 1969. 301p.

On his cruise the author did not go ashore at Dominica, but in chapter eight, 'Sabbath Island' (p. 88-99), he describes the island and the Carib Indians from other printed sources, especially John Imray's *Edinburgh Medical and Surgical Journal* article, 'Observations on the characters of endemic fever in the island of Dominica . . .' printed in 1848 (vol. 70, no. 177, p. 253-87).

30 Lands of the inner sea: the West Indies and Bermuda.
W[alter] Adolphe Roberts. New York: Coward-McCann, 1948. 285p. map.

The Jamaica-born author wrote extensively about the region and in this travelogue managed to effectively portray the island's geography and history with brevity (p. 202-08), including a poignant description by Lafcadio Hearn in *Two years in the French West Indies* (New York: Harper, 1890).

31 Dies Dominica: a publication commemorating Dominica Day.
Written and compiled by Edward Scobie. Roseau: Government Printery, 1965. 71p. map.

A diverse collection of fiction, non-fiction, photographs and illustrations published to commemorate Dominica Day, 3 November 1965. The contents include: 'Conquest and colonisation', 'Constitutional development of Dominica', and 'RIP la peau cabrit', all by Scobie; 'Dangers of a one crop economy', by A. Gregory; 'Educating our youth', by W. S. Stevens; 'Dominica's domestic market', by A. Gregory; 'Hurricane', by P. K. Agar; 'Our national future', by N. A. N. Ducreay; 'Dominica's national dress'; and other short articles and poems. The Dominica-born author was Mayor of Roseau and editor of several newspapers and magazines.

32 Cruising among the Caribbees: summer days in winter months.
Charles Augustus Stoddard.   New York: Charles Scribner's Sons, 1895. 198p. map.
The author was charmed by 'Sabbath Day Island' and describes its physical beauty and agricultural products (p. 108-18) as well as 'The Caribs of Dominica and St. Vincent' (p. 119-25). A photograph of an indigo plantation in Dominica is included.

33 The cradle of the deep: an account of a voyage to the West Indies.
Sir Frederick Treves.   London: Smith, Elder; New York: E. P. Dutton, 1908. 378p. maps. bibliog.
From Martinique the author visited Dominica, about which he relates a brief historical and contemporary account. In another chapter he reconstructs images of the Caribs, past and present (p. 162-73). A photograph of the Roseau Valley is included.

34 Background notes: Dominica.
United States Department of State, Bureau of Public Affairs.   Washington, DC: Government Printing Office, Nov. 1981. 4p. 2 maps. (Department of State Publication 9235, Background Notes Series).
A practical, succinct publication giving a profile of the island and a sketch of its geography, history, government, economy, defence, foreign relations in general and US–Dominican relations in particular, together with brief travel notes.

35 The book of the West Indies.
A[lpheus] Hyatt Verrill.   New York: E. P. Dutton, 1917. 458p.
The author and his brother, G. E. Verrill, visited Dominica in 1890 to make ornithological collections and observations. Chapter seven, 'Dominica, the Caribbean wonderland' (p. 72-80), containing photographs of Soufrière, a Carib girl, and the entrance to the Botanic Gardens, recounts the visit to Roseau and its nearby environs.

36 Thirty years in the jungle.
A[lpheus] Hyatt Verrill.   London: John Lane, Bodley Head, 1929. 281p. map.
An account of the author's more than thirty years of explorations and scientific investigations in the West Indies, Central and South America. Verrill's first trip took him to the Lesser Antilles, where he was captivated by Dominica's

rainforests in 1888. He returned numerous times to 'wondrous Dominica' but here details his first tropical ventures with the excitement of a 'veritable tenderfoot' in recounting his discoveries and interactions with Dominicans (p. 2-45).

37 Dominica: diving for yesterday.
Stephen M. Voynick. *Américas*, vol. 31, no. 10 (Oct. 1979), p. 19-24. map.

The underwater archaeology of 17th- and 18th-century wrecks off Dominica is described in this article, which includes several photographs. According to Lloyd's List in London, sixty-five wrecks, including the Spanish treasure fleet of 1567, are located off the island's coast. The author, an experienced diver and professional photographer, is Vice President of Seaborne Ventures, Inc.

38 Golden islands of the Caribbean.
Fred Ward. New York: Crown, [1972]. 160p. maps.

A popular, historical overview of the forces which shaped the Lesser Antilles. More than forty historical prints, maps and photographs, and more than one hundred photographs by the author and Ted Spiegel supplement the book's five chapters. 'Dominica & the planter isles' (p. 65-96) contrasts the unexploited beauty of Dominica with the intensely-cultivated sugar islands of Antigua, Montserrat, Nevis and St. Kitts in prose and pictures.

39 Hot countries.
Alec Waugh, with woodcuts by Lynd Ward. New York: Literary Guild, 1930. 304p.

The first of several pieces by the author about Dominica appears in this collection of travel articles on Tahiti, Martinique, Siam, Ceylon, the New Hebrides and Haiti. Waugh writes of the carnival (p. 106-09), and, in 'The Englishman in the tropics' (p. 205-17), of visiting a retired English judge in Dominica in 1928. He describes Dominica as the Ireland of the Antilles: 'it is the loveliest of the islands and it is the most difficult to manage' (p. 106).

40 The sugar islands: a Caribbean travelogue.
Alec Waugh. New York: Farrar, Straus, 1949. 278p.

The prolific author visited Dominica in 1928, 1939 and 1948, and developed a fascination with the island. He describes this attitude in the context of his visits to friends Elma Napier and John Archbold who lived on Dominica, and through recounting the island's contradictory history of agricultural booms and busts. The phrase 'typical Dominica', referring to the complications of island life, forms the title of a chapter in this book (p. 89-134) which was reprinted in a later collection, *Love and the Caribbean: tales, characters and scenes of the West Indies* (New York: Farrar, Straus, Cudahy, 1958. p. 273-307), updated with observations from a more recent visit. The essay is one of the most literate and perceptive on this aspect of the island's history and its residents.

41 The sense of time, the social construction of reality, and the foundations of nationhood in Dominica and the Faroe Islands.
Jonathan Wylie. *Comparative Studies in Society and History*, vol. 24, no. 3 (1982), p. 438-66. bibliog.

This well-written, unusual article is based on the author's thirteen months' residence in a Dominican fishing village in 1977-78, and ten months' stay in a fishing village in the Faroe Islands in 1971-72. He draws a sharp contrast between Afro-Caribbean society, in which the 'past is shallow and unimportant', 'reality is shiftingly construed, often through argument', and where people regard one another suspiciously, with Scandinavian society, where the past is 'deep and a topic of general interest', historical truths and the order of nature underlie reality, and where people go out of their way to get along with one another (p. 439). What the islands share is that 'modernization has destroyed much of a traditional way of life' (p. 466).

Birnbaum's Caribbean, Bermuda, and the Bahamas 1986.
See item no. 70.

Baedeker's Caribbean including Bermuda.
See item no. 71.

Fodor's Caribbean 1987.
See item no. 72.

The traveller's tree: a journey through the Caribbean islands.
See item no. 74.

Dramatic Dominica.
See item no. 75.

Caribbean Dominica: an island primeval.
See item no. 77.

Frommer's dollarwise guide to the Caribbean, 1986-87 edition.
See item no. 78.

The Caribbean.
See item no. 79.

Dominica the unique.
See item no. 80.

Fielding's Caribbean 1987.
See item no. 82.

The wildlife of Dominica.
See item no. 128.

Columbus saw them first.
See item no. 164.

The Dominica story: a history of the island.
See item no. 216.

Periodicals

42 Report on Dominica for the Year . . .
Great Britain, Colonial Office.   London: HM Stationery Office,
1947-65. map. bibliog.
An extremely informative series of official reports, each about fifty to sixty pages
long, issued annually, biannually and triannually. Standardized chapters cover:
population; occupations, wages and labour organization; public finance and
taxation; currency and banking; commerce; production; social services; legislation; justice, police and prisons; public utilities and public roads; communications;
press, broadcasting, films and government information services; geography and
climate; history; administration; and weights and measures. There is also a
reading list. Varied appendixes and photographs round out this broad portrait of
the island.

Geography, Geology and Climate

Geography

43 Dominica: a wet tropical human habitat.
Lucia Carolyn Harrison.   *Economic Geography*, vol. 11, no. 1
(Jan. 1935), p. 62-76. 3 maps.
An article giving an admirably-sketched cultural and economic geography of the island, using rainfall data, export statistics and well-chosen photographs. The author surveys topographical influences on the population and transportation patterns, and on the island's economic development in terms of the rise and fall of the coffee, sugar-cane, cacao and lime industries.

44 Caribbean lands.
John Macpherson.   Trinidad, Jamaica: Longman Caribbean, 1980.
4th ed. 200p. maps.
A highly-instructive survey, especially intended for GCE (O) Level candidates, but very useful for anyone seeking an understanding of the cultural and physical geography of the region. The author asserts that Dominica is 'undoubtedly the wildest and most complex' of the Lesser Antilles. 'Indeed it is such a mass of peaks, ridges and ravines that in proportion to area it is more rugged than Switzerland' (p. 107). Maps of rainfall, relief and land use, and a photograph of the Layou River Valley supplement the descriptive section on Dominica (p. 107-10).

Geography, Geology and Climate. Geography

45 West Indian memories: the Lesser Antilles and the 'Boiling Lake'.
W. Gifford Palgrave. *MacMillan's Magazine*, vol. 35, no. 209
(March 1877), p. 361-74.
With raptured prose the author recounts his visits to Martinique and Dominica,
where in spring 1877, he ventured to the Boiling Lake with Dr. Henry Nicholls
and others. Theirs was the third recorded expedition by Europeans to the island's
'Grand Soufrière' region, 'a strange sight to see, and not less awful than strange'
where the 'lake rages and roars like a wild beast in its cage' (p. 372).

46 Caribbean isles.
Peter Wood and the editors of Time-Life Books. New York:
Time-Life Books, 1975. 184p. map. bibliog. (The American
Wilderness Series).
A selective tour of the 'glistening archipelago's' natural terrain and wildlife,
featuring underwater scenery, Jamaica, Bonaire, Aves Island, Mount Pelée, 'the
inner world of Dominica' (p. 50-65), and a photographic essay of 'the watery
wilds' of Dominica by John Dominis (p. 166-79). The author describes his trek
through the rainforest to the Valley of Desolation on the 'one island in the
Antilles that Columbus would still recognize', and his encounters with
Dominicans who describe themselves as 'the people who live behind God's back'
(p. 50). The volume is illustrated with dramatic colour photographs of Dominica
throughout.

Isles of the Caribbees.
See item no. 24.

Isles of the Caribbean.
See item no. 26.

Thirty years in the jungle.
See item no. 36.

Golden islands of the Caribbean.
See item no. 38.

The mouth of hell.
See item no. 49.

The island of Dominica.
See item no. 50.

The mountains of Dominica.
See item no. 52.

Dominica.
See item no. 67.

**A forest lover in the Caribbee Islands. IV. The cloud-capped wilderness
of Dominica.**
See item no. 87.

14

Photographer in the rain-forests.
See item no. 90.

Camps in the Caribbees: the adventures of a naturalist in the Lesser Antilles.
See item no. 93.

The history of the island of Dominica, containing a description of its situation, extent, climate, mountains, rivers, natural productions, etc., etc., together with an account of the civil government, trade, laws, customs, and manners of the different inhabitants of that island. Its conquest by the French, and restoration to the British dominions.
See item no. 191.

The Dominica story: a history of the island.
See item no. 216.

Names on Dominica.
See item no. 275.

A resource guide to Dominica, 1493-1986.
See item no. 489.

Geology

47 The Lesser Antilles.
William Morris Davis. New York: American Geographical Society, 1926. 207p. maps. bibliog. (American Geographical Society Map of Hispanic America Publication, no. 2).
A geological and geographical survey of the Lesser Antilles, which discusses Dominica as 'a superb example of an elaborately dissected, composite volcanic island' (p. 63). Three maps and a sketch of the south-western coast illustrate the description of Dominica (p. 63-73).

48 Geological notes on the island of Dominica, B. W. I.
Kenneth W. Earle. *Geological Magazine*, vol. 65, no. 4 (April 1928), p. 169-87. 2 maps. bibliog.
A professional account of the island's geological characteristics. The author describes the older volcanic rocks, marine deposits, later lava flows, and recent deposits and volcanic phenomena, including the Valley of Desolation and the Boiling Lake, of which he provides a sketched map. Included are lists of rock types and fossils from limestone deposits on the leeward coast.

49 The mouth of hell.
Stuart E. Elliott. *Natural History*, vol. 60, no. 10 (Dec. 1951),
p. 440-45, 476.
A sensationalistic account of the author's trek to the Valley of Desolation and the
Boiling Lake, the source of the article's title. His guide was a grandson of the
guide for the ill-fated Clive, whose trip some fifty years earlier and death from
sulphurous gases at the lake are described.

50 The island of Dominica.
Frederick M[iller] Endlich. *American Naturalist*, no. 14, no. 11
(Nov. 1880), p. 761-72.
An account, emphasizing geography and geology, of the author's visit to the
Boiling Lake, the Valley of Desolation and Wotten Waven, all well-known
sources of volcanic activity in Dominica, in February 1880, several weeks after the
4 January activity which covered much of the island in ash. The author reports
temperature measurements and minerological observations, and determines the
4 January event to have been an 'explosion' rather than an 'eruption'.

51 Volcanism and vegetation in the Lesser Antilles.
Richard A. Howard. *Journal of the Arnold Arboretum*, vol. 43,
no. 3 (July 1962), p. 279-311. map. bibliog.
A survey of volcanic history and its effects on surrounding flora from Grenada to
St. Kitts, based on field observations made in 1950 and 1961. Volcanic areas on
each island, including Dominica, are described in the 'catalogue of the fumarole
areas of the Lesser Antilles' (p. 296-305). Detailed historical references and
twenty-one relevant photographs make this a particularly useful article. The
author is Director of the Arnold Arboretum at Harvard University, Cambridge,
Massachusetts.

52 The mountains of Dominica.
Paul Griswold Howes. *Natural History*, vol. 29, no. 6 (Nov.-Dec.
1929), p. 595-610.
An account of the author's expedition up Morne Diablotin, Dominica's highest
mountain at 4,747 feet (mistakenly reported as the highest in the Lesser Antilles),
with a commentary on the flora and fauna. Twenty-one photographs by the
author and Dickenson S. Cummings, including the first photograph taken from
the summit of Diablotin, are of particular interest.

53 A summary of the geology of the Lesser Antilles.
P. H. A. Martin-Kaye. *Overseas Geology and Mineral Resources*,
vol. 10 (1971), p. 172-206. map. bibliog.
An excellent, and perhaps the best, overview of the geological history of all the
islands of the Lesser Antilles, which consist of two closely-related arcs of different
geologic age. The outer eastern arc, extending from Sombrero Island to Grenada,
was formed in the early Tertiary, and the inner arc, of which Dominica is a part,
was formed in the later Miocene and Pliocene. In addition to two photographs of
Dominican mountains, the article contains a 'Stratigraphic correlation chart for

the islands of the Lesser Antilles', a large 'Structural map of the Lesser Antilles', and an extensive bibliography. The author was formerly Geologist for the Windward Islands.

54 The volcanic eruption in Dominica.
H[enry] A[lfred] Alford Nicholls. *Nature* (London), vol. 21, (19 Feb. 1880), p. 372-73.
The best published first-hand account of Dominica's only volcanic eruption in historic times. Dr. Henry Nicholls describes the 4 January 1880 eruption in detail as well as his observations on 12 January at the site of the explosion about eight miles from Roseau, which had been covered by 2-3 inches of ash.

55 Partly welded pyroclast flow deposits in Dominica, Lesser Antilles.
Haraldur Sigurdsson. *Bulletin of Volcanology*, vol. 36 (1972), p. 148-63. map. bibliog.
Although technical in nature, this is the only article published in recent years on the geology of Dominica. The author, then a geologist in the Seismic Research Unit at the University of the West Indies, St. Augustine, Trinidad, now a Professor of Oceanography at the University of Rhode Island, Kingston, Rhode Island, analyses data on an extensive Pleistocene pyroclast flow in the Roseau Valley, the first known occurrence of welded tuff in the Lesser Antilles. These deposits from Morne Micotrin are from eruptions of the *nuée ardente* type, the same type as the famous eruption of nearby Mount Pelée on Martinique in 1902, and have yielded radio-carbon dates of between 50,000 and 10,000 years ago. This article was also published in the *Proceedings of the sixth Caribbean geological conference*, Margarita, Venezuela (St. Augustine, Trinidad: University of the West Indies, Seismic Research Unit, 1972. p. 307-12).

56 The Boiling Lake of Dominica.
Philip B. Whelpley. *Nature Magazine*, vol. 7, no. 2 (Feb. 1926), p. 89-90.
The brief description of a visit to the island's 'steaming caldron', with some mention of an earlier visit which resulted in tragic deaths in 1901, with two photographs by the author. The Boiling Lake is reportedly the second largest in the world, next to one found in New Zealand.

Caribbean lands.
See item no. 44.

Dominica's national park: geology and soils.
See item no. 399.

Soil and land use

57 The development of natural resources in Dominica.
Lewis G. Campbell. Cave Hill, Barbados: University of the West Indies, Institute of Social and Economic Research (Eastern Caribbean), Dec. 1965. 341p. map. bibliog.

A discussion of natural resources, the development of land resources, and selected enterprises and land-development requirements, by the author, a Lecturer in Agricultural Engineering at the University of the West Indies, St. Augustine, Trinidad. A brief foreword by economist Carleen O'Loughlin and a provisional general soil map are included.

58 Patterns of land tenure in the Leeward and Windward Islands and their relevance to problems of agricultural development in the West Indies.
Herman J. Finkel. *Economic Geography*, vol. 40, no. 2 (1964), p. 163-72. Reprinted in: *Peoples and cultures of the Caribbean. An anthropological reader*. Edited by Michael M. Horowitz. New York: Natural History Press, 1971, p. 291-304.

Presents a set of comparisons of St. Kitts and Nevis in the Leewards, and Dominica and St. Lucia in the Windwards as a study of 'agricultural development for the region with special emphasis on the utilization of soil and water resources' (p. 291). Each island is characterized by a different pattern of land settlement, and distinctive patterns of land tenure and land use. The author offers an analysis of the proportions of landholdings of various sizes in Dominica based on a census made in 1958, and recommends changes in the present patterns of land tenure in which 'The 85 large estates (100 acres+) include 40,000 acres of a total land area in farms of 72,408 acres, or 55 per cent, which are operated by less than 1 per cent of the farmers. At the other end of the scale there are 8,027 farmers with less than 5 acres each, totalling 16,293 acres. This represents 91 per cent of the farmers and 22.4 per cent of the land.' (p. 297-98).

59 Studies in West Indian soils: the soils of Dominica, their genesis and fertility considered in relation to reaction.
F. Hardy. *West Indian Bulletin*, vol. 19, no. 1 (30 Sept. 1921), p. 86-123. map. bibliog.

The author, a chemist on the staff of the Imperial Department of Agriculture for the West Indies, visited Dominica from 29 October to 6 December 1920, and provides a comprehensive report on Dominica soils. He describes the main geological features and origin of the soils, provides data on chemical composition, the chief soil-types of the Central Uplands and the Windward and Leeward Coastal Belts, and reports the results of experimental cacao and lime plots at the island's Botanic Station.

60 Report on squatter problem and land use: island of Dominica.
Arthur Thelwell. Kingston: Lands Department, 16 June 1950. 33p.

During the banana 'boom' of 1950, estate owners wanted to reclaim more of their land from squatters in order to produce more bananas, which resulted in disagreements with the tenants and shortages of food crops as well. The author was invited to survey the situation and to make recommendations, which he did following a visit to Dominica from 24 March to 16 April 1950. The report provides a valuable glimpse of land tenure and crop production for that time.

Climate and hurricanes

61 Two days in Dominica.
Patrick Hoyos. *Bajan*, vol. 311 (Oct. 1979), p. 10, 12, 14.

A special report and cover feature on Dominica, two weeks after Hurricane David struck, with nine photographs of the damage. The article includes a description of the relief efforts and the labours of individual Dominicans.

62 Hurricane: death and devastation.
Jeremy Taylor. *Caribbean & West Indies Chronicle*, vol. 94, no. 1552 (Oct.-Nov. 1979), p. 8-9, 29.

An account, with photographs, of the impact of hurricanes David and Frederick on Dominica and neighbouring islands. On Dominica, David's 150-mph winds killed 40, injured about 9,000 and left 60,000 people homeless. Estimates put damage to the banana crop at 50 per cent, coconuts at 95 per cent, citrus at 40 per cent, and timber resources at 90 per cent; 60 per cent of the roads and 80 per cent of the schools were destroyed by the island's worst hurricane of the century.

63 Dominica.
Fred Ward. *National Geographic*, vol. 158, no. 3 (Sept. 1980), p. 354-59.

Dramatic photographs of Dominica before and after Hurricane David by the author and *National Geographic* photographer Joseph J. Scherschel, with an account by Ward of the devastation. The same issue contains related articles 'Hurricane!' by Ben Funk (p. 346-53, 360-67, 372-79) and 'Into the eye of David' by John L. Eliot (p. 368-71) which place Hurricane David in a broader perspective.

64 The unsung heroes.
John L. Webster. *Bajan*, vol. 311 (Nov. 1979), p. 36-40.

Discusses the role of the amateur radio operators during and after Hurricane David. Dominican ham operator Fred White kept the island in touch with the outside world for two weeks because all other communications equipment was destroyed. The author, an amateur radio operator in Trinidad and Barbados, went to Dominica to assist during the recovery efforts, and supplements the article with his own photographs.

Maps and atlases

65 Caribbean history in maps.
Peter Ashdown. Trinidad, Jamaica: Longman Caribbean, 1979. 84p.

A wealth of maps, diagrams, tables and lists present a chronological view of Caribbean history from the Amerindian migrations to the political and social events of the late 1970s. The book is especially useful for its presentation of events and conditions on Dominica in the context of the political economy of the Lesser Antilles. Special sections display data on religion, politics, economy and tourism in the 1970s, and provide lists of 'Notable West Indians old and new' and 'Culture in the English-speaking Caribbean'.

66 The atlas of Central America and the Caribbean.
The Diagram Group. New York: Macmillan; London: Collier Macmillan, 1985. 144p. maps. bibliog.

A beautifully-produced, information-packed book of maps on the region. Part 3 concerns the Caribbean region and contains charts on demography, land use, economy, politics, government finances and individual country profiles. 'Dominica and St. Lucia' are portrayed and discussed together (p. 128-29), providing useful comparisons and statistical data in a variety of categories.

67 Dominica.
Lands and Surveys Division, Ministry of Agriculture, Lands and Fisheries. Surbiton, Surrey, England: Directorate of Overseas Surveys for the Dominica Government, 1982. map.

Attractive, colourful maps of the island are readily obtainable from the Lands and Surveys Division, Ministry of Agriculture, Lands and Fisheries, Roseau, Dominica, or from Edward Stanford Ltd., 12/14 Long Acre, London WC2E 9LP. Current maps include three of the entire island and one of Roseau. The largest map is in three sheets, 'Dominica', scale 1:25,000 (5th ed. 1978). 'Dominica', scale 1:50,000 (3rd ed. 1982) includes a colour inset of Roseau, scale 1:10,000. 'Dominica', scale 1:125,000 (Directorate of Overseas Surveys 998 Edition 2, 1982) includes a small inset of the eastern Caribbean. 'Roseau and environs', scale 1:5,000 (DOS Series 151 Edition 2) provides excellent detail of the town and nearby areas.

68 **Maps and charts of North America and the West Indies, 1750-1789: a guide to collections in the Library of Congress.**
Compiled by John R. Sellers, Patricia Molen Van Ee.
Washington, DC: Library of Congress, 1981. 495p.
An annotated listing of the Library of Congress map collection for the brief period covered. Twenty maps of the Lesser Antilles are described (p. 417-20), as are fourteen for Dominica, including Archibald Campbell's 'Sketch of the coast' [1761] and Robert Brereton's 'Plan of Prince Rupert's & Douglas Bays . . .' [1785] (p. 430-33). Seven of the maps of Dominica are elaborate depictions of the Rosalie Estate by Isaac Werden [1776], one of which is reproduced as a full-page illustration (p. 431).

69 **The printed maps of Dominica and Grenada.**
Ronald Vere Tooley. Durrant House, London: Map Collectors' Circle, 1970. 15p. bibliog. maps. (No. 62).
A descriptive list of thirty-six maps of Dominica from the one by Emanuel Bowen [1745], the earliest published individual map of the island, to the 1898 War Office map used in C. O. Naftel's *Report on the agricultural capabilities of Dominica* (London, 1898). Plates of six Dominica maps supplement the list: Thomas Jefferys, [1775]; Thomas Bowen, [1778]; LeRouge, [1779]; Thomson, [1814]; Society for the Diffusion of Useful Knowledge, [1835]; and George Phillip & Son, [1856].

Travel Guides and Tourism

Travel guides

70 Birnbaum's Caribbean, Bermuda, and the Bahamas 1986.
Edited by Stephen Birnbaum, Marcia Wallace, area editor.
Boston, Massachusetts: Houghton Mifflin, 1985. 721p. maps.

One of the best, annually-updated, guides on the region. The chapter on Dominica (p. 357-67) has reliable standard sections on 'The island at-a-glance', 'Sources and resources' and 'Best on the island'.

71 Baedeker's Caribbean including Bermuda.
Helmut Blume, Hans Dieter Haas, W. Hassenpflug, U. Moll.
Englewood Cliffs, New Jersey: Prentice-Hall, n.d. 339p. 69 maps.

This colourful, well-illustrated guide, translated from the German, provides good coverage of each island, including more historical and sociological information than most travel guides. The account of Dominica (p. 114-18, 320, 324) contains the basic information, a map, and colour photographs of the island.

72 Fodor's Caribbean 1987.
Edited by Gail Chasan. New York, London: Fodor's Travel Guides, 1986. 545p. maps.

Fodor's travel guides, updated annually, provide some of the most reliable information in standardized categories for visitors to the region. The chapter on Dominica (p. 163-73) written by New York freelance writer David P. Schulz, offers advice on 'exploring Dominica', as well as an assortment of practical information on where to stay, what to eat, and what to do. A companion volume each year, *Fodor's budget Caribbean*, condenses most of the essential tourist facts but emphasizes 'moderate' and 'inexpensive' hotels and restaurants. The 1987 edition (Fodor's Travel Guides, 1987. 244p.) proclaims that 'for sheer unadulterated green, lush tropics, this place is tops' (p. 216).

73 Retiring to the Caribbean.
Wesley Edson. Garden City, New York: Doubleday, 1964. 324p. maps.

In twenty-five chapters on islands and island groups, plus 'Finding the right island' (p. 5-13), 'Houses for the West Indies' (p. 312-16) and 'Making a living in the islands' (p. 317-24), the author offers insights and advice on successful retirement, much of it remaining valid since the book's publication. Dominica receives special attention in a chapter (p. 179-205) describing roads, health care, amenities, flora and fauna, shopping, handicrafts, accommodation, living costs, food, banking and land prices ('just about the lowest in all the Caribbean', p. 199). The author spent two 'depressing' months living in Dominica's rainy mountains before finding happiness living on the coast (p. 6). To him, Dominica is 'a backward, exotic isle', 'in some respects a hundred years behind the French and British islands to the north and south of it', but 'no other island in the Caribbean quite matches the wild untamed beauty of Dominica' (p. 7, 179).

74 The traveller's tree: a journey through the Caribbean islands.
Patrick Leigh Fermor. New York: Harper & Row, 1950. 403p. map.

A well-written description of fifteen islands with numerous black-and-white photographs by A. Costa. Fermor's visit to Dominica (p. 98-130) focuses on an account of Roseau, the hospitality of writer Elma Napier, and his horseback ride through the dense forest, 'a vague, steaming and antediluvian world' (p. 123), to visit the Carib Indians. Before this book, Major Leigh Fermor was better known for his wartime exploits in the Balkans and Crete.

75 Dramatic Dominica.
Victor Haagen. *Travel*, vol. 130, no. 4 (Oct. 1968), p. 30-34.

The author describes the island's geographic and romantic appeal, accommodation and tourist opportunities, which are illustrated by the cover photography and several other pictures.

76 Crossroads of the buccaneers.
Hendrik de Leeuw. Philadelphia: J. B. Lippincott, 1937. 414p.

A descriptive travel book relating the author's tour of several islands with their histories. 'Dominica and its uncrowned king' (Dr. Henry Nicholls, p. 207-26), gives an historical sketch of the island and the works of physicians John Imray and Henry Nicholls, followed by an account of the author's excursion to the Boiling Lake. The author's line-drawings are interspersed with the text.

77 **Caribbean Dominica: an island primeval.**

Lawrence Millman. *Travel-Holiday*, vol. 166, no. 1 (July 1986), p. 26-28.

An enthusiastic general survey of island ambiance, covering the main sights and recommending Reigate Hall Hotel as the island's best. The author is a Massachusetts-based freelance writer.

78 **Frommer's dollarwise guide to the Caribbean, 1986-87 edition.**

Darwin Porter, assisted by Danforth Prince. New York: Frommer/Pasmantier, Simon & Schuster, 1986. 686p. 19 maps.

This reliable, comprehensive, annual guide to the region covers all the islands, and describes Dominica as 'the most original island in the Caribbean' (p. 514). Standard sections for Dominica (p. 514-23), include background and factual information, hotels and restaurants, tourist sights, sports, shopping and nightlife.

79 **The Caribbean.**

Selden Rodman, drawings by Bill Negron. New York: Hawthorn Books, 1968. 320p. maps.

A personal, descriptive tour of the island by a prolific writer and art critic with long experience in the region. For this book the author visited all the islands in late 1966. While in Dominica he was based at Peter Brand's Island House Hotel and included a visit to the Carib Reserve (p. 80-91).

80 **Dominica the unique.**

David P. Schulz. *Stores*, vol. 67, no. 7 (July 1985), p. 50-54. map.

An interesting, succinct survey of Dominican tourist opportunities and facilities, with several photographs.

81 **The Caribbean bed & breakfast book.**

Kathy Strong. Charlotte, North Carolina: East Woods Press, 1985. 268p. maps.

A selective guide to more than 150 inns and guest houses in the Caribbean, emphasizing those places offering special touches such as historical significance, unique settings or notable service. In Dominica (p. 218-23), the author recommends four guesthouses/hotels: the Anchorage, Castaways, Papillote and Springfield.

82 **Fielding's Caribbean 1987.**

Margaret Zellers. New York: Fielding Travel Books, c/o William Morrow, 1987. 840p. maps.

A detailed account of tourist facilities and attractions on all the islands, considered by many to be the most informative guide to the region. In the Dominica chapter (p. 251-62), the author rates the hotels and restaurants and notes the political picture, lifestyle, touring tips, 'places worth finding', and 'treasures and trifles'. Dominica is a 'fiercely individualistic country', 'not a place for the fainthearted or the carsick crowd' (p. 253, 255). 1986 prices are included.

An annual, shorter companion volume, *Fielding's economy Caribbean 1987* (New York: Fielding Travel Books/Morrow, 1986. 272p.) describes a less expensive way to see the region. The Dominica chapter (p. 111-15) includes a description of five guesthouses.

83 The inn way.
   Margaret Zellers.   Stockbridge, Massachusetts: Berkshire Traveller Press, 1978. 192p.
A guide to 109 of the small, intimate inns scattered throughout most of the Caribbean islands. For Dominica (p. 57-64), the experienced author singles out five special places to stay: the Anchorage Hotel; the Fort Young Hotel (subsequently destroyed by Hurricane David in 1979); the Island House; the Rivière La Croix Estate Hotel; and the Castaways Hotel. A new edition was published in 1981 (Geomedia Productions), which also covered Dominica (p. 73-78).

The pocket guide to the West Indies.
See item no. 1.

Ports of the sun: a guide to the Caribbean, Bermuda, Nassau, Havana and Panama.
See item no. 12.

Our island culture.
See item no. 18.

Isles of the Caribbees.
See item no. 24.

Isles of the Caribbean.
See item no. 26.

West Indian odyssey: the complete guide to the islands of the Caribbean.
See item no. 28.

Golden islands of the Caribbean.
See item no. 38.

Sailing and cruising guides

84 Islands to windward: cruising the Caribbees.
   Carleton Mitchell.   New York: D. van Norstrand, 1948. 287p.
The author reports on sailing and anchoring conditions at Dominica (p. 264) while recounting details of his cruise in the *Carib* and his visits ashore in Roseau

and Portsmouth. Four photographs are included in the chapter 'Dominica' (p. 86-97). The voyage is vividly portrayed in the author's *National Geographic* article, '*Carib* cruises the West Indies', vol. 93, no. 1 (Jan. 1948), p. 1-56.

85   Street's cruising guide to the eastern Caribbean.
    Donald M. Street, Jr.   New York: Norton, 1980-86. 4 vols. maps.
    bibliog.

The most detailed and authoritative cruising guide, enabling one to sail safely from Puerto Rico to Venezuela. Vol. I (1981, 246p.) is an introduction, discussing laws and regulations, chartering, wind, weather, tides and sailing basics. Vol. II, part 1, (1985, 150p.) covers *Puerto Rico, the passage islands, the U.S. and British Virgin Islands*. Vol. III (1980, 142p.) describes *Martinique to Trinidad*. Vol. IV (1980, 129p.) explores coastal *Venezuela*. Vol. II, part 2, (1986, 148p.), completely revised and updated in January 1986, and entitled *Anguilla to Dominica*, provides pertinent information on Dominica (p. 131-38). The author discusses the difficulties of anchoring in Woodbridge Bay, Roseau's roadstead, as well as his difficulties with island youths during a visit to Prince Rupert's Bay in March 1984. This new guide replaces the author's *A cruising guide to the Lesser Antilles* (New York: Norton, 1964, 1974).

Tourist development

86   Dominica. A tourist development strategy.
    Shankland Cox and associates.   Liverpool, England: Seel House,
    Aug. 1971. 3 vols. maps.

The Government of Dominica retained this firm of town planners and architects based in London and Kingston to assess the ways in which Dominica could develop a modern tourist economy, exploiting its own distinctive beaches, forests and historical sites. The resulting report is a three-volume complex plan profusely illustrated with photographs, maps, plans and artists' conceptions of tourist facilities. Vol. I is the 'technical report' (209p.); vol. II is the 'planning and policy report' (147p.); and vol. III is a brief summary of the twenty-year project (15p.). The Government ultimately decided against developing an economy based on tourism.

Flora and Fauna

General

87 A forest lover in the Caribbee Islands. IV. The cloud-capped wilderness of Dominica.
J[ohn] S[tewart] Beard. *Journal of the New York Botanical Garden*, vol. 46, no. 550 (Oct. 1945), p. 237-48.
A useful general account of the island's rich natural resources, with a description of the Valley of Desolation and of the major vegetation zones: littoral woodland; seasonal forests; rainforests; elfin (mossy) woodland; and secondary forests. Six photographs accompany the article.

88 A botanist's Dominica diary.
W[alter] H[enricks] Hodge. *Scientific Monthly*, vol. 58, no. 3 (March 1944), p. 185-94; no. 4 (April 1944), p. 281-91. map.
Two popular articles by one of the foremost students of the island's flora and fauna. Part one, 'In and about Roseau', recounts the author's landing at, and perceptions of Roseau, as well as of the Botanic Gardens and his trip into the interior. Part two, 'Off the beaten path', describes his visits to the Boiling Lake, Carib Reserve, Sylvania Estate and Morne Trois Pitons. Throughout are his botanical observations, often illustrated with his photographs.

89 Anomaly island.
Paul Griswold Howes. *Scientific American*, vol. 139, no. 6 (Dec. 1928), p. 516-18.
The author, Curator of Natural History at the Bruce Museum, Greenwich, Connecticut, extolls the 'strange or unique story' of Dominica's flora and fauna, suggesting that scientists need not go to South America for 'unexplored wilderness'. Several photographs illustrate the article.

90 Photographer in the rain-forests.
Paul Griswold Howes. Chicago: Adams Press, 1970. 218p. bibliog.
The author, Curator Emeritus of the Bruce Museum of Natural History, History and Art, Greenwich, Connecticut, describes his expeditions to the rainforests of British Guiana, Dominica and the Colombian Andes. Six of the twenty chapters are devoted to his accounts of the geography, flora and fauna of Dominica (p. 79-134), and are supplemented with thirty-two pages of photographs by the author. Birds, bats, reptiles and amphibians, the 'stinking hole' and an expedition to the summit of Morne Diablotin are featured.

91 Flora and fauna of the Cabrits Peninsula.
Arlington A. James. Roseau: Forestry and Wildlife Division, Ministry of Agriculture, Cabrits Project, 1985. 34p. 2 maps. bibliog.
An excellent description of the plants and animals of a relatively undisturbed portion of Dominica. Appendixes contain local and scientific names of all wildlife mentioned. The author is Forest Officer and Cabrits National Park Project Officer. The booklet, amply illustrated with photographs and drawings, is available from the Superintendent, National Parks, Botanic Gardens, Roseau, Dominica.

92 A naturalist's excursion in Dominica.
Fr. Johow. *Popular Science Monthly*, vol. 26 (March 1885), p. 679-87.
A translation for *Popular Science Monthly* of part of the author's *Vegetationsbilder aus Westindien und Venezuela* (Views of vegetation in the West Indies and Venezuela) in *Kosmos*, vol. 15 (1884), p. 112-30, 270-85, recounting his botanical excursion from Roseau to Laudat and the Boiling Lake. He describes the floral sights along the way. The visit occurred in 1882 or 1883.

93 Camps in the Caribbees: the adventures of a naturalist in the Lesser Antilles.
Frederick A. Ober. Boston: Lee & Shepard, 1886. 366p.
Between 1876 and 1878, under the auspices of the Smithsonian Institution, the author explored the Lesser Antilles, focusing especially on the avifauna, but also including other aspects of natural history. Here he recounts his visits to Martinique, Guadeloupe, Grenada and the Grenadines, St. Vincent, Antigua and Barbuda. More than any other island (p. 1-169), he describes Dominica, its birds, its fauna, natural setting, Boiling Lake, and his experiences among the Caribs, including their social life, appearance and language (p. 90-111).

Flora

94   Mosses of Dominica, British West Indies.
Edwin B. Bartram.   *Bulletin of the British Museum (Natural
History) Botany*, vol. 2, no. 2 (Dec. 1955), p. 37-49.
The first report on Dominican mosses, based on the extensive collection made by
W. R. Elliott between 1892 and 1896 of about 800 specimens. The 155 species and
sixty-eight genera represented are preserved in the British Museum (Natural
History) and represent ninety per cent of the island's moss flora, 'a substantial
contribution to our knowledge of Caribbean moss flora' (p. 37).

95   The natural vegetation of the Windward and Leeward Islands.
J[ohn] S[tewart] Beard.   Oxford: Clarendon Press, 1949. 192p.
maps. bibliog. (Oxford Forestry Memoirs, no. 21, 1948).
A thorough description of the vegetation of the former British and currently
French islands of the eastern Caribbean, based on surveys conducted in 1942-46
by the author as a member of the Colonial Forest Service. The study is divided
into a preliminary discussion, 'Factors of the environment', 'Plant geography',
'Classification of plant communities', 'Description of communities' and 'Comparative studies'. The chapter on Dominica (p. 107-22) 'the most mountainous island
in the Lesser Antilles and the most heavily forested at the present day' (p. 107),
includes lists of sixty species making up the average composition of ten acres of
rainforest (p. 111), fifty-six species, the average in ten acres of lower montane
rainforest (p. 114), and twenty-five species for one acre of montane thicket
(p. 117). Maps, diagrams and photographs enrich this useful volume.

**96   The *Pteridophyta* of the island of Dominica, with notes on various
ferns from tropical America.**
Karel Domin.   Prague: Ed. Grégr & Son, 1929. 259p. bibliog.
(Memoirs of the Royal Czech Society of Sciences, Division of
Natural History and Mathematics, New Series, no. 2).
A major work on Dominica's ferns, resulting from the author's study in 1926 of
plant associations and general ecological conditions. In 'Climatological notes',
'Botanical exploration' and 'Botanical literature' (p. 5-28), the author reviews the
publications and findings of all botanists who had worked on Dominica, and thus
presents a synopsis of 'everything that so far is known about the flora and
vegetation of Dominica' (Preface, p. 1). All specimens cited here are in the Royal
Botanic Gardens herbarium at Kew, England. Forty leaves of plates supplement
the text. The author's two-volume work in Czech, *Travels in West Indies* (Prague,
1928-29) contains extensive information on the history, geography, vegetation and
agriculture of Dominica, plus numerous plates illustrating the island and its
vegetation. Accompanying his English volume *Trinidad and the West Indies*
(Brünn, Czechoslovakia, 1929) is a volume of one hundred photographs of island
vegetation mounted on unbound pages.

97 **Bredin-Archbold-Smithsonian biological survey of Dominica: Myxomycetes from Dominica.**
Marie L. Farr. *Contributions from the United States National Museum*, vol. 37, pt. 6 (1969), p. 397-440. bibliog. map.
From January to March 1966, the author collected over 500 slime mould specimens in the field and sixty-three from 187 moist chamber cultures yielding ninety-six taxa, of which two were new species. This was the first extensive investigation of slime moulds in Dominica. The author's description of collecting on Dominica, comparisons of the findings with those known from other islands, and a map of collection locations broaden the value of this scientific contribution to the study of the island's floral life.

98 **Miscellaneous contributions towards a flora of Dominica, British West Indies.**
Walter Henricks Hodge. PhD thesis, Harvard University, Cambridge, Massachusetts, 1941. 218 leaves.
This study of island flora was the first doctoral dissertation based on fieldwork in Dominica. The author collected plant specimens during 1937, 1938 and 1940, some of which are seen in this work's twenty-six plates. This study and its fieldwork served as the basis for the author's numerous future botanical reports.

99 **A synopsis of the palms of Dominica.**
Walter Henricks Hodge. *Caribbean Forester*, vol. 3, no. 3 (April 1942), p. 103-09.
A description of the palm flora of the island, composed of seven species representing five genera, only one of which was previously recorded for Dominica. Six photographs illustrate the descriptions.

100 **Plants used by the Dominica Caribs.**
W. H. Hodge. *Journal of the New York Botanical Garden*, vol. 43, no. 512 (Aug. 1942), p. 189-201. map.
An account, supplemented with photographs by the author, of the numerous uses made of plants by the Carib Indians, including those plants used for dugout canoes, baskets, fish poisons, household articles and cultivation. The author was in the Department of Botany at Massachusetts State College at the time of publication.

101 **The vegetation of Dominica.**
W[alter] H[enricks] Hodge. *Geographical Review*, vol. 33, no. 3 (July 1943), p. 349-75. 2 maps. bibliog.
A botanical tour of the island's flora, using a climatic basis for plant classification. A discussion of the vegetation is organized around four major zones: the pantropical or xerophytic vegetation of the coastal strip, the transitional zone; the mesophytic or rainforest zone; and the mossy or elfin forest of the mountains above 3,000 feet. Twenty-two photographs of vegetation illustrate the article.

102 Flora of Dominica, B.W.I.
W[alter] H[enricks] Hodge. *Lloydia*, vol. 17, no. 1 (March 1954), p. 1-238. 3 maps. bibliog.

The most comprehensive survey of Dominica's flora published. The author, who began fieldwork on the island in 1937 and wrote his PhD thesis on the subject in 1941 (*Miscellaneous contributions towards a flora of Dominica, British West Indies*, Harvard University, Cambridge, Massachusetts), sets forth a systematic description of five types of plant community: swamp forest; dry evergreen; seasonal; rainforest; and montane. The majority of the work consists of a catalogue of the vascular plants. Especially interesting to the non-specialist is the brief history of botanical exploration in the island (p. 44-50), followed by a bibliographic listing (p. 50-52). Rainfall tables, figures and photographs supplement the text.

103 The ethnobotany of the Island Caribs of Dominica.
W[alter] H[enricks] Hodge, Douglas Taylor. *Webbia*, vol. 12, no. 2 (March 1957), p. 513-644. 2 maps. bibliog.

An excellent collaboration between the authorities on the subjects aiming 'to provide accurate botanical and ethnological information about species gathered or cultivated by the Caribs of Dominica not only today but also (as far as possible) in the past' (p. 518). Historical notes, indexes to scientific, French-based Creole and Island Carib names of plants, and forty figures complete a full description of the plants' uses. This work is also reproduced in the Human Relations Area Files under ST 13 Callinago, no. 13.

104 Caribbean wild plants and their uses: an illustrated guide to some medicinal and wild ornamental plants of the West Indies.
Penelope N[arodny] Honychurch. London; Basingstoke, England: Macmillan Caribbean, 1986. 166p.

The best guide to common and uncommon wild plants in Dominica, with botanical and medicinal aspects of each plant described, and with 212 line-drawings by the author. Included and increasing the usefulness of the volume are several appendixes: 'Compounds of medicinal interest'; 'Summary of medicinal plants'; 'Plants used for fodder'; 'Sources of nectar for honeybees'; 'Glossary'; 'Reference list'; 'Index to French and patois names'; 'Index to English names'; and 'Index to scientific names'. A slightly different edition was published in 1980 (Barbados: Letchworth Press. 163p.).

105 Flora of the Lesser Antilles: Leeward and Windward Islands.
Edited by Richard A. Howard. Jamaica Plain, Massachusetts: Arnold Arboretum, Harvard University, 1974-79. 3 vols. bibliog.

A landmark study of Lesser Antillean flora, by the Director of the Arnold Arboretum at Harvard University, Cambridge, Massachusetts. It comprises three volumes: Volume 1, *Orchidaceae*, by Leslie A. Garay and Herman R. Sweet, 1974; Volume 2, *Pteridophyta*, by George R. Proctor, 1977; and Volume 3, *Monocotyledonae*, by Richard A. Howard, 1979. Extensive formal accounts of Dominica's vegetation run throughout the volumes, which are illustrated and contain maps and bibliographies.

106 **Studies on soil microfungi of Nigeria and Dominica.**
Liang Hsiung Huang. PhD thesis, University of Wisconsin,
Madison, Wisconsin, 1971. 413p. bibliog. (Available from University
Microfilms, Ann Arbor, Michigan, 1972. Order no. 72-2014).
In a pioneer study of 4,480 soil samples from twenty-six uncultivated sites in
Nigeria and nine undisturbed rainforest sites in Dominica, 182 soil fungi were
recorded for Nigeria and thirty-six for Dominica, with sixteen species found
common to both tropical areas. As a result, several new species were discovered
and the known geographic ranges for several more were substantially extended.

107 **Freshwater swamps and mangrove species in Dominica.**
Arlington James. [Roseau]: Forestry Division, Ministry of
Agriculture, 1980. 37p. 2 maps. bibliog.
The author describes the three major types of swamp formation (the freshwater
swamp, the rainforest swamp and the herbaceous swamp) and their associated
mangrove species, seeking to 'generate an appreciation among readers for our wet
lands and their role in the ecology of their immediate environment' (p. [iii]). The
majority of the discussion is on the freshwater swamp and its dominant species of
tree 'Bois Mang' (*Pterocarpus officinalis*). The booklet provides an important
addition to the botanical literature on the island, since it contains descriptions of
the black-and-white maritime mangrove species whose existence had been
overlooked by earlier botanists. Drawings and photographs by the author
illustrate the text.

108 **Cabrits plants and their uses.**
Compiled by Arlington A. James. Roseau: Forestry and Wildlife
Division, Ministry of Agriculture, 1986. 48p. map. bibliog. (Cabrits
Project Report).
This publication describes the uses of sixty-seven of the ninety-two species
identified by an intensive study of the Cabrits Peninsula in north-western
Dominica, part of the developing national park system. The report is divided into
two sections: 'Uses of shrubs, herbs, grasses and vines' (p. 1-15), twenty-seven
species; and 'Uses of trees' (p. 17-39), forty species. Appendixes give summaries
of plant uses, list families and genera, and local and common names of the
species. Photographs and line-drawings by Lennox Honychurch identify many of
the species, the uses of each of which are described in the text. It is available from
the Superintendent, National Parks, Botanic Gardens, Roseau, Dominica.

109 **Official guide to the Botanic Gardens, Dominica, (illustrated) with
an index of the principal plants.**
[Joseph Jones]. Barbados: Advocate Company, n.d. [1915?]. 44p.
map.
An excellent guide for visitors to what many once considered the finest botanic
garden in the region, by the man most responsible for creating it. The guide
combines a history and general description of the gardens with a detailed walking

tour. Both exotic and common flora are quickly located by the index and many are identified by photographs. The author was Curator of the Botanic Gardens from 1892 to 1924.

Thirty years in the jungle.
See item no. 36.

Caribbean isles.
See item no. 46.

Volcanism and vegetation in the Lesser Antilles.
See item no. 51.

The mountains of Dominica.
See item no. 52.

Dominica.
See item no. 63.

The history of the island of Dominica, containing a description of its situation, extent, climate, mountains, rivers, natural productions, etc., etc., together with an account of the civil government, trade, laws, customs, and manners of the different inhabitants of that island. Its conquest by the French, and restoration to the British dominions.
See item no. 191.

Relation of crown diameter to stem diameter in forests of Puerto Rico, Dominica, and Thailand.
See item no. 387.

A comparison of environments of rain forests in Dominica, British West Indies, and Puerto Rico.
See item no. 388.

Dominica forest and park system plan.
See item no. 389.

Is Dominica's forest doomed?
See item no. 390.

Dominica: a chance for a choice. Some considerations and recommendations on conservation on the island's natural resources.
See item no. 393.

Dominica multiple land use project.
See item no. 394.

Dominica's national park: vegetation.
See item no. 399.

Dominica's Morne Trois Pitons National Park.
See item no. 401.

A resource guide to Dominica, 1493-1986.

See item no. 489.

Dominica.

See item no. 490.

Fauna

110 Zoogeography of Antillean bats.

Robert J. Baker, Hugh H. Genoways. In: *Zoogeography in the Caribbean: the 1975 Leidy Medal Symposium.* Edited by F. B. Gill. Philadelphia: Academy of Natural Sciences of Philadelphia, 1978, vol. 13, p. 1-128. 7 maps. bibliog.

In this comprehensive article on bat zoogeography, the authors discuss the genera and species present, models of faunal origin, geographic origins of fauna, distributional patterns, endemism, and similarity of insular faunas for the Lesser and Greater Antilles. Each island's bat species, including the twelve species in Dominica, are identified and compared in extensive tables and in maps.

111 Nidification of the birds of Dominica, B. W. I.

James Bond. *The Auk*, vol. 58, no. 3 (9 July 1941), p. 364-75.

The expert on Caribbean birds describes the fifty-four species supposed to nest on Dominica. His descriptions are based not only on his visit in 1927 and on collections made by Frederick Ober and the Verrills in the last century, but especially upon specimens, eggs and nests of no less than forty-two species, sent to the Academy of Natural Sciences of Philadelphia by Percival Agar of Dominica. The author describes the island as 'better known ornithologically than any other island of the group' (p. 364).

112 Birds of the West Indies.

James Bond. Boston, Massachusetts: Houghton Mifflin, 1985. 5th American ed. 256p. maps.

This standard reference work on more than four hundred bird species known to occur in the West Indies is based on the author's research which began in 1926. Ranges, island locations, descriptions, sounds and local names for each bird are noted, and ninety-four colour illustrations by Don R. Eckelberry and 186 line-drawings by Earl L. Poole are included, making this a very useful field guide. The author, whose name was appropriated for the character created by Ian Fleming, is Curator of Birds at the Academy of Natural Sciences of Philadelphia. This is a revised edition based on *Birds of the West Indies* (Philadelphia: Academy of Natural Sciences of Philadelphia, 1936) and *Field Guide to the Birds of the West Indies* (New York: Macmillan, 1947).

Flora and Fauna. Fauna

113   Bredin-Archbold-Smithsonian biological survey of Dominica: the
      Phoridae of Dominica (Diptera).
      Thomas Borgmeier.   *Smithsonian Contributions to Zoology*,
      no. 23 (1969), p. 1-69. bibliog.
A description of the collection of phorid flies made in 1964 by members of the
biological survey team and sent to the author, a priest in Rio de Janeiro, Brazil.
Phorid flies usually run along the ground and many species live underground in
ants' or termites' nests. This collection consists of eighty-two species, of which
forty-three are new.

114   Bredin-Archbold-Smithsonian biological survey of Dominica: the
      freshwater and terrestrial decapod crustaceans of the West Indies
      with special reference to Dominica.
      Fenner A. Chace, Jr., Horton H. Hobbs, Jr.   *United States
      National Museum Bulletin*, no. 292 (1969), p. 1-258. 2 maps.
      bibliog.
Everything you might want to know about the land crabs and freshwater shrimps
of Dominica is presented in this comprehensive monograph. The study identifies
and details the habits and habitats of twenty-nine species from Dominica through
text, eight photographs and numerous line-drawings; in addition, ninety-two
species from the broader West Indian region are included. The second author
collected 7,225 specimens during his visits in January-April 1964 and 1966; both
authors are Senior Zoologists in the Department of Invertebrate Zoology at the
Smithsonian Institution, Washington, DC.

115   Bredin-Archbold-Smithsonian biological survey of Dominica: the
      Trichoptera (Caddisflies) of the Lesser Antilles.
      Oliver S. Flint, Jr.   In: *Proceedings of the United States National
      Museum*, vol. 125, no. 3665 (1968), p. 1-86. bibliog. 2 maps.
The author's participation in the biological survey of Dominica in 1963 allowed
him to collect thirty-six species of these moth-like flies, triple the number found
on other Lesser Antillean islands. He describes these in detail and explains the
distribution of the caddisflies in the region.

116   On the terrestrial mollusca of Dominica and Grenada; with an
      account of some new species from Trinidad.
      R. J. Lechmere Guppy.   *Annals and Magazine of Natural History*,
      vol. 4, no. 1 (1868), p. 429-42.
The first scientific account of twenty species of land mollusc from Dominica, nine
of them for the first time anywhere. The author's notes, however, are said to be
'extremely erroneous' by A. D. Brown in his 'Notes on the land-shells of
Dominica', *American Naturalist*, vol. 15, no. 1 (Jan. 1881), p. 56-57. Next to
birds, land molluscs were the most collected and studied faunal types on
Dominica. George French Angas reported on twenty species in 'On the terrestrial
mollusca of Dominica, collected during a recent visit to that island' in *Proceedings
of the Zoological Society of London* (4 Dec. 1883, p. 594-97). Henry A. Pilsbry
described fourteen species found at 1,000-2,500 feet elevations in March, April

35

Flora and Fauna. Fauna

and May, 1890, in 'On a collection of land mollusca from the island of Dominica, West Indies', *Transactions of the Connecticut Academy of Arts and Sciences* (vol. 8, April 1892, p. 356-58).

117 Wild life in Dominica.
Paul Griswold Howes. *Natural History*, vol. 30, no. 1 (Jan.-Feb. 1930), p. 90-103.
Two brief expeditions in 1926 and 1929 provided the author with a wealth of plants and animals to study. He describes a range of fauna from earthworms and crustaceans to agouti and bats, providing photographs of many specimens.

118 Boa constrictors and other pets.
Paul Griswold Howes. *Natural History*, vol. 31, no. 3 (May-June 1931), p. 300-09.
The author's 1930 expedition focused on Dominica's reptiles. He describes several species of snake, gecko and lizard, and there are photographs of these, as well as of island scenes.

119 A record of *Eptesicus fuscus* (Chiroptera: Vespertilionidae) from Dominica, West Indies.
J. E. Hill, P. G. H. Evans. *Mammalia*, vol. 49, no. 1 (1985), p. 133-36.
This article is a product of the ecological studies of bats, the most numerous mammals by far in Dominica, carried out from 1982 to 1984 by Evans. The Big Brown bat *Eptesicus fuscus* had not been recorded in Dominica before this report, and the authors describe this and other species of bat captured on the island. This data supplements the broader description of twelve Dominican bat species in R. J. Baker and H. H. Genoways's 'Zoogeography of Antillean bats' in *Zoogeography in the Caribbean*, edited by F. B. Gill. (Philadelphia: Academy of Natural Sciences of Philadelphia, Special publication 13, p. 53-97).

120 Monkeys in the West Indies.
John Imray. *Nature* (London), vol. 21 (19 Feb. 1880), p. 371-72.
Dr. Imray describes the introduction of monkeys to Trinidad, St. Kitts and Nevis, and compares this to the accidental introduction of opossums to Dominica about forty years earlier. The opossums flourished and nearly caused the disappearance of the crapaud, Dominica's large edible frog.

121 Bredin-Archbold-Smithsonian biological survey of Dominica: 1. The echinoids of Dominica.
Porter M. Kier. *Proceedings of the United States National Museum*, vol. 121, no. 3577 (1966), p. 1-10. map. bibliog.
The first in a series of faunal studies resulting from the biological survey of Dominica. The author describes ten species of sea urchin collected in April 1964 mostly on the Caribbean side of Dominica down to depths of eighty-five feet. A

locator map and photographs accompany the text. The author was Associate Curator, Division of Invertebrate Paleontology, Smithsonian Institution, at the time.

122 Catalogue of the birds of Dominica from collections made for the Smithsonian Institution by Frederick A. Ober, together with his notes and observations.
George N[ewbold] Lawrence. *Proceedings of the United States National Museum*, vol. 1 (31 July 1878), p. 48-69.
Ornithologist G. N. Lawrence corresponded extensively with naturalist Frederick A. Ober. During Ober's second visit to the island in 1877, he had an attack of fever. Lawrence organized the collections Ober sent back, and described fifty-six species as well as the island itself from Ober's notes and observations. After making his collections, Ober reports that he went to live with the Caribs for six weeks, where he procured more birds.

123 The Lesser Antillean representatives of *Bothrops* and *Constrictor*.
James D. Lazell, Jr. *Bulletin of the Museum of Comparative Zoology, Harvard University*, vol. 132, no. 3 (Dec. 1964), p. 245-73. 2 maps. bibliog.
The author re-evaluates the taxonomic relationship of the largest Lesser Antillean snakes: two species of the poisonous 'Fer-de-lance' or *Bothrops*, found on St. Lucia and Martinique; and two subspecies of *Constrictor*, from St. Lucia and Dominica, where it is called 'Tet'chien'. Each snake is illustrated, and its range, habitat, habits and physical characteristics are described. On Dominica this two-metre-long reptile is described as 'amazingly abundant' (p. 266).

124 Bredin-Archbold-Smithsonian biological survey of Dominica: the family Dolichopodidae with some related Antillean and Panamanian species (Diptera).
Harold Robinson. *Smithsonian Contributions to Zoology*, no. 185 (1975), p. 1-141. bibliog.
An especially full account of the long-legged flies of Dominica. Of the thirty genera and 113 species described, three genera and sixty-nine species are new. The author is in the Department of Botany at the National Museum of Natural History, Smithsonian Institution, Washington, DC, and collected on Dominica between January and April 1965.

125 The black flies of Dominica.
Alan Stone. *Proceedings of the Entomological Society of Washington*, vol. 71, no. 3 (Sept. 1969), p. 312-18. bibliog.
A description of three species of black fly, none previously reported from Dominica, and one a new species, based on data and specimens collected by several scientists on Dominica from 1956 to 1966 as members of the Bredin-Archbold-Smithsonian biological survey.

126 **Bredin-Archbold-Smithsonian biological survey of Dominica: the mosquitoes of Dominica (Diptera: Culicidae).**
Alan Stone. *Smithsonian Contributions to Zoology*, no. 16 (1969), p. 1-8. bibliog.
The author describes the distribution and biology, and lists collection data for twenty-two species of mosquito in Dominica, seventeen of which were reported on the island for the first time. The species described were collected not only by members of this biological survey, but also by others as far back as 1905. The author works in the Systematic Entomology Laboratory of the US Department of Agriculture at the Smithsonian Institution.

127 **Notes on the fauna of the island of Dominica, British West Indies, with lists of the species obtained and observed by G. E. and A. H. Verrill.**
G[eorge] E[lliott] Verrill. *Transactions of the Connecticut Academy of Arts and Sciences*, vol. 8, no. 42 (April 1892), p. 315-55. bibliog.
The observations and collections of the Verrill brothers in Dominica from March to May 1890. Twenty-six birds are described in detail, and a check-list of sixty-three species, all those recorded by visiting naturalists and ornithologists, including E. C. Taylor (1863), F. A. Ober (1877) and G. Ramage (1887-88) is included. Fourteen batrachians and reptiles are described, as are four land and freshwater crustaceans. Three photo-lithographic plates illustrate twenty specimens.

128 **The wildlife of Dominica.**
Michael P. Zamore. Roseau: Forestry Division, Ministry of Agriculture, n.d. 32p. map. bibliog.
This recent conservation-oriented booklet, available from the Forestry Division, Ministry of Agriculture, Botanical Garden, Roseau, Dominica, was published to educate the public on the island's most familiar wildlife. The agouti, opossum, wild pig, crapaud, iguana, thirteen bird species, three kinds of shrimp and three freshwater or land crabs are discussed, and many are illustrated. The author is Assistant Forest Officer and officer-in-charge of the Forestry Protection Service.

129 **The jungle crusade of 'Holly Parrot'.**
David R. Zimmerman. *New York Times Magazine*, (6 Aug. 1978), p. 13, 14, 16, 18, 42-43, 45, 56, 58. map.
A profile, amply illustrated with photographs, of American Holly Nichols who, with her husband Tom, has worked to save Dominica's endangered species of parrot from poachers and parrot smugglers.

130   **Ecology and adaptations of the trembler on the island of Dominica.**
       Richard L. Zusi. *Living Bird*, vol. 8 (1 Nov. 1969), p. 137-64.
       bibliog. (Eighth Annual of the Cornell Laboratory of
       Ornithology).
Report on a study of this tropical evergreen forest resident on Dominica 'the last
of the islands within its range to remain extensively forested and thus the last
island on which the species in widespread and common' (p. 137). It is based on
the author's researches from January to April 1964 and March to April 1968, as a
member of the Bredin-Archbold-Smithsonian biological survey of Dominica.
Drawings from field sketches and photographs accompany the article.

Mount Joy.
See item no. 17.

The mountains of Dominica.
See item no. 52.

Dominica multiple land use project.
See item no. 394.

**The dilemma of the *Amazona imperialis* and *Amazona arausiaca* parrots in
Dominica following Hurricane David in 1979.**
See item no. 395.

Endangered parrots.
See item no. 397.

Dominica's national park: wildlife.
See item no. 399.

**The complete Caribbeana 1900-1975: a bibliographic guide to the
scholarly literature.**
See item no. 482.

A resource guide to Dominica, 1493-1986.
See item no. 489.

Amerindians

Prehistory and archaeology

131 On the historicity of Carib migrations in the Lesser Antilles.
Louis Allaire. *American Antiquity*, vol. 45, no. 2 (April 1980),
p. 238-45. map. bibliog.
By a critical examination of the documentary and archaeological evidence, the
author questions the historicity of Carib migrations to the Lesser Antilles. Neither
pottery nor historical accounts is adequate in dating a migration to the islands.
The term 'Island Carib', he suggests, is valid only as a linguistic term; 'it cannot
claim to apply to cultural or ethnic realities' (p. 243). He proposes a very late
migration of Arawakan peoples rapidly acculturated to mainland Carib culture.
The author is in the Department of Anthropology at the University of Manitoba,
Edmonton, Canada.

132 The lack of archeology on Dominica.
Clifford Evans.   In: *Proceedings of the Second International
Congress for the Study of Pre-Columbian Cultures of the Lesser
Antilles*. Edited by Ripley P. Bullen. St. Ann's Garrison,
Barbados: Barbados Museum and Historical Society, 1968, p. 93-
102. map. bibliog.
The first published article specifically concerned with the archaeological aspects of
Dominica. A one-month archaeological survey of the island in 1966 by the author,
a respected anthropologist from the Smithsonian Institution, produced evidence
of three phases of occupation: pre-Arawak; Arawak; and historical Carib.
Because the sites are shallow, and because an important foodsource for shellfish
for the early inhabitants, mangroves, is absent, the author concludes that
ecological conditions made Dominica a useful temporary place of settlement, but

Amerindians. Prehistory and archaeology

that it was 'unattractive as a permanent place of habitation' compared to larger nearby islands (p. 101). The survey was conducted as part of the Bredin-Archbold-Smithsonian biological survey of Dominica.

133 A prehistoric island culture area of America.
J. Walter Fewkes. In: *Thirty-fourth annual report of the Bureau of American Ethnology*. Washington, DC: United States Government Printing Office, 1922, p. 35-271.
A detailed archaeological report based on the author's visits to the West Indies in the winter of 1912-13, to several European museums in the winter of 1913-14, and his analysis of some 9,500 prehistoric objects from the West Indies in the collection of the Museum of the American Indian (Heye Foundation). The account of his brief time in Dominica and the implements from that island (p. 123-28) provides one of the few early 20th-century discussions of Dominica prehistory. Line-drawings and photographs of implements, and numerous photographic plates supplement the report.

134 Archaeological materials from Dominica in North American and European museums.
Robert A. Myers. In: *Proceedings of the Eighth International Congress for the Study of the Pre-Columbian Cultures of the Lesser Antilles*. Edited by Suzanne M. Lewenstein. Tempe, Arizona: Arizona State University, 1980, p. 473-80. bibliog.
(Anthropological Research Papers, no. 22).
As part of an effort to establish the size of the pre-European Amerindian population of Dominica, the author surveyed twenty museums and collections in the United States and Britain. The survey turned up relatively few specimens, although materials in many museums are labelled 'West Indian' without specifying the particular island.

135 Note descriptive de la collection d'objets lithiques de la librairie publique de Roseau-Dominique (W. I.). (A descriptive note on the collection of stone objects in the Roseau Public Library.)
Henry Petitjean Roget. In: *Proceedings of the Seventh International Congress for the Study of Pre-Colombian [sic] Cultures of the Lesser Antilles, Caracas, Venezuela, 11-16 July 1977*. Edited by Jean Benoist, Francine-M. Mayer. Montreal: Centre de recherches caraïbes, Université de Montréal, 1978, p. 117-35. map. bibliog.
A description, with photographs, diagrams and a location map, of the only collection of Amerindian stone artefacts on Dominica. Of the 159 objects, the discovery site is known for only fifty-four. Forty-seven stone pieces appear in photographs.

41

136 **Reconnaissance archéologique à l'île de la Dominique (West Indies).**
(Archaeological reconnaissance of the island of Dominica, West Indies.)
Henry Petitjean Roget.   In: *Proceedings of the Seventh International Congress for the Study of Pre-Colombian [sic] Cultures of the Lesser Antilles, Caracas, Venezuela, 11-16 July 1977.* Edited by Jean Benoist, Francine-M. Mayer. Montreal: Centre de recherches caraïbes, Université de Montréal, 1978, p. 81-97. 18 maps. bibliog.

The most extensive archaeological survey of the island. The author, an archaeologist resident in Martinique, located twenty-four sites in May 1976 and March 1977. He provides descriptions and location maps of seventeen sites, and photographs of the ceramic artefacts found. The author describes the brief archaeological investigations of others in Dominica, and suggests that additional efforts will be very productive.

Historical and contemporary Island Caribs

137 **An inquiry into the structure of Island Carib culture.**
Eugene Pendleton Banks.   PhD thesis, Harvard University, Cambridge, Massachusetts, 1954. 263 leaves. 2 maps. bibliog.

This well-written anthropological study directed by Clyde Kluckhohn was based on ten months' fieldwork in 1950-51. This is the second doctoral dissertation written about a Dominican topic and the first written on the Island Caribs, whose culture is described. Twenty photographs supplement the text. The author is Professor of Anthropology at Wake Forest University, Winston-Salem, North Carolina.

138 **Island Carib folktales.**
E[ugene] P[endleton] Banks.   *Caribbean Quarterly*, vol. 4, no. 1 (Jan. 1955), p. 32-39.

The author discusses the reasons for studying Island Carib tales, and describes some of the work of Raymond Breton, Jacques Bouton and Douglas Taylor on the Caribs. To this he adds three tales collected in 1951, places them in a broader regional folklore perspective and encourages others to collect Carib tales before they disappear completely.

139   A Carib village in Dominica.
E[ugene] P[endleton] Banks. *Social and Economic Studies*,
vol. 5, no. 1 (March 1956), p. 74-86. map. bibliog.

A description of the village of Bataka, the largest Carib community in Dominica's
Carib Reserve, based on fieldwork done in 1950-51. Among the 201 residents of
thirty-five households, the author discusses the importance of kin relations,
marriage patterns, the extended family, work patterns and village structure.

140   The Caribs of Dominica.
H[enry] Hesketh Bell. *Journal of the Barbados Museum and
Historical Society*, vol. 5, no. 1 (Nov. 1937), p. 18-31.

An abridged version of Administrator Bell's 29 July 1902 official 'Report on the
Caribs of Dominica', introduced by C. N. C. Roach. Bell contrasts the historical
Caribs with those living in 1902, and proposes the establishment of a Carib
Reserve on 3,700 acres officially surveyed by A. P. Skeat, with a small stipend for
the Carib Chief. Roach recounts his interview with a Carib recruit in December
1916. The original report, with a map showing the Carib Reserve, appears in
Colonial Reports, Miscellaneous, no. 21, Cd. 1298 (London: HM Stationery
Office).

141   The memoirs of Père Labat, 1693-1705.
[Jean Baptiste Labat], translated and abridged by John Eaden.
Introduction by Philip Gosse. London: Constable, 1931.
Reprinted, London: Cass, 1970. 263p. (Cass Library of West
Indian Studies, no. 8).

A useful translation and abridgement of one of the important early French
accounts of the Lesser Antilles, *Nouveau voyage aux isles de l'Amérique* (Paris:
Giffart, 1722). Jean Baptiste Labat (1663-1738) left Marseilles in 1693, spent
several years in the French islands, and in January 1700 stayed for seventeen days
among the Dominica Caribs, who numbered perhaps 2,000 by his estimate. His
accounts of the visit and of the Caribs in general are rendered in three chapters:
'Carib Indians' (p. 70-84); 'A Carib carbet' (p. 85-91); and 'Dominica Caribs'
(p. 92-115).

142   Les derniers Caraïbes, leur vie dans une réserve de la Dominique.
(The last Caribs, their life in a Dominican reservation.)
Jean-Baptiste Delawarde. *Journal de la Société des Américanistes
de Paris*, vol. 30 (1938), p. 167-204. 2 maps. bibliog.

An account of Carib culture in April-May 1936. The author, a priest, provides
historical and contemporary information, describing the Caribs' lack of religion
and traditions, farming and hunting activities, material culture, daily activities,
fishing, trading and legends. Sketches by the author and nineteen photographs
supplement the text.

Amerindians. Historical and contemporary Island Caribs

143 Histoire générale des Antilles habitées par les françois. (General history of the French Antilles.)
Jean-Baptiste Du Tertre. Paris: Thomas Jolly, 1667. 2 vols.

The earliest and perhaps most valuable of the ethnographic works by 17th-century French missionaries. Where the Island Caribs are concerned, information is derived primarily from Father Raymond Breton's work. This is fortunate because Breton's descriptive study was lost and only his annotated linguistic work remains. Marshall McKusick and Pierre Verin translated the portion from Du Tertre's *History* on the Amerindians as 'Concerning the natives of the Antilles', for inclusion in the Human Relations Area Files, ST 13 Callinago, no. 4, p. 1-42. This describes the Island Caribs' origins, religion, life cycle, occupations, commerce, feasts, food and treatment of visitors, ornaments, material culture, warfare, weapons and attitudes toward disease, death and funerals.

144 The Caribs of Dominica.
Patrick Leigh Fermor. *Geographical Magazine*, vol. 23, no. 6 (Oct. 1950), p. 256-64. map.

An account of Island Carib life on the Reserve as it appeared to the author during his visit. Photographs of Chief George Frederick and of daily activities enrich the article, which is partially composed of extracts from the author's *The traveller's tree* (New York: Harper & Row, 1950).

145 In our Carib Indian village.
Faustulus Joseph Frederick with Elizabeth Shepherd. New York: Lothrop, Lee & Shepard, 1971. 96p. 4 maps. bibliog.

The only children's book about Dominica, and the only book written and illustrated by a Dominican Island Carib. An excellent introduction for primary grades to the historical Carib Indians and to their way of life in the Reserve in Dominica today. Line-drawings by brothers Faustulus and Mas Clem Frederick portray house styles and daily activities, while reproductions of prints from the New York Public Library give historical depth to the introductory section by writer Elizabeth Shepherd. Instructions on how to make a 'finger catcher' and a glossary of French-based Creole terms are included.

146 The Caribs and their colonizers: the problem of land.
Chief Hilary Frederick. Tripoli: International Organization for the Elimination of All Forms of Racial Discrimination (EAFORD), [1981]. 20p. map. bibliog. (Paper no. 23).

This paper, prepared by Yusuf M. Hamid, General Secretary of the Caribbean branch of EAFORD, was presented by the Carib Chief at the NGO Conference on the Rights of Indigenous People and Their Land at Geneva, 15-18 September 1981. The paper discusses the legal history of the Carib Reserve boundaries, and argues that the Reserve is being encroached upon on its southern and western boundaries. The publication is available from EAFORD's London office at 35-37 Ludgate Hill, London EC4M 7JN or EAFORD-CARIB, PO Box 159, Roseau, Dominica.

147 **The Carib population of Dominica.**
Anthony Layng. PhD thesis, Case Western Reserve University, Cleveland, Ohio, 1976. 243 leaves. 2 maps. bibliog. (Available from University Microfilms, Ann Arbor, Michigan, 1978. Order no. 7803906).

An ethnographic description of the Island Caribs during the author's 1974-75 fieldwork, with emphasis on historical and structural contexts, and the ways in which residence on the Reserve forms the foundation to Carib identity and economic activity. This study served as the basis for the author's *The Carib Reserve* (Washington, DC: University Press of America, 1983).

148 **Religion among the Caribs.**
Anthony Layng. *Caribbean Review*, vol. 8, no. 2 (spring 1979), p. 36-41.

An account of religion, including both Roman Catholic and folk beliefs, among Dominica's Island Caribs, and its role in maintaining social boundaries between the Caribs and their Afro-Dominican neighbours. Three photographs by the author supplement the article.

149 **The Carib Reserve: identity and security in the West Indies.**
Anthony Layng, foreword by Leo A. Despres. Washington, DC: University Press of America, 1983, 177p. 3 maps. bibliog.

The first book-length account of Dominica's Island Caribs. The author, Professor of Anthropology at Elmira College, Elmira, New York, stresses the role of the Reserve in maintaining a distinct Carib ethnic identity. He views continuation of reservation status as an adaptive strategy reducing competition with non-Caribs for land. The book is based on nine months' fieldwork in 1974-75 and supplemented by eight black-and-white photographs and eight tables.

150 **The Caribs of Dominica: prospects for structural assimilation of a territorial minority.**
Anthony Layng. *Ethnic Groups*, vol. 6, no. 2-3 (1985), p. 209-21. map. bibliog.

Following a sketch of their history, the author discusses the Island Caribs as a distinct minority group characterized by differential access to material resources, prejudicial treatment and stereotypes, endogamy, assumed identifiability, and common fate identity. He argues that they will 'decide that retaining a reservation status is no longer in their own interests' (p. 218) and that, 'early in the next century, Caribs will willingly relinquish both their reservation status and, consequently, their minority status' (p. 219). This article complements the author's earlier 'Ethnic identity, population growth, and economic security on a West Indian reservation' in *Revista/Review Interamericana*, vol. 9, no. 4 (winter 1979/80), p. 577-84.

151 **Ethnohistorical vs. ecological considerations: the case of Dominica's Amerindians.**
Robert A. Myers. In: *Proceedings of the Seventh International Congress for the Study of Pre-Colombian [sic] Cultures of the Lesser Antilles, Caracas, Venezuela, 11-16 July 1977.* Edited by Jean Benoist, Francine-M. Mayer. Montreal: Centre de recherches caraïbes, Université de Montréal, 1978, p. 325-41. bibliog.

An article arguing for more extensive Amerindian settlement of Dominica than is claimed in Clifford Evans's 'The lack of archeology on Dominica' (Barbados, 1968). The author traces historical accounts of European-Amerindian contact, describes the archaeological collection in the Victoria Museum in Roseau, and suggests that archaeological investigation of the island is still at an early stage, with the most important sites located under contemporary towns and villages.

152 **Island Carib cannibalism.**
Robert A. Myers. *Nieuwe West-Indische Gids/New West Indian Guide*, vol. 58, no. 3/4 (1984), p. 147-84. bibliog.

A review of the literature debating the existence of Island Carib cannibalism, as well as the earliest documentary evidence for the act. Each claim of observed cannibalism is examined as is archaeological evidence (none), linguistic evidence (none), and relevant historical cartography. The author concludes that William Arens's thesis in *The man-eating myth* (New York, London: Oxford University Press, 1979) about the mythology of anthropophagy is true for the region occupied by the Island Caribs.

153 **Les Caraïbes des Antilles: leur représentants actuels dans l'île de la Dominique.** (The Caribs of the Antilles: their present-day representatives on the island of Dominica.)
M. Neveu-Lemaire. *La Géographie*, vol. 35, no. 2 (1921), p. 127-46. 2 maps. bibliog.

An early 20th-century summary account of the Dominican Island Caribs which includes a comparison of the Carib vocabulary collected by Dr. Daniel Thaly in 1916 and 1918 with the mid-17th-century vocabulary from Raymond Breton's Carib–French dictionary. The author includes photographs of Chief J. B. Corriette and of a 'stone hatchet attributed to the Caribs'. This article, originally published by the Société de Géographie of Paris, was translated into English by Marie Dickerman and included in the Human Relations Area Files, ST 13 Callinago, no. 10, p. 1-15.

154 **Aborigines of the West Indies.**
Frederick A. Ober. *Proceedings of the American Antiquarian Society*, vol. 9 (1895), p. 270-313. bibliog.

Based on the author's exploration of the Lesser Antilles and extensive historical research, this article describes the Amerindians of the Bahamas, the Greater and Lesser Antilles, their origins, contacts with Europeans and their artefacts. The author sent the first collection of Island Carib artefacts to the United States. Pages 295-313 of this article concern the Island Carib of Dominica and are printed in the Human Relations Area Files, ST 13 Callinago, no. 9.

155 **Land and politics in a Carib Indian community: a study of ethnicity.**
Nancy Hammack Owen. PhD thesis, University of
Massachusetts, Amherst, Massachusetts, 1974. 230 leaves. bibliog.
(Available from University Microfilms, Ann Arbor, Michigan,
1975. Order no. 75-6066).

This anthropological study, based on thirteen months' fieldwork in 1970 and 1972, examines the mechanisms by which the Caribs have created and maintained an ethnic identity, despite cultural and physical similarities to the Afro-Dominican Creole population. The author analyses the Dominican situation, suggesting that a 'cultural pool of traits' model is more useful than the 'cultural pluralism' model in explaining persistent Carib ethnicity.

156 **Land, politics, and ethnicity in a Carib Indian community.**
Nancy H[ammack] Owen. *Ethnology*, vol. 14, no. 4 (Oct. 1975),
p. 385-93. bibliog.

An analysis of the complexities of Carib ethnicity on Dominica. Carib group membership is based on physical appearance, the chieftaincy, legends and control of the Reserve lands, asserts the author, using data collected during thirteen months of fieldwork on the Carib Reserve in 1970 and 1972.

157 **Conflict and ethnic boundaries: a study of Carib-Black relations.**
Nancy Hammack Owen. *Social and Economic Studies*, vol. 29,
no. 2-3 (June-Sept. 1980), p. 264-74. bibliog.

An exploration of the sometimes hostile relations between Island Caribs and Afro-Dominicans living on the Carib Reserve, using the concept of ethnic boundaries. The ways in which the Caribs assert their ethnic identity as a way of attempting to maintain group boundaries and the consequences of this within the Reserve boundaries are discussed.

158 **Conditions in the Carib Reserve, and the disturbance of 19th
September, 1930, Dominica: report of a commission appointed by
His Excellency the Governor of the Leeward Islands, July, 1931.**
J. Stanley Rae, Sydney A. Armitage-Smith. London: HM
Stationery Office, 1932. 29p. map. (Great Britain, Sessional
Papers, House of Commons, Cmd. 3990).

The results of the investigation into the incident in which two Caribs were killed, two wounded and policemen beaten, when the latter attempted to arrest a group of Caribs suspected of smuggling. The Commissioners visited the Reserve between 21-24 May and examined twenty-seven witnesses. In addition to the details of the incident and the suggested 'measures for amelioration of the social and economic condition of the Caribs' (p. 22-29), the report is valuable for its history of the legal relations between the British and the Island Caribs of Dominica.

159 Caribs and Arawaks.
Charlesworth Ross. *Caribbean Quarterly*, vol. 16, no. 3 (Sept. 1970), p. 52-59.

A popular, personal account by the author who was once 'Officer in charge of Caribs' (p. 55), as well as Chief Magistrate of Antigua and Commissioner of Montserrat. The article is an excerpt from a projected autobiography, *Island son.*

160 The Carib.
Irving Rouse. In: *Handbook of South American Indians.* Edited by Julian H. Steward. *The Circum-Caribbean tribes.* Washington, DC: United States Government Printing Office, 1948, vol. 4, p. 547-65. (Smithsonian Institution, Bureau of American Ethnology. Bulletin 143).

A survey article summarizing numerous earlier sources. Following brief discussions of archaeology, history and sources, most of the article concerns Island Carib ethnography, covering subsistence activities, villages and houses, dress and adornment, transport, manufactures, social and political organization, life cycle, warfare, aesthetic and recreational activities, religion and shamanism, mythology, and lore and learning. Six plates illustrate historical Carib artefacts and contemporary descendants. Douglas Taylor critiques the article in 'The interpretation of some documentary evidence on Carib culture', *Southwestern Journal of Anthropology*, vol. 5 (1949), p. 379-92.

161 The Island Caribs of Dominica, B. W. I.
Douglas Taylor. *American Anthropologist*, vol. 37, no. 2, pt. 1 (April-June 1935), p. 265-72. bibliog.

The first of the author's numerous ethnographic and linguistic accounts of the Island Carib. This report includes a commentary on the customs, traditions, industry and language, and is based on 'meagre scraps, gleaned by me in the course of about half a dozen visits of from one to five days in the Reserve, made at long intervals between 1930 and 1934' (p. 265). The article is reprinted in *Aspects of Dominican history* (Roseau: Dominica Government, 1972), p. 61-66.

162 The Caribs of Dominica.
Douglas [MacRae] Taylor. Washington, DC: United States Government Printing Office, 1938. p. 103-59. map. (Bureau of American Ethnology, Bulletin 119, Anthropological Papers, no. 3).

The most extensive professional ethnography of the Island Caribs to date, based on the author's prolonged contact with the Caribs which began in 1930. The author describes most aspects of everyday life and the life cycle on the Reserve, including childhood games, sexuality, shelters and houses, fishing, canoe-building, cultivation and legends. Word- and phrase-lists preserve a now-lost language. Six photographic plates and twenty-seven line-drawings illustrate the text. The entire study is reproduced in the Human Relations Area Files, ST 13 Callinago, no. 6.

Amerindians. Historical and contemporary Island Caribs

163 Additional notes on the Island Carib of Dominica, B.W.I.
Douglas Taylor. *American Anthropologist*, vol. 38, no. 3, pt. 1
(July-Sept. 1936), p. 462-68.
Numerous customs and remnants of the Carib language are described in this
article, the author's second published ethnographic work, supplementing his first,
'The Island Carib of Dominica, B.W.I.', *American Anthropologist*, vol. 37
(1935), p. 265-72. In his conclusion, Taylor refers to the disappearance of Carib
language, tradition and culture due to a 'stupid policy of interferance and
absorption', the need to preserve the Caribs as they existed then (1936), and the
need to 'make a representative collection of the ancient weapons and implements
with which the soil of the island abounds' (p. 468).

164 Columbus saw them first.
Douglas Taylor. *Natural History*, vol. 48, no. 1 (June 1941),
p. 40-49. map.
A popular survey of Island Carib history, culture and lifestyle amply
supplemented with drawings by Hester Merwin and photographs by H. M. and
E. L. Ayres. It is reprinted without the illustrations in *Aspects of Dominican
history* (Roseau: Dominica Government, 1972), p. 1-7.

165 Carib folk-beliefs and customs from Dominica, B.W.I.
Douglas Taylor. *Southwestern Journal of Anthropology*, vol. 1,
no. 4 (winter 1945), p. 507-30. bibliog.
The fullest descriptive catalogue of Carib beliefs and customs, particularly
regarding the supernatural world. Discussion is organized around the beliefs
about the origin of man; magicians; spiritual entities, or zombi, which include
disembodied souls; ghosts of the dead and nine types of individual spiritual
beings; dreams and daydreams; reminiscences; customs related to life-cycle
phases; omens; sickness; and charms.

166 Notes on the star lore of the Caribbees.
Douglas Taylor. *American Anthropologist*, vol. 48, no. 2 (April-
June 1946), p. 215-22. bibliog.
Island Carib beliefs concerning the sun, moon, stars and planets. The Pleiades is
by far the best known, but the author salvages considerable lore about several
other constellations and heavenly bodies.

167 Kinship and social structure of the Island Carib.
Douglas Taylor. *Southwestern Journal of Anthropology*, vol. 2,
no. 2 (summer 1946), p. 180-212. bibliog.
A remarkably detailed article in the author's ethnographic series on the Island
Carib, or Callinago, to whom he devoted his professional life. Using the 17th-
century French works of Raymond Breton, Jean-Baptiste Du Tertre, R. P. De la
Borde and César de Rochefort in addition to his own extensive field observations,
Taylor describes the traditional and contemporary Island Carib culture, especially
with respect to social practices in the field of kinship relations. The article

49

includes a list and discussion of one hundred kinship terms. *Aspects of Dominican history* (Roseau: Dominica Government, 1972), p. 18-43, and the Human Relations Area Files, ST 13 Callinago, no. 11, both include this important article.

168   The interpretation of some documentary evidence on Carib culture.
Douglas Taylor. *Southwestern Journal of Anthropology*, vol. 5, no. 4 (winter 1949), p. 379-92. bibliog.

Using primary source materials from the 17th century, the ethnologist author provides a series of corrective commentaries on Irving Rouse's chapter, 'The Carib', in vol. 4, *The Circum-Caribbean Tribes* of the *Handbook of South American Indians* (Washington, DC, 1948, p. 547-65). This important article is reproduced in *Aspects of Dominican history* (Roseau: Dominica Government, 1972), p. 8-17, and in the Human Relations Area Files, ST 13 Callinago, no. 12.

169   The meaning of dietary and occupational restrictions among the Island Carib.
Douglas Taylor. *American Anthropologist*, vol. 52, no. 3 (July-Sept. 1950), p. 343-49. bibliog.

The author describes the 17th-century priests' accounts of dietary and occupational restrictions, and the remnants of such practices among the contemporary Island Carib and the Black Carib of British Honduras. He explains the famous Carib custom of *couvade* in which the husband fasts and goes into seclusion during his wife's delivery and confinement, as well as other ritual practices in terms of beliefs in contagious magic reducing individuals' vulnerability during critical passages of life. The article is reproduced in the Human Relations Area Files, ST 13 Callinago, no. 8.

170   The Black Carib of British Honduras.
Douglas MacRae Taylor.   New York: Wenner-Gren Foundation for Anthropological Research, 1951. 176p. 2 maps. bibliog. (Viking Fund Publications in Anthropology, no. 17).

An ethnography of the descendants of St. Vincentian Caribs deported to Roatan Island, British Honduras, in 1797, including chapters on language, subsistence, social organization, life cycle, supernatural beliefs, rites and practices, with appendixes on basketry, lore and learning, a glossary, an extensive bibliography and seven plates. This study is based on twelve months' fieldwork in 1947-48 and six months' library research at Northwestern University, Evanston, Illinois, in 1949. The Black Carib provided the author with a wealth of ethnographic data amplifying and complementing his knowledge of the Island Carib. The Introduction (p. 15-36) discussing the Black Caribs' historical background and literary sources is equally valuable for the study of Dominica's Island Caribs.

171   Tales and legends of the Dominica Caribs.
Douglas Taylor. *Journal of American Folklore*, vol. 65, no. 257 (July-Sept. 1952), p. 267-79. bibliog.

Eight folktales collected by the author between 1938 and 1941, with commentary. According to Taylor, 'four of the seven raconteurs . . . are now dead; and it is unlikely that their tales are known to surviving Caribs' (p. 267). The stories fall into three groups: shreds of celestial myths; local or localized legends; and tales told just for entertainment. This article was reprinted in *Aspects of Dominican history* (Roseau: Dominica Government, 1972), p. 44-55.

172 **A note on marriage and kinship among the Island Carib.**
Douglas Taylor. *Man*, vol. 53, art. 175 (Aug. 1953), p. 117-19.
bibliog.

A short account clarifying the marriage and kinship practices which were reported differently by the French missionaries visiting Dominica in the 17th-century. Breton and R. P. De la Borde are credited with understanding traditional Carib culture and language better than anyone else. The paper was reprinted in *Aspects of Dominican history* (Roseau: Dominica Government, 1972), p. 56-60.

173 **Conquerors of the Caribbean.**
Anthony Weller, Alen MacWeeney. *Geo*, vol. 5 (April 1983), p. 68-76, 102, 105-06. map.

A descriptive account of the current life and socio-economic difficulties of the 'approximate 100 pure Caribs' left on Dominica (p. 73). Dramatic colour photographs by Alen MacWeeney illustrate the article. Anthony Weller, a New York-based poet and novelist, lived in the Caribbean and gives his impressions of Salybia and Bataka villages in this popularly-written article.

In old Roseau: reminiscences of life as I found it in the island of Dominica, and among the Carib Indians.
See item no. 3.

Dominica.
See item no. 6.

The English in the West Indies: or, the bow of Ulysses.
See item no. 14.

Our island culture.
See item no. 18.

Caribbean circuit.
See item no. 21.

Isles of the Caribbees.
See item no. 24.

Isles of the Caribbean.
See item no. 26.

Cruising among the Caribbees: summer days in winter months.
See item no. 32.

The cradle of the deep: an account of a voyage to the West Indies.
See item no. 33.

Camps in the Caribbees: the adventures of a naturalist in the Lesser Antilles.
See item no. 93.

Plants used by the Dominica Caribs.
See item no. 100.

The ethnobotany of the Island Caribs of Dominica.
See item no. 103.

The Caribbean people.
See item no. 184.

The Dominica story: a history of the island.
See item no. 216.

Broken atoms.
See item no. 333.

How Dominicans view political independence: no nation is an island.
See item no. 339.

Planning the Waitikubuli Institute of Learning and Community Development.
See item no. 409.

The cooking of the Caribbean islands.
See item no. 453.

The complete Caribbeana 1900-1975: a bibliographic guide to the scholarly literature.
See item no. 482.

Amerindians of the Lesser Antilles: a bibliography.
See item no. 488.

A resource guide to Dominica, 1493-1986.
See item no. 489.

Biology

174 Recherches sur les hémoglobines des populations indiennes de l'amérique de sud. (Research on South American Indian haemoglobins.)
M. R. Cabannes, A. Schmidt-Beurrier. *L'Anthropologie* (Paris), vol. 70, no. 3-4 (1966), p. 331-42. map. bibliog.

A comparative study of five haemoglobin types among primarily Indian populations of Dominica (130 subjects), French Guiana (545 subjects) and Bolivia (2,623 subjects).

175 Étude hémotypologique de la population indienne de l'île Dominique. (A blood-group study of the Dominica Indian population.)
Chilling-Rathford, G. Larrouy, R. Mille, J. Ruffié.
L'Anthropologie (Paris), vol. 70, no. 3-4 (1966), p. 319-30. map. bibliog.

General descriptions of the island situation and of the Carib Reserve, followed by an analysis of the ABO, Rhesus, MN, P and Kell blood groups of 135 individuals. The study was conducted in August 1964 by the Centre d'Hémotypologie du CNRS de Toulouse, and the Institute Pasteur de la Martinique. The first author's name is misspelled and should be D. Shillingford, then Dominica's Chief Medical Officer.

176 Frequency of genetic traits in the Caribs of Dominica.
R. G. Harvey, Marilyn J. Godber, A. C. Kopeć, A. E. Mourant, D. Tills. *Human Biology*, vol. 41, no. 3 (Sept. 1969), p. 342-64. 2 maps. bibliog.

Blood specimens were taken from 126 individuals during a three-week study in 1966. Analysis of some three dozen blood components shows the prominent Amerindian ancestry of Dominica's Island Caribs. The authors are from the Serological Population Genetics Laboratory of the Medical Research Council in London.

Amerindian languages

177 Dictionaire Caraïbe-Français. (Carib–French dictionary.)
R. P. Raymond Breton. Leipzig: B.G. Teubner, 1892. 480p.
Reprinted by Jules Platzmann. Facsimile ed.

A facsimile edition of the first account of the Island Carib language published in 1665 (Auxerre, France: Gilles Bouquet). This is the work upon which our

Amerindians. Amerindian languages

understanding of Island Carib and Arawak languages, and much about their culture, rests. Following a brief dedication and introduction, the author proceeds in standard dictionary form, listing the Carib work, followed by a French translation. For many words, Breton has added explanatory descriptions which enrich the volume immeasureably. Part of the valuable work has been reorganized and translated by Marshall McKusick and Pierre Verin as 'Father Raymond Breton's observations of the Island Carib: a compilation of ethnographic notes taken from Breton's Carib–French dictionary' and published in the Human Relations Area Files, ST 13 Callinago, no. 2, p. 1-48.

178 Grammaire Caraïbe suivi du catéchisme Caraïbe. (A Carib grammar followed by a Carib catechism.) R. P. Raymond Breton, introduced by Lucien Adam. Paris: Maisonneuve Cᶦᵉ, 1877. 73p, 54p. New ed. published by Lucien Adam, Ch. LeClerc. (Bibliothèque linguistique américaine, t. III). Reprinted, Nendeln, Lichtenstein: Kraus Reprints, 1968.

The editors performed an important service by reprinting, following an extended introduction (28p.) by Lucien Adam, two of the three original publications of missionary Raymond Breton, who spent years among the Dominica Island Caribs during 1641-53. Breton's ethnographic records were lost and without this primary material, knowledge of the language and culture of the Amerindians would be minimal. *Grammaire Caraïbe* (Auxerre, France: Gilles Bouquet, 1667, 73p.) is a formal description of the structure of Island Carib as Breton understood it. *Petit catéchisme ou sommaire des trois premières parties de la doctrine Chrestienne* (Little catechism, or a summary of the first three parts of Christian doctrine) (Auxerre, France: Gilles Bouquet, 1664, 54p.) is a catechism printed in double columns of French and Carib addressed to 'the Caribs of Dominica' and followed by a sonnet 'to the savages' (p. 49-54).

179 The Carib language as now spoken in Dominica, West Indies. Joseph Numa Rat. *Journal of the Anthropological Institute of Great Britain and Ireland*, vol. 27 (Feb. 1897), p. 293-315.

The first formal effort at describing Dominican Island Carib speech since Raymond Breton's work in the mid-17th-century. Orthography, articles, adjectives, substantives, number, gender, pronouns, possessive, demonstrative, interrogatives, numerals, verbs, peculiarities of the language and borrowed words are discussed. Four brief paragraphs are given in Carib and translated into English. The author, an assistant surgeon in Dominica from 1890 to 1908, provides no information on how or when he collected his information, and is better known for his work on yaws.

180 Carib, Caliban, cannibal.

Douglas Taylor. *International Journal of American Linguistics*, vol. 24, no. 2 (April 1958), p. 156-57.

A brief discussion of Taino, Arawak and Island Carib influences to explain why 'Carib, Caribe, Caraïbe' became such common terms while 'Arawak, Aruaca and Arrouague' never did. The ethnological linguist author proposes that 'our "cannibal" and "Carib" go back to Arawakan designations describing some tribe or clan as *manioc people*' (p. 157).

181 Loan words in Dominica Island Carib.

Douglas Taylor. *International Journal of American Linguistics*, vol. 12, no. 4 (Oct. 1946), p. 213-16.

A fascinating account of the words borrowed from Spanish, French and English and their assimilation into Island Carib. Contains lists of loan-words with translations.

182 The linguistic repertory of the Island-Carib in the seventeenth century: the men's language – a Carib pidgin?

Douglas R. [sic] Taylor, Berend J. Hoff. *International Journal of American Linguistics*, vol. 46, no. 4 (Oct. 1980), p. 301-12. bibliog.

An analysis of the Island Carib men's language showing that the Island Carib were not divided by a men's language and a women's language as is commonly represented, but that the so-called women's language was the native language of both sexes, a typical Arawakan language. The 'men's language', a Carib pidgin, never became anyone's mother tongue, was learned in adolescence and was useful to the islanders in their dealings with Caribs on the South American mainland. This was the last article published by the first author, who had studied the Island Carib of Dominica and their language for forty-five years.

History

Regional

183 Caribbean story. Book one: foundations, Book two: the inheritors.
William Claypole, John Robottom.   Trinidad, Jamaica: Longman
Caribbean, 1980-81. 2 vols. 55 maps. bibliog.

An excellent historical survey, written especially to provide a Caribbean
perspective for the CXC (Caribbean Examinations Council) history syllabus, with
numerous illustrations and exercises for each chapter. Volume one, *Foundations*,
covers Caribbean history from the Amerindian occupation to emancipation, with
a final chapter on 19th-century immigration. Volume two, *The inheritors*, brings
the history from emancipation to the post-independence period. Dominica is
mentioned only in passing, but the introductory chapters on Amerindian
settlement provide a useful background for the history of the island.

184   The Caribbean people.
Lennox Honychurch.   Kingston; Walton-on-Thames, Surrey:
Nelson Caribbean, 1979-81. 3 vols. maps. bibliog.

The three books in this historical series for secondary-school children focus on the
origins and development of Caribbean society from the Amerindian times to the
present. Volume one covers the 'Earliest times to 1492' with chapters on the
Arawaks and Island Caribs. Volume two describes the period 1492-1770 with
emphasis on colonization and plantation society. Volume three concerns the
insular region from 1770 to the 1970s. Throughout the well-illustrated volumes the
Dominica-born author presents an excellent context for the general and often
specific historical background on his island home.

185   A historical geography of the British colonies. Vol. II. The West
       Indies.
       Charles Prestwood Lucas.   Oxford: Clarendon Press, 1905.
       2nd ed. 348p. maps. bibliog.
An informative historical survey of Dominica as one of the Leeward Islands
Colony, also including St. Kitts, Nevis, Montserrat and the Virgin Islands (p. 137-
70). This work is particularly useful for West Indian political events of the 17th
and 18th centuries.

186   Chronological history of the West Indies.
       Thomas Southey.   London: Longman, Rees, Orme, Brown, &
       Green, 1827. 3 vols. Reprinted, London: Cass, 1969. (Cass Library
       of West Indian Studies, no. 4).
A year-by-year account compiled from books, journals and government
documents, referenced at the bottom of each page, of events in the islands by
Captain Southey, a Commander in the Royal Navy and brother of Poet Laureat
Robert Southey. Prominent events on Dominica are described throughout each
volume. Volume one covers the years 1492-1655; volume two covers 1655-1783;
and volume three, 1784-1816. For example, a full account by General George
Prevost, Governor of Dominica, of the French General La Grange's attack on
Roseau in 1805 is in Volume three, p. 312-16. At the end of his work, Captain
Southey concludes that 'the history of the West Indies presents little more than a
melancholy series of calamities and crimes' (vol. 3, p. 616), but he looks forward
to the 'mitigation and gradual removal' of the slave system.

187   A family of islands: a history of the West Indies from 1492 to 1898,
       with an epilogue sketching events from the Spanish–American War
       to the 1960's.
       Alec Waugh.   Garden City, New York: Doubleday, 1964. 348p.
       maps.
A highly-readable history by the well-known novelist whose experience in the
region dates back to the 1920s. Numerous references to the roles of the Island
Caribs and of Dominica in this sweep of nearly five centuries reflect the author's
interest in the island.

188   From Columbus to Castro: the history of the Caribbean, 1492-1969.
       Eric Williams.   New York: Harper & Row, 1973; London: André
       Deutsch, 1976. 576p. maps. bibliog.
The panorama of Caribbean history, coherently presented. This volume is one of
the most comprehensive studies of the complex island region and provides
extensive tables, illustrations and a lengthy 'Select bibliography' (p. 516-58). The
place of Dominica in the region's history is clearly presented with numerous
references to the island. The late author was a prolific historian, as well as Prime
Minister of Trinidad and Tobago.

West Indian societies.
See item no. 20.

Golden islands of the Caribbean.
See item no. 38.

General and social

189 Aspects of Dominican history.
Issued by the Government of Dominica to commemorate the Fifth
Anniversary of Associated Statehood with Britain, November 3,
1972. Foreword by E[dward] O[liver] LeBlanc. [Roseau]:
Government Printing Division, 1972. 172p. bibliog.
A collection of twelve articles, six by Douglas Taylor, four by Joseph Boromé,
and one each by Cecil A. Goodridge and Rev. Father Raymond Proesmans,
focusing especially on the Island Caribs and on island history throughout the 19th
century. Each article (except for the last two) was first published elsewhere, and
each is annotated in the present bibliography. E. O. LeBlanc was Premier at the
time of publication.

190 West Indian tales of old.
Algernon E. Aspinall. London: Duckworth, 1915. Reprinted,
Westport, Connecticut: Negro Universities Press, 1969. 259p.
One of these tales is an account of the period in Dominican history known as 'La
Grange' (p. 163-70), the last attempt by French forces to take the island. In
February 1805, General La Grange landed near Roseau but was prevented from
capturing the town. Instead, he departed after extorting £12,000 ransom from the
inhabitants. Unfortunately, during the town's defence, wadding from the English
cannon caused a major fire, destroying much of Roseau and burning many
valuable documents of the period. A photograph of a street scene in Roseau
accompanies the text.

**191 The history of the island of Dominica, containing a description of its
situation, extent, climate, mountains, rivers, natural productions,
etc., etc., together with an account of the civil government, trade,
laws, customs, and manners of the different inhabitants of that
island. Its conquest by the French, and restoration to the British
dominions.**
Thomas Atwood. London: J. Johnson, 1791. Reprinted, London:
Cass, 1971. 285p. (Cass Library of West Indian Studies, no. 27).
A first-hand view of 18th-century events and life on Dominica, and the best
general description of the island until the 1970s. The author, planter and Chief
Justice in both Dominica and the Bahamas, gives an enthusiastic survey of the

island's history, flora and fauna, government, and population groups. Atwood wrote to stimulate British government interest in the well-positioned colony and to attract British immigrants. A German translation was published in 1795 as *Geschichte der Insel Dominica* (Göttingen, FRG: J. C. Dieterich), two years after Atwood died in King's Bench prison in Dominica where he was sentenced for corrupt practices. As a result of his twenty-one years' residence in the West Indies, Atwood published in 1789 'Observations on the true methods of treatment & usage of the negro slaves, in the British West-India Islands. And a refutation of the gross misrepresentations calculated to impose on the nation on that subject' (London: John Mott, 15p.).

192 Sources of West Indian history.
Compiled by F. R. Augier, Shirley C. Gordon. Trinidad, Jamaica: Longman Caribbean, 1962. 308p.

A collection of brief accounts and excerpts from a wide variety of sources organized in seven chapters: 'People of the Caribbean'; 'Economic life'; 'Religion and education before emancipation'; 'Slavery and its abolition'; 'Emancipation and apprenticeship'; 'Social conditions since emancipation'; and 'Government and politics'. The book, updated in 1969, is 'primarily intended for use in the senior forms of secondary schools' (Foreword, p. ix) but others will find it useful. Accounts from or about Dominica are numerous.

193 Spain and Dominica, 1493-1647.
Joseph [Alfred] Barome [sic]. *Caribbean Quarterly*, vol. 12, no. 4 (Dec. 1966), p. 30-46. bibliog.

The only article on the earliest period of European contact with Dominica, from the island's discovery by Columbus to Spain's diversion of the West Indian armada away from the Lesser Antilles in 1647. Professor Boromé consulted archives in England, France and Spain to reconstruct this history detailing both aggressive and peaceful interactions between the Amerindians and the Europeans. It is reprinted in *Aspects of Dominican history* (Roseau: Dominica Government, 1972, p. 67-79).

194 Four years' residence in the West Indies, during the years 1826, 7, 8, and 9; to which is now added, a faithful narrative, derived from official documents and private letters, of the dreadful hurricanes in Barbados, St. Vincent, and St. Lucia, in August, M.DCCC.XXXI.
F[rederic] W[illiam] N[aylor] Bayley. London: William Kidd, 1832. 742p. 'A new ed.' [3rd ed.]

The author spent his late teens and early twenties in the West Indies with his parents, and wrote this account when he returned to England. Dominica is described melodramatically through his dialogue with a visiting 'Lieutenant S— of the Royal Engineers' (p. 256-62). Chapter VI of the Appendix (p. 648-58) contains a 'Chronology of Dominica, from its first discovery to A.D. 1814' based on colonial returns, Atwood's *History of the island of Dominica*, Coke, Edwards and Southey. The first edition was published in 1830.

195 The Imperial Road in Dominica.
H[enry] Hesketh Bell. *West India Committee Circular*, vol. 19,
no. 128 (28 June 1904), p. 257-60.

The author, one of the most popular administrators of Dominica, discusses island
history. In particular he emphasizes the significance of opening up new lands to
settlement and cultivation along the recently constructed 'Imperial Road', so-
named because it was built with parliamentary funding. A photograph by E.
Fenton of the narrow road illustrates the article.

196 Notes on Dominica and hints to intending settlers.
H[enry] Hesketh Bell. [Barbados]: Imperial Department of
Agriculture for the West Indies, 1903. 24p. (Pamphlet Series,
no. 24).

One of the island administrator's efforts to attract new settlers included the
publication of this pamphlet describing agricultural and social conditions and
opportunities. The pamphlet was revised and enlarged by Administrator G. W.
Douglas Young in 1909 (Barbados: Advocate Company, 34p.) and again in 1919
by H. A. Alford Nicholls (Barbados: Advocate Company, 62p.). The last edition
included thirteen photographs, a map, and a list of 177 useful timbers on the
island. The pamphlets were distributed to hotels and waiting rooms in England to
stimulate interest in Dominica.

197 George Charles Falconer.
Joseph Alfred Boromé. *Caribbean Quarterly*, vol. 6, no. 1 (fall
1960), p. 11-17. bibliog.

A biographical article about one of the most prominent 19th-century Dominicans.
George Charles Falconer (1819-72), born in Barbados, arrived in Dominica in
1839 and in the same year founded the newspaper *Dominican*, through which he
defended freedom of speech and the press. He taught briefly in Mico Charity
schools (which supplemented the Protestant schools in Dominica in 1839) and
became prominent in the Methodist Church, but is chiefly remembered as an
editor and vigorous liberal legislator.

198 The French and Dominica, 1699-1763.
Joseph A[lfred] Boromé. *Jamaican Historical Review*, vol. 7,
no. 1-2 (1967), p. 9-39. bibliog.

Sixty-five years of Dominican history, from the landing of Col. Tobias Frere's
lumbering colony in October 1699 to the Treaty of Paris, 10 February 1763, which
ceded the island to Britain. Although declared neutral by agreements between
France and Britain in 1686 and the Treaty of Aix-la-Chapelle in 1748, the island
was the site of continuous French and sometimes English settlement. The author
thoroughly documents these developments using American, French and British
archival materials. The article is reproduced in *Aspects of Dominican history*
(Roseau: Dominica Government, 1972, p. 80-102).

199 Dominica during French occupation, 1778-1784.
Joseph A[lfred] Boromé. *English Historical Review*, vol. 84,
no. 330 (Jan. 1969), p. 36-58. bibliog.
Between 6 September 1778 and 8 January 1784, Dominica was occupied by
French forces. During this period of French and English warfare, trade to and
from Dominica virtually stopped, the island was raked by a hurricane and a major
fire destroyed Roseau. The author presents a detailed account of the events with
careful documentation in his extensive footnotes. The account is reprinted in
Aspects of Dominican history (Roseau: Dominica Government, 1972, p. 103-19).

200 How Crown Colony government came to Dominica by 1898.
Joseph A[lfred] Boromé. *Caribbean Studies*, vol. 9, no. 3 (Oct.
1969), p. 26-67. bibliog.
An excellent history of island government and politics from the early 19th century
to the early 20th century. The author, Professor of History at the City College of
the City University of New York, provides scrupulous documentation for the
contentious personalities shaping political events throughout the 1800s. It is
reprinted in *Aspects of Dominican history* (Roseau: Dominica Government, 1972,
p. 120-50).

201 The Senhouse papers.
Edited by James C. Brandow. *Journal of the Barbados Museum
and Historical Society*, vol. 37, no. 3 (1985), p. 276-95. map.
bibliog.
Introduction and excerpts from the diary of Joseph Senhouse (1743-1829) written
between June and August 1776. Senhouse was Collector and Comptroller of
Customs in Dominica, 1771-73, and visited the island again briefly in 1776.

**202 The elusive deodand: a study of the fortified refuges of the Lesser
Antilles.**
David Buisseret. *Journal of Caribbean History*, vol. 6 (May
1973), p. 43-80. bibliog. 12 maps.
An account of the Lesser Antillean deodands, or fortified refuges, built in the
17th and 18th centuries. For this historical study, the author visited St. Kitts,
Nevis, Antigua, Montserrat, Guadeloupe, Dominica, St. Lucia, St. Vincent,
Grenada, Tobago and Barbados, and describes briefly the refuges 'for non-
combatants (and final citadel for combatants) in time of war' (p. 43). Morne
Bruce overlooking Roseau is discussed (p. 59-62) and, as is the case for each
deodand, a sketch map is included. The author is at the Herman Dunlap Smith
Center for the History of Cartography of the Newberry Library, Chicago,
Illinois.

203   References to the plan of the island of Dominica, as surveyed from the year 1765 to 1773.

John Byres.   London: S. Hooper, 1777. 30p.

To accompany his large-scale map of the island published in 1776, Chief Surveyor John Byres compiled a list of all properties on the island. The list, complete with alphabetical index, shows the acreage of each lot with its original and present purchaser or lessee for each parish.

204   John Candler's visit to Martinique, Dominica, and Guadeloupe.

John Candler.   *Caribbean Studies*, vol. 5, no. 2 (July 1965), p. 56-63.

John Candler and his wife, Protestant missionaries, toured the islands and reported their observations of economic and labour conditions. Their brief comments for Dominica date from their ten-day visit in February 1850.

205   A treatise on the yellow fever as it appeared in the island of Dominica in the years 1793-4-5-6: to which are added, observations on the bilious remittent fever, on intermittents, dysentery, and some other West India diseases; also the chemical analysis and medical properties of the hot mineral waters in the same island.

James Clark.   London: J. Murray, S. Highley, 1797. 168p.

After Thomas Atwood's *History of the island of Dominica* (London, 1791), this is the only 18th-century book about Dominica, although the book is less about the island than about the aetiology, symptoms and treatment of particular diseases. The author, a physician in Dominica from 1771-88, 1789-96, and 1804-18, presents a history of yellow fever on the island linking its appearance with the influx of 3-4,000 emigrants from Martinique in June 1793, coincident with a 'deranged state of the atmosphere' (p. 63) and 'mephitic effluvia' (p. 25). During the next three months, at least 1,000 died (p. 2). He also describes bilious remittent fever (now known to be falciparum malaria), typhus fever, dysentery, dry belly-ache, cholera and tetanus. Finally, he analyses the water of the hot baths at Soufrière. The appendix contains 'Experiments on the cinchona brachycarpa by Mr. Brande' (p. 161-68). A lengthy synopsis of the work appears in *Annals of Medicine*, vol. 2 (1797), p. 155-83.

206   A history of the West Indies, containing the natural, civil, and ecclesiastical history of each island: with an account of the missions instituted in those islands, from the commencement of their civilizations; but more especially of the missions which have been established in that archipelago by the society late in connexion with the Rev. John Wesley.

Thomas Coke.   London: A. Paris, 1808-11. 3 vols. Reprinted, London: Cass, 1971. (Cass Library of West Indian Studies, no. 21).

The history of the Methodists in the West Indies. Two chapters of Volume two (1810) are devoted to the history of Dominica, the first (p. 332-49) containing a more general account of the island and the second (p. 350-83), a detailed history of Methodism in Dominica. The author first visited Dominica in January 1787 but was unable to establish the first mission until December of the next year. The accounts contain lengthy excerpts from missionaries' letters and serve as a valuable record of Dominica during the period 1787-1806.

207   Six months in the West Indies in 1825.
[Henry Nelson Coleridge].   London: John Murray, 1826. 332p.

The author, nephew and son-in-law of the poet Samuel Coleridge, went to the West Indies for his health with another uncle, William H. Coleridge, Bishop of Barbados. On Dominica they met Captain John Bent, an old friend from the fifth form at Eton, and visited estates. Much of the chapter on the visit (p. 150-68) relates the privateering exploits of a former Anglican vicar, Mr. Audain. The volume was published anonymously in its first two editions; Coleridge added his name to the 1832 3rd ed. and the 1841 4th ed.

208   Cinderella of the Antilles: Dominica's plight and remedy.
Samuel Henry Davies.   *West India Committee Circular*, vol. 36, no. 587 (31 March 1921), p. 120-22. map.

In this précis the author outlines three serious problems confronting Dominica: lack of population; low standard of education; and insufficient revenue for road maintenance and expansion, proper medical services, school staffs, agricultural development and administration. He proposes a Colonial Office loan to develop a colonization scheme from other islands and to fund necessary improvements in roads, education and administration. He strongly supports a West Indian federation.

209   Five years' residence in the West Indies.
Charles William Day.   London: Colburn, 1852. 2 vols.

The author visited Dominica twice, between 16 March and 31 May, and between 12 June and 5 September 1850, and gives a rather detailed, if prejudiced and anti-Roman Catholic account of life in the litigious colony, 'one of the poorest spots, perhaps, on the face of the globe' (p. 177). Day travelled about the island visiting Portsmouth and Scott's Head as well as the hot springs of Wotton Waven and Soufrière. Almost three chapters are devoted to his visits (p. 171-203, 227-67).

210   The West Indies before and since slave emancipation, comprising the Windward and Leeward Islands' military command, founded on notes and observations collected during three years' residence in the Antilles.
John Day.   London: W. & F. G. Cash, 1854. Reprinted, London: Cass, 1971. 551p. map. (Cass Library of West Indian Studies, no. 22).

Davy, an MD and Inspector General of Army Hospitals, presents succinct, useful accounts of the islands. Drawing from earlier writers, especially Thomas Atwood, he gives a brief description of Dominican geography and history, including population and trade statistics from the 1840s (p. 492-509).

211 **The history, civil and commercial, of the British West Indies, with a continuation to the present time.**
Bryan Edwards. London: G. & W. B. Whitaker, 1819. Reprinted, New York: AMS Press, 1966. 5th ed. 5 vols.

A valuable expanded edition of the three-volume 1801 history providing the best review of its time of island events. The chapter about Dominica in Volume one of the 5th edition (p. 431-47) is identical to the chapter in the 1st edition which draws heavily from Thomas Atwood's *History of the island of Dominica* (London, 1791), but in Volume five the author brings events up to the 1814 Maroon War in Dominica. Volume two contains the entire 1797 memoir by William Urban Buée, 'Some account of the cultivation of the clove tree' in Dominica (p. 374-83) and Volume five's Appendix contains several Dominican slave laws (p. 118-24). The Island Caribs are discussed in Volumes one and three.

212 **Dominica – the French connection.**
Cecil A. Goodridge. In: *Aspects of Dominican history*. Dominica Government. [Roseau]: Government Printing Division, 1972, p. 151-62. bibliog.

A brief history of French contacts with and influence over Dominica, from the first French settlement in 1632 throughout the 19th century, with special attention to the *métayage* system. The author holds a PhD in history from the University of Edinburgh, was once Headmaster of the Dominica Grammar School, and at the time of publication was on the staff of the University of the West Indies, Mona, Jamaica.

213 **A winter in the West Indies, described in familiar letters to Henry Clay, of Kentucky.**
Joseph John Gurney. London: John Murray, 1840. Reprinted, New York: Negro Universities Press, 1969. 2nd ed. 282p.

A series of letters describing the generally improved conditions in the West Indies and the industry of the former slaves, by a Quaker missionary hoping to influence opinions of slaveholders in the United States. 'Letter VI' (p. 70-87) from Dominica emphasizes positive commercial aspects of the island, the Mico Charity schools, successful non-white individuals and a perceived new attitude towards field labour.

214 **Report of the Royal Commission (appointed in September, 1893) to inquire into the condition and affairs of the island of Dominica and correspondence relating thereto.**
Sir Robert [George Crookshank] Hamilton. London: HM Stationery Office, Eyre & Spottiswoode, 1894. 204p. (House of Commons, Sessional Papers, Cd. 7477).

The most comprehensive official report on the island of Dominica in the 19th century, prepared by a former Governor of Tasmania. Following disorders in Dominica, Hamilton was sent to evaluate general conditions and to suggest ways to improve the situation. Between 21 November and 28 December 1893, he held hearings in Roseau and seven other towns and villages. He recorded the testimony of seventy-nine people, from merchants, government officials, and large estate-owners to priests, peasant proprietors, tenants and labourers. Among his many recommendations were changes in the island's taxation system, a restructuring of the Executive Council and the Legislative Assembly, and the removal of Dominica from the Leeward Islands Confederation and appointment of a Lieutenant-Governor for the island. The report attributed Dominica's lack of development to economic and geographic factors rather than to political ones.

215 The General Assembly of the Leeward Islands.
C. S. S. Higham. *English Historical Review*, vol. 41, nos. 162, 163 (April, July 1926), p. 190-209, 366-88. bibliog.

The political history of the Leeward Islands (Antigua, St. Kitts, Nevis, Montserrat and, later, Dominica) from the General Assembly of 1674 to the Leeward Islands Federation of 1871. A particularly useful discussion of the ceded islands of Dominica, Grenada, St. Vincent, and Tobago is included, as well as an account of the earliest British administration under Robert Melville of Dominica from 1763 to 1770, when the island became separate from Granadian administration.

216 The Dominica story: a history of the island.
Lennox Honychurch. Roseau: Dominica Institute, 1984. 2nd ed. 225p. 13 maps. bibliog.

The multi-talented author rewrote his series of dramatized radio broadcasts to produce the first history of the island by a native son (Barbados: Letchworth Press, 1975. 111p.) in which he surveys events on Dominica from Amerindian settlement to Associated Statehood in 1967. The second edition expands earlier chapters and recounts the turbulent first years of independence, from 1978 up to 1983. This is a popular history, written first and foremost for the people of Dominica, rather than a heavily-documented history written for scholars. Honychurch, who served in the Dominica House of Assembly from 1975-79, tells the story with confidence and insight, remaining objective but still conveying intimacy with the subjects. This generously-illustrated book contains numerous photographs, figures and his own sketches, and can be obtained from The Dominica Institute, PO Box 89, Roseau, Dominica.

217 Dominica, an island in need of an historian.
Anthony Layng. *Caribbean Quarterly*, vol. 19, no. 4 (Dec. 1973), p. 36-41.

A brief sketch of the island's past 'offered as an illustration of the problems involved in compiling a comprehensive history' (p. 38) and a plea for an historian to sort it all out.

218   Leeward Islands almanac, with which is incorporated the Dominica almanac.

Compiled by Alexander Rumsey Lockhart.   Roseau: Official Gazette, 1879. 233p.

Lockhart published the *Dominica almanac and year book* annually, beginning in 1874 and continuing the *Dominica almanac* published by Charles August Fillan as early as 1862. The volumes provide a wealth of information on the island. In the *Leeward Islands almanac*, the Dominica section (p. 120-88) contains chronological notes, a list of estates and John Imray's 'Useful woods of the island of Dominica'.

219   A letter to a friend relative to the present state of the island of Dominica.

Langford Lovell.   Winchester, England: James Robbins, 1818. 39p.

A long-term resident describes the dismal state of affairs in Dominica since the restrictions on trade with Americans following the Revolution and the War of 1812, the doubling of prices after the hurricanes of 1814 and 1816, and the depressed state of religion in the colony, and pleads vigorously for an end to the restrictions.

220   The Empire at war.

Sir Charles Lucas.   London: Oxford University, 1923. vol. 2. maps.

In Part three, 'The West Indies', the chapter 'The Leeward Islands' (p. 373-87) describing Antigua, St. Kitts-Nevis and Dominica was condensed by the author from materials supplied by F. H. Watkins, J. A. Burdon and H. A. Alford Nicholls, Dominica's Senior Medical Officer. This is the most substantial account of Dominica's participation in World War I. Dominica sent 700 men to the war, meeting not only her own quota, but also making up the shortage of recruits from Antigua and St. Kitts. 'In Dominica alone of all the Presidencies no recruiting meetings were necessary . . .' (p. 378). Dominica claims to have been the first colony to present fighting 'aeroplanes' to the war effort. The severe hurricane of 8 August 1916, in which fifty-seven people were killed, is also described.

221 History of the colonies of the British Empire in the West Indies,
South America, North America, Asia, Austral-Asia, Africa, and
Europe; comprising the area, agriculture, commerce, manufactures,
shipping custom duties, population, education, religion, crime,
government, finances, laws, military defense, cultivated and waste
lands, emigration, rates of wages, prices of provisions, banks, coins,
staple products, stock, moveable and immoveable property, public
companies, etc. of each colony; with the charters and the engraved
seals.
Robert Montgomery Martin. London: Dawsons of Pall Mall,
1843. Reprinted, London: Dawsons, 1967. 602, 304p. map.
Taken from the official records of the Colonial Office, Martin's compendium of
information is an indispensable source of data on the Empire. Charts and tables
provide extensive data supplementing the account on Dominica (p. 73-79). A
lengthy 'Appendix of official documents relative to the commerce, agriculture,
social state, etc. of the Colonies of the British Empire' for the West Indies (p. 1-
25) includes a wealth of data on Dominica.

222 The British Colonial library, comprising a popular and authentic
description of all the colonies of the British Empire, their history –
physical geography – geology – climate – animal, vegetable, and
mineral kingdoms – government – finance – military defense –
commerce – shipping – monetary system – religion – population,
white and coloured – education and the press – emigration, social
state, &.
Robert Montgomery Martin. London: Henry G. Bohn, 1844.
10 vols.
In Volume V, the author provides one of the best surveys of Dominica in the
1820s and 1830s (p. 270-88), with information on all the categories mentioned in
the title. Several tables offer data on population, exports, shipping and finances.
This material complements rather than duplicates data in Martin's 1843 *History of
the colonies of the British Empire in the West Indies . . .* (q.v.).

223 The uncrowned king of Dominica.
J. H. Menzies. *United Empire. Journal of the Royal Colonial
Institute*, vol. 17 (April 1926), p. 203-05.
An obituary for Sir Henry Alfred Alford Nicholls, MD, CMG, who died on 9
February 1926. Rather than dwelling on the details of Dr. Nicholls's life, the
author traces his general influence on the island, quoting extensively from James
Anthony Froude's *The English in the West Indies* (London, 1888) on Nicholls's
agricultural accomplishments on St. Aromant Estate. The article was partially
reprinted in the *Canada-West India Magazine*, vol. 15, no. 7 (July 1926), p. 156.

224 O, call back yesterday.
Elma Napier. *BIM*, vol. 11, nos. 43, 44 (1966), p. 200-04, 242-44.
In a two-part article, the novelist-politician author gives a sensitive personal account of Dominica during World War II. She describes how Dominica provided a haven to several thousand Free French from Guadeloupe and Martinique. Because they received free food and lodging, the French islanders became a burden, causing a serious protein shortage that lasted for years after the war ended.

225 Dominica: the loveliest and grandest island of the Caribbean archipelago.
H[enry] A[lfred] Alford Nicholls, with views of the island taken by José Anjo. St. John's, Antigua: José Anjo, n.d. [1905?]. 32p.
The author, distinguished Senior Medical Officer of Dominica at the time, describes the natural, agricultural and human assets of the island in glowing terms. The ten photographs by the Antiguan photographer José Anjo accomplish their purpose, giving 'some idea of the grandeur and loveliness of the scenery' (p. 32) and are among the best views existing of the island at the beginning of the century.

226 A brief memoir of Sir Henry Alfred Alford Nicholls, K.B., C.M.G.
(His Honour Mr. Justice) Noble. Roseau: Bulletin Office, 1928, 29p.
The fullest biography of one of the most influential figures in Dominica's history. The memoir describes Sir Henry Nicholls (27 Sept. 1851-9 Feb. 1926) as medical man, as an expert on tropical agriculture, and as a man devoted to his adopted island home. Included are excerpts from obituary notices in the *Dominica Chronicle*, *The Times* and from the memorial service held in Roseau at his death.

227 Dominica, a fertile island.
F. Sterns-Fadelle. Roseau: A. T. Righton, 1902. 28p.
Written just after the eruption of Mount Pelée in Martinique, the Paris University-educated author sought to rescue 'our island from the anomalous position of a highly gifted country in a very backward state' (p. 1). The booklet contains a discursive history of the island, emphasizing agriculture and economics, and uses extensive extracts from Thomas Atwood's *History of the island of Dominica*, (London, 1791) and government reports. In promoting Dominica, the author compares it to other nearby islands. A supplementary section offers practical and touristic advice. Thirteen pages of advertisement may interest a historian of the island's merchant community. This pamphlet was later published as a chapter in Francis Dodsworth's *Book of the West Indies* (London: George Routledge, 1904, p. 168-85). In 1903, Sterns-Fadelle published an account of the island's best-known natural feature, *The Boiling Lake of Dominica: a historical and descriptive account of a unique phenomenon.* (Roseau: Dominican Office, 1903, 26p.).

228 **The West Indies in 1837; being the journal of a visit to Antigua, Montserrat, Dominica, St.** Lucia, Barbados and Jamaica; undertaken for the purpose of ascertaining the actual condition of the Negro population of those islands.
Joseph Sturge, Thomas Harvey. London: Hamilton, Adams, 1838. Reprinted, London: Dawsons of Pall Mall; Cass, 1968. 380p. (Cass Library of African Studies. Slavery Series, no. 6).

Two members of the Society of Friends toured the Antilles and reported on conditions following the abolition of slavery. Although their visit was brief, their descriptive account gives a valuable view of the social and agricultural conditions in Dominica in December 1836 (p. 90-107). The Appendix (p. xvi-xxi) includes 'A table, shewing the increase and decrease of slaves on three estates of RESIDENT proprietors, and on three others of NON-RESIDENT proprietors, from 1817 to 1834', comments on the local government and the late Governor, Sir Evan MacGregor, and the comparative condition of the apprentices, concluding 'It appears evident that the negros in this Colony have gained nothing by the exchange of Slavery for Apprenticeship.' (p. xx-xxi). The facsimile edition published by Dawsons of Pall Mall has an index and an introduction by Philip Wright.

229 **Handbook of the Leeward Islands.**
Compiled by Frederick Henry Watkins. London: Waterlow & Sons, for the West India Committee, 1924. 308p. map. bibliog.

The author provides a wealth of information on the Leeward Islands, to which Dominica belonged until 1940. A description of the island (p. 113-31), including two photographs, a chronological outline history of the Leeward Islands, and a list of estates with acreage and owner for each island are included.

The pocket guide to the West Indies.
See item no. 1.

Dominica.
See item no. 6.

Notes on the island of Dominica, West Indies.
See item no. 8.

The English in the West Indies: or, the bow of Ulysses.
See item no. 14.

The West Indies illustrated, including the Isthmus of Panama and Bermuda: historical and descriptive, commercial and industrial facts, figures, & resources.
See item no. 22.

Dominica: diving for yesterday.
See item no. 37.

The sense of time, the social construction of reality, and the foundations of nationhood in Dominica and the Faroe Islands.
See item no. 41.

The volcanic eruption in Dominica.
See item no. 54.

Island Carib cannibalism.
See item no. 152.

Conditions in the Carib Reserve, and the disturbance of 19th September 1930, Dominica: report of a commission appointed by His Excellency the Governor of the Leeward Islands, July, 1931.
See item no. 158.

'I love my home bad, but . . .': the historical and contemporary contexts of migration on Dominica, West Indies.
See item no. 251.

Post-emancipation migrations and population change in Dominica: 1834-1950.
See item no. 252.

Place names as a reflection of cultural change: an example from the Lesser Antilles.
See item no. 276.

Social structural changes in Dominica.
See item no. 295.

Peasants and capital: Dominica in the world economy.
See item no. 298.

Two centuries of health care in Dominica.
See item no. 302.

Glimpses of a governor's life from diaries, letters and memoranda.
See item no. 332.

Broken atoms.
See item no. 333.

From a colonial governor's notebook.
See item no. 336.

From Crown Colony to Associated Statehood: political change in Dominica, the Commonwealth West Indies.
See item no. 337.

The consitutional history of the Windwards.
See item no. 348.

Dominica's ill-fated lime industry.
See item no. 374.

Report of C. O. Naftel, Esqr., **(late inspector of plantations in Ceylon) on the forest lands and estates of Dominica, and on the agricultural capabilities of the island.**
See item no. 377.

A century of West Indian education.
See item no. 405.

Agostino Brunias, Romano: Robert Adam's 'bred painter'.
See item no. 445.

Step by step from livré to douillette.
See item no 447.

A guide to records in the Windward Islands.
See item no. 455.

Guide to British West Indian archive materials, in London and in the islands, for the history of the United States.
See item no. 456.

Origin and growth of the public libraries of Dominica.
See item no. 457.

The first printing in Dominica.
See item no. 462.

Dominica Official Gazette.
See item no. 466.

The complete Caribbeana 1900-1975: a bibliographic guide to the scholarly literature.
See item no. 482.

Research guide to Central America and the Caribbean.
See item no. 483.

Sources for West Indian studies: a supplementary listing, with particular reference to manuscript sources.
See item no. 484.

A resource guide to Dominica, 1493-1986.
See item no. 489.

A guide for the study of British Caribbean history, 1763-1834, including the abolition and emancipation movements.
See item no. 491.

A guide to manuscript sources for the history of Latin America and the Caribbean in the British Isles.
See item no. 492.

Slavery and the Maroons

230 Dominique, terre de refuge. (Dominica, land of refuge.)
Raphaël Bogat. *Bulletin de la Société d'Histoire Guadeloupe*,
no. 8 (deuxième semestre 1967), p. 79-94; no. 11-12 (1969), p. 149-
54.
Two articles stressing the theme of Dominica as a refuge, recounting the intimate
historical associations between Dominica and the French islands between which it
lies. The first article consists of two parts, 'Dominica, Carib Reserve' and
'Dominica, asylum for Antillean patriots during the French Revolution'. The
second is subtitled 'Dominica, haven of slaves during the last years of their
servitude', and focuses on events in the 1830s and 1840s.

**231 'Black man' – the mutiny of the 8th (British) West India regiment: a
microcosm of war and slavery in the Caribbean.**
Roger N. Buckley. *Jamaican Historical Review*, vol. 12 (1980),
p. 52-74. bibliog.
In April 1802, the 8th West India Regiment, stationed in Dominica, and one of
twelve imperial black corps recruited from plantations slaves in the Caribbean,
mutinied, resulting in over a hundred casualties. The documentary evidence
concerning this mutiny is important as 'it represents one of the very few recorded,
albeit brief, testimonies of West Indian slaves in which they comment on their
own personal condition' (p. 60). The author, Professor of History at Varnier
College, Montreal, sets the event in the contemporary social and military
contexts.

**232 A collection of plain authentic documents, in justification of the
conduct of Governor Ainslie; in the reduction of a formidable
rebellion among the Negro slaves in the island of Dominica, at a
crisis of the most imminent danger to the lives and properties of the
inhabitants.**
London: C. Lowndes, 1815. 47p.
Testimonials and petitions delivered in 1814 and 1815 by members of the Council,
the House of Assembly, planters and merchants, including many free men of
colour, in support of Dominica Governor George Robert Ainslie who had been
summoned to England regarding charges associated with his expeditions against
the Maroons. The documents include extracts from the House of Assembly
minutes of 15 August 1815 and other accounts providing a valuable glimpse of
events in the colony in 1815. Ainslie was later exonerated from the charges.

233 Testing the chains: resistance to slavery in the British West Indies.
Michael Craton. Ithaca, New York: Cornell University Press,
1982. 389p. maps. bibliog.
A social history of slave resistance in the British West Indies, with considerable
material directly relevant to the history of Dominica. The introduction discusses

the Amerindian response to European colonization. Two chapters, entitled 'New colonies, traditional resistance, 1763-1802' and 'The subjugation of Dominica and Trinidad, 1791-1814' recount the first and second Maroon wars of Dominica, led by Balla, Pharcell, Quashie, Apollo, Jacko and others. The author includes reproductions of paintings by Agostino Brunias and a useful map showing areas of Maroon activity (p. 142). The author is Professor of History at the University of Waterloo, Ontario, Canada.

234 Slave populations of the British Caribbean, 1807-1834.
Barry W. Higman. Baltimore, Maryland: Johns Hopkins
University Press, 1984. 781p. bibliog.

An invaluable work of scholarship, the most comprehensive study of British Caribbean slavery available for the years covered. The author presents and analyses extensive demographic data on Dominican slavery, using primary archival materials examined during his visit to the island. Lengthy appendixes contain a wealth of data on slavery for most of the former British islands.

**235 The report of the Committee of the Legislature of Dominica,
appointed to enquire into and report on certain queries relative to
the condition, treatment, rights & privileges of the Negro population
of that island.**
John Laidlaw, William Blanc, Henry J. Glanville, Joseph Court,
Robert Burt. London: Charles M. Willich, June 1823. Reprinted
in: *West Indian slavery. Selected pamphlets.* Westport, Connecticut:
Negro Universities Press, 1970, no. 5, p. 1-43.

For this report the committee members procured 'from the most respectable and authentic sources, a mass of information, which completely establishes that every care and attention is paid to the happiness and comforts, as well as to the moral and religious instruction of the Slaves' (p. 1). To support their claim that the state of slavery 'is soothed and ameliorated by the kindness and humanity of the West Indian Proprietor' (p. 2), statements are presented from physicans, officials and missionaries, which reveal their views on slavery in Dominica and include data on marriages, baptisms and manumissions for 1821-23.

**236 Maronage in slave plantation societies: a case study of Dominica,
1785-1815.**
Bernard A. Marshall. *Caribbean Quarterly*, vol. 22, no. 2 & 3
(June-Sept. 1976), p. 26-32. bibliog.

An account of Maroon activities on Dominica and their role in destablizing the plantation economy. An estimated 300 Maroons in 1785 and at least 559 in 1814 lived in remote parts of the mountainous island and used guerrilla tactics against the planters. The author reconstructs the history from Colonial Office records.

237 Slave resistance and white reaction in the British Windward Islands, 1763-1833.
Bernard [A]. Marshall. *Caribbean Quarterly*, vol. 28, no. 3 (Sept. 1982), p. 33-46. bibliog.
Studies slave resistance in the forms of murder, revolt and maronage in Tobago, St. Vincent, Grenada and Dominica. Dominica's Maroons were second in strength and organization only to their counterparts in Jamaica, and remained active longer than runaway slaves in the other Windward Islands. The author, an historian, presented a doctoral dissertation entitled 'Society and economy in the British Windward Islands, 1763-1823' to the University of the West Indies, Mona, Jamaica, in 1972.

238 Doctors and slaves: a medical and demographic history of slavery in the British West Indies, 1680-1834.
Richard B. Sheridan. New York, London: Cambridge University Press, 1985. 420p. map. bibliog.
A ground-breaking historical study of medicine and demography in the pre-emancipation British islands. Considerations include not only diseases and health care, but also labour and nutrition, using a world-systems approach and offering an explanation for the region's slave population decline. Dominica is mentioned throughout, and the work of Dr. Jonathan Troup of Dominica in 1789-90 is profiled as exemplary of difficult contemporary medical conditions (p. 302-05). The author is Professor Emeritus in the Department of Economics, University of Kansas, Lawrence, Kansas.

239 Notes on the slaves of the French.
Rev. Father R[aymond] Proesmans. In: *Aspects of Dominican history*. Dominica Government. Roseau: Government Printing Division, 1972, p. 163-72.
The only published article on Dominican history by the late Belgian-born author, parish priest of Pt. Michel, Dominica, for forty years and unofficial historian of the island. The author, using French, English and Roman Catholic Church records, documents the French laws governing behaviour towards slaves, incorporating accounts by John Barbot, Fr. Gombaud, Fr. Vidaud and Father William Martel.

240 Labour and emancipation in Dominica: contribution to a debate.
Michel-Rolph Trouillot. *Caribbean Quarterly*, vol. 30 (1984), p. 73-84. bibliog.
The author analyses data collected by William Lynch, Stipendiary Magistrate, on forty-one Dominican estates during the four months immediately following the end of Apprenticeship in 1838. He demonstrates that more than 1,000 slaves or thirty-nine per cent of the forty-one estates' labour force fled, that the flight was most severe during the first two months, and that many of these labourers returned to work, but generally on different estates, during the next two months.

West Indian societies.
See item no. 20.

Caribbean story. . .
See item no. 183.

The Caribbean people.
See item no. 184.

From Columbus to Castro: the history of the Caribbean, 1492-1969.
See item no. 188.

Aspects of Dominican history.
See item no. 189.

The history of the island of Dominica, containing a description of its situation, extent, climate, mountains, rivers, natural productions, etc., etc., together with an account of the civil government, trade, laws, customs, and manners of the different inhabitants of that island. Its conquest by the French, and restoration to the British dominions.
See item no. 191.

The history, civil and commercial, of the British West Indies, with a continuation to the present time.
See item no. 211.

A winter in the West Indies, described in familiar letters to Henry Clay, of Kentucky.
See item no. 213.

The Dominica story: a history of the island.
See item no. 216.

The West Indies in 1837; being the journal of a visit to Antigua, Montserrat, Dominica, St. Lucia, Barbados and Jamaica; undertaken for the purpose of ascertaining the actual condition of the Negro population of those islands.
See item no. 228.

Population, Migration and Demography

General

241 Demographic survey of the British Colonial Empire.
Robert René Kuczynski. London, New York: Oxford University Press, 1953. 493p. bibliog.

Volume three, *West Indian and American Territories*, completed after Kuczynski's death by his daughter Brigitte Long, provides an unusually comprehensive account of the demography of the British West Indies. A complete discussion of the Dominica censuses of 1921 and 1946 is provided, including a history of census-taking since 1891 (p. 28-51). Analyses are also presented of the composition of the population, birth and death registration, and birth and death statistics with data reported for each year from 1919 to 1948 (p. 378-87). An earlier chapter compares the demographic features of all British Colonies in America, 1921-46.

Census reports

242 Census taken November 1871, tables. Dominica.
Registrar-General [Theo. F. Lockhart]. Roseau: New Dominican Office, 1 Aug. 1872. [9]p.

Report, with summary tables by Theo. F. Lockhart, Registrar-General, of the census taken on 27 November 1871 in the Presidency of Dominica. Comparisons of the populations of Roseau and the parishes are made between the 1871 and 1860 population returns. The series of Dominica population censuses which this begins are crucial documents for the understanding of the demographic history of the country. The census of 1844 remains available only in less accessible official colonial documents.

243 Census of Dominica, 1881.
Dominica. Registrar-General [Cavendish Boyle's] office.   Roseau:
A. T. Righton, 1881. [8]p.

Twelve tables report the island's population on 4 April 1881, showing town and parish populations by sex (also compared to 1871 figures), colour, numbers of infirm people, religion, marital status, institutional populations, Caribs, place of birth, occupation and age structure. Cavendish Boyle, Registrar-General, provides a brief summary of the census.

**244 [Census reports: Leeward Islands census 1891; St. Kitts-Nevis,
1911; St. Kitts-Nevis, 1921; Montserrat, 1921; Dominica, 1921].**
University of the West Indies. Census Research Programme.
[Port of Spain], Trinidad: Central Statistical Office, Aug. 1964.
[124]p.

A reissue by the Census Research Programme, in one volume lacking a title page, of five census reports: Leeward Islands, 1891; St. Kitts-Nevis 1911; St. Kitts-Nevis, 1921; Montserrat, 1921; Dominica, 1921. The 5 April 1891 census of the Leeward Islands included Dominica and provides especially complete information on sex, race, marital status, housing size and age structure in five-year cohorts for each parish, as well as place of birth and occupation. The Dominica census for 24 April 1921 is reprinted from the Supplement to the 21 November 1921 *Official Gazette*, and is summarized by E. H. E. Dalrymple, Chief Clerk, General Register Office. Fifteen tables display data for categories which include occupation, age structure, birthplace, religion, nationality, education, infirmity, 'relationship to head of family', race, and population of public institutions. This volume, which is introduced briefly by George W. Roberts of the University of the West Indies, Mona, Jamaica, and Jack Harewood, Central Statistical Officer, Trinidad, makes important demographic information on these islands readily available.

245 Census 1911. Dominica.
Dominica. Registrar-General [N. C. Ruggles's] office.   Roseau:
Bulletin Office, 1911. 11p.

A report by the acting Registrar-General, N. C. Ruggles, summarizes the accompanying tables which cover population in towns, villages and parishes, sex, age, marital status, occupation, birthplace and nationality, religion, education, infirmities, relationship to head of family, 'complexion', and population of public institutions. Several population totals are compared to those from the censuses of 1871, 1881, 1891 and 1901.

**246 West Indian census 1946. Census of the Windward Islands
(Dominica – Grenada – St. Lucia – St. Vincent). 9th April, 1946.**
Central Board of Statistics.   Kingston: Government Printer, 1950.
79p. 4 maps.

The vital statistics for the four islands, with analyses of distribution and growth of population, households, dwellings and rooms, race and sex, age, conjugal condition, 'motherhood and fertility', 'religion, birthplace, literacy and language', and 'industry, status and occupation'. The administrative report for Dominica by T. A. Boyd, Census Officer (p. lxv-lxvii), gives a history of census-taking on the island. Data for the four islands is integrated in tables by category throughout.

247 **Windward Islands. Dominica. Population census 1960. 7th April 1960.**
Population Census Division.   Port of Spain: Central Statistical Office, 1963, 1965, 1969. 3 vols.

Three volumes present a wealth of data from the census taken on 7 April 1960. Volume one, published in March 1965, describes 'the planning of the entire census, of the approaches and concepts adopted and of the methods used in processing the data. This volume contains as well a comprehensive description of the boundaries of each enumeration district' (Preface, p. v). Volume two, published in August 1963, contains summary tabulations giving information for each enumeration district about household and family, age and race, religion, migration, education, marital status, fertility and union status, and working population and union force. Volume three, published in March 1969, contains a second major set of tabulations with special reference to cross-classifications by the principal characteristics of the population: 'individuals by type of households; and internal and external migration'; 'marital and union status'; 'age, ethnic origin and religion'; 'households and families'; 'educational attainment'; and 'working population'.

248 **Associated State of Dominica. 1970 population census: preliminary report (provisional).**
Dominica. Division of Statistics.   Roseau: Division of Statistics, Ministry of Finance. Trade and Industry, March 1971. 112p.
2 maps.

A much briefer presentation of census data than either the 1960 or 1981 censuses. The Administrative Report by Olwyn M. Norris, Census and Statistical Officer, describes the planning and enumeration as well as basic summary population results, sex ratios and housing figures (p. 1-19). The four appendixes give more detailed breakdowns of these categories and provide comparisons with findings from the 1946 and 1960 censuses. A copy of the census questionnaire, a colour map of Dominica (scale 1:122,500) and a plan of Roseau are bound into the volume.

249 **1980-1981 population census of the Commonwealth Caribbean. Dominica.**
CARICOM; Hubert Barker, Regional Census Co-ordinating Committee Chairman.   Jamaica: Statistical Institute of Jamaica, n.d. 2 vols.

Contains the details of the census conducted in Dominica on 7 April 1981 which had been postponed from the previous year due to political unrest. Volume one analyses the population according to sex, age, enumeration district, economic activity, immigration, internal migration, education, vocational training, race and religion, marital and union status and fertility, housing, services and household. Volume two goes into a more detailed counting of the population in several of the same categories: economic activity, education, vocational training, race and religion, marriage, fertility and union status, housing, services, household and income. This is the only census conducted since 1970. A copy of the census questionnaire is appended to each volume. Copies can be obtained from the Statistical Division, Ministry of Finance, 22 Bath Road, Roseau, Commonweath of Dominica.

Migration

250 Report of the delegation appointed to visit Dominica to examine the possibilities of a land settlement scheme there for Barbadians.
M. E. Cox, D. D. Garner, J. M. Cave, D. Harris, Mrs. D. Harris, T. O. Lashley, L. A. Pinard, J. C. King. Bridgetown: Government Printing Office, June 1960. 7p.

In May 1960, a committee composed of Barbadians and former Dominican officials visited Dominica, often considered to be an underpopulated island, to evaluate it as a site for Barbadian emigrants. The committee reviewed the agricultural outlook, infrastructure, social services, labour situation, the fishing industry, industrial outlook and attitude towards migrants. Although advantages were likely to accrue for both islands from a settlement scheme, the committee reported that lack of amenities, unfavourable terrain and lower living standards in Dominica were likely to be significant obstacles to new settlers. The scheme was abandoned following the report.

251 'I love my home bad, but . . .': the historical and contemporary contexts of migration on Dominica, West Indies.
Robert A. Myers. PhD thesis, University of North Carolina, Chapel Hill, North Carolina, 1976. 518 leaves. 8 maps. bibliog. (Available from University Microfilms, Ann Arbor, Michigan, 1977. Order no. BWH76-28313).

Based on fieldwork in Dominica in 1972-73, this study consists of two parts: 'The context of Dominican migrations', a history of the ebb and flow of populations on the island from prehistoric times to 1970, and 'the community of Fond Colé and migration', the impact of migration on one small impoverished community. Findings are integrated in Part III, 'the study of West Indian migrations'. Appendixes contain questionnaires used, as well as detailed health and population statistics. Twenty-five photographs illustrate the thesis.

252 Post-emancipation migrations and population change in Dominica: 1834-1950.
Robert A. Myers. *Revista/Review Interamericana*, vol. XI, no. 1 (spring 1981), p. 87-109. bibliog.

An historical and demographic account drawing upon censuses, government reports and first-hand accounts of the period covered. The article is divided into three periods: 'Stagnation and stability: 1834-1870' characterized by gradual increase of the largely former-slave population; 'The rush to the gold fields: 1870-1900', during which thousands emigrated to Venezuela causing a labour shortage on the island; and 'Twentieth century migrations', which included a small influx of British and an outflux of workers to the oil refineries of Aruba. These population movements are set in the context of the island's fluctuating economy.

253 West Indian migration to Britain: a social geography.
Ceri Peach. London, New York: Oxford University Press for the Institute of Race Relations, London, 1968. 122p. 2 maps. bibliog.

An analysis of the large-scale West Indian emigration to Britain during the 1950s. The author, Lecturer in Geography at Oxford University, considers the conditions in Britain and the islands and concludes Britain's need for labour was the primary cause. He shows that the migrants moved into areas of lesser labour demand as a replacement population for whites leaving second-rate jobs and decaying urban living areas. Dominica is conspicuous in the analysis as the island, after Montserrat, with the second highest rate of emigration. Between 1955-61 more than thirteen per cent of the island's population emigrated.

254 Population movements in the Caribbean.
Malcolm J[arvis] Proudfoot. Port of Spain: Caribbean Commission Central Secretariat, 1950. 187p. bibliog. Reprinted, New York: Negro Universities Press, 1970.

A study commissioned by the Caribbean Commission Central Secretariat to establish existing evidence of population pressure, rate of population growth, prospective growth, major migratory movements affecting the Caribbean dependencies and the present outlook for migration. The author has assembled a mass of data on the entire region, of which Dominica is one unit. Among many statistics for Dominica are the annual rates of increase and decrease between 1921 and 1948. The author was Professor of Geography, Northwestern University, Evanston, Illinois. The study is introduced with a brief foreword by Eric Williams, late Prime Minister of Trinidad and Tobago.

255 Population density and emigration in Dominica.
Barbara Welch. *Geographical Journal*, vol. 134, no. 2 (June 1968), p. 227-35. map. bibliog.

The author explores reasons for the high rate of emigration from Dominica to the United Kingdom when Dominica, relative to other Caribbean islands, has a low population density. Rugged terrain, poor soil, limited development and difficult economic conditions are seen as important factors behind the out-migration. The author spent fifteen months in the eastern Caribbean during 1966 and 1967, and was a Lecturer in Geography at McGill University, Montreal.

Family planning

256 Contraceptive prevalence surveys: a comparative study of contraceptive prevalence in Antigua, Dominica, St. Lucia and St. Vincent.
Barbados Family Planning Association. Columbia, Maryland: Westinghouse Health Systems, Sept. 1983. 83p.

An analysis of interviews with a sample of about 1,000 women, aged 15-44 years, in each country. The study contains a wealth of information on fertility, potential demand for contraceptive services, contraceptive knowledge, use and supplies, and awareness and use of family planning services. The analysis of responses from 1,017 women in Dominica (p. 32-48), written by Jack Harewood, is accompanied by sixteen tables. The study was partially funded by the US Agency for International Development.

257 The need for a family planning programme in Dominica, West Indies.
Karl A. Smith. *West Indian Medical Journal*, vol. 21, no. 2 (June 1972), p. 125-34. bibliog.

A discussion of the need for family planning in Dominica in light of a rapidly-growing population (seventeen per cent growth in the decade 1960-70), low per capita annual income (EC$418 in 1968) and various other economic and social problems. The author wrote his MD thesis at Aberdeen University in 1977 on *Family planning in Dominica, West Indies.*

Language, Dialect and Names

General

258   A lifelong exercise in linguistic anthropology.

Penny Honychurch. *Bajan*, (June 1979), p. 24, 26-28.

An interview with Douglas Taylor in Dominica on the occasion of his receiving an honorary doctoral degree from the University of the West Indies at Cave Hill, Barbados. The article includes a short biography of Taylor who was born in 1901 (and died in 1980) and read Modern Languages at Cambridge before devoting his life to the study of the Caribs and Caribbean languages.

259   Language contacts in the West Indies.

Douglas Taylor. *Word*, vol. 12, no. 3 (Dec. 1956), p. 399-414. bibliog.

Part one of this article describes the 'intimate borrowing' which occurred between Carib-speaking men and their Arawak-speaking women in Dominica. Taylor uses Swadesh's lexicostatistical test list of one hundred terms to demonstrate the convergence of male and female vocabularies over three centuries. Part two analyses the relatedness of Caribbean and West African languages proposing that 'the modern Creole languages of the West Indies were formed in an effort to achieve mutual intelligibility between slaves at least as much as between master and slave' (p. 412).

260   Use and disuse of languages in the West Indies.

Douglas Taylor. *Caribbean Quarterly*, vol. 5, no. 2 (Feb. 1958), p. 67-77.

Survey article on West Indian languages with particular emphasis on constructions from French Creole and Island Carib, and comparisons of these with Indo-European linguistic | examples. There is some general discussion on the relationship between cultural context and language.

261 Language shift or changing relationship?
Douglas Taylor. *International Journal of American Linguistics*,
vol. 26, no. 2 (April 1960), p. 155-61. bibliog.

A theoretical discussion of the relationship among Caribbean Creoles, and
between them and their European mother languages, emphasizing structural
similarities among the Creoles. Examples from Dominican French Creole,
Haitian Creole, Papiamentu and Sranan, the English Creole of Surinam, bolster
the arguments. Taylor suggests that an early Portuguese pidgin used in coastal
West Africa may have provided the essential grammatical structure, but not the
vocabulary, of the Caribbean Creoles.

262 New languages for old in the West Indies.
Douglas Taylor. *Comparative Studies in Society and History,*
vol. 3, no. 3 (April 1961), p. 277-88. bibliog. Reprinted in: *Peoples*
and cultures of the Caribbean. An anthropological reader. Edited
and introduced by Michael M. Horowitz. Garden City, New York:
Natural History Press, 1971. p. 77-91.

An excellent overview of the creation of Creole languages in the region through
the culture contacts among Amerindians, African slaves and Europeans.
Numerous examples from the languages are given, with emphasis on the
formation of French and English Creoles.

263 The origin of West Indian Creole languages: evidence from
grammatical categories.
Douglas Taylor. *American Anthropologist*, vol. 65, no. 4 (Dec.
1963), p. 800-14. bibliog.

Through comparisons of Martinican Creole (and by extension, Dominican
Creole), Haitian Creole and Sranan, the English-vocabulary Creole of Surinam,
the author argues 'There is reason to believe that many of the Africans brought to
the West Indies as slaves during the latter half of the seventeenth and the first half
of the eighteenth centuries were already familiar, at the time of their arrival, with
an Afro-Portuguese pidgin; and that this pidgin provided the framework upon
which subsequent West Indian pidgins were built by a process of lexical
replacement.' (p. 812-13).

English- and French-based Creole

264 Dominican Creole phonology.

Jon Edward Amastae. PhD thesis, University of Oregon,
Eugene, Oregon, 1975. 194 leaves. bibliog. (Available from
University Microfilms, Ann Arbor, Michigan, 1976. Order
no. 76-5137).

This study of Dominican French Creole explores issues germain to phonological
theory and the nature of Creole languages. It consists of four sections: an
historical and social background; a survey of basic syntax and morphology; a
grammar of the phonological system; and a section on markedness. The
phonological analysis is conducted within the framework of generative phonology.

265 Dominican English Creole phonology: an initial sketch.

Jon [Edward] Amastae. *Anthropological Linguistics*, vol. 21,
no. 4 (April 1979), p. 182-204. bibliog.

A detailed beginning description of the English spoken on Dominica, arguing that
it is a Creole language just as is the French Creole spoken there. The author
compares Dominican English Creole with Dominican French Creole, with other
West Indian English Creoles and with standard English to bolster his case.

266 Dominican Creole phonology I, II.

Jon [Edward] Amastae. *Georgetown University Papers on
Languages and Linguistics*, vol. 15 (spring 1979), p. 83-122; vol. 16
(fall 1979), p. 1-32. bibliog.

An analysis, within a generative phonological framework, of the phonological
system of Dominican 'patois' or French Creole. Part one establishes the
'underlying segments of the language and the rules necessary to relate' them 'to
their surface realizations'. Part two argues 'that the segment inventory and rule
types are nearly optimal' (p. 83), that the Creole phonological system tends to be
maximally unmarked and that the concept of markedness should be part of the
definition of 'creole language'. The author collected data for this analysis in 1968-
70 and in 1974; he was at Pan American University when it was published.

267 Agentless constructions in Dominican Creole.

Jon [Edward] Amastae. *Lingua*, vol. 59, no. 1 (Jan. 1983),
p. 47-75. bibliog.

The author, who is at the University of Texas at El Paso, examines the agentless
(semi-passive) constructions with transitive verbs in Dominican French Creole as
a means of explaining other problems in the description of that Creole: the
nature of verbs and adjectives; the verb 'be'; and the distribution and
intepretation of tense-aspect markers. The analysis also provides a description of
Indian Ocean French Creole which is similar to but morphologically more
complex than Dominican French Creole.

268 Deviations from standard English in the speech of primary school children in St. Lucia and Dominica: a preliminary survey. Part I.
Lawrence D. Carrington. *International Review of Applied Linguistics in Language Teaching*, vol. VII, no. 3 (Aug. 1969), p. 165-84. bibliog.

This study of non-standard English is based on an analysis of the tape-recorded speech in 1966 of 59 children, 37 from six schools in St. Lucia and 22 from three schools in Dominica. Here the focus is on phonological deviations: vowels; differences in the Creole and standard English vocalic systems; treatment of English vowel phonemes; and consonants. Eleven appendixes expand on the author's conclusions. The author was at the Institute of Education, University of the West Indies, St. Augustine, Trinidad.

269 Language maintenance and language shift in Dominica.
Pauline Christie. *Caribbean Quarterly*, vol. 28, no. 4 (Dec. 1982), p. 41-51. bibliog.

An historical and linguistic explanation of the survival of French-lexicon Creole and the demise of Island Carib. The author attributes the resilience of Dominican Creole to a consciousness among its speakers of Creole culture and the extinction of Island Carib to the Caribs' loss of faith in their own culture as they were 'hopelessly outnumbered by the fast increasing Creole-speaking population' (p. 50).

270 Certain Carib morphological influences on Creole.
Douglas Taylor. *International Journal of American Linguistics*, vol. 11, no. 3 (July 1945), p. 140-55.

With detailed comparisons the author meticulously argues that there are historical, lexical and phonological grounds for his hypothesis that Island Carib influenced the formation of Caribbean Creole (the French Creole of Dominica). Numerous words, phrases and sentences are rendered in Carib, Creole and English.

271 Phonemes of Caribbean Creole.
Douglas Taylor. *Word*, vol. 3, no. 3 (Dec. 1947), p. 173-79.

A phonemic analysis of the 'average middle-aged country-folk of the island of Dominica, whose speech so far has been little influenced by contacts with the local, largely English-speaking town on the one hand, or with the neighboring French islands on the other' (p. 173). The author notes Carib as well as French influences on the twenty-two consonant and eleven vowel phonemes he describes. As is characteristic of his articles, the author includes numerous examples and translations of words in Caribbean Creole.

272 Structural outline of Caribbean Creole.
Douglas Taylor. *Word*, vol. 7, no. 1 (April 1951), p. 43-59.

A formal description of the morphology and syntax of Caribbean (French-based) Creole, emphasizing its difference from French, with numerous words and phrases translated as examples.

273 **Phonic interference in Dominican Creole.**
Douglas Taylor. *Word*, vol. 11, no. 1 (April 1955), p. 45-52.
An elaboration and refinement of the author's earlier description of Dominican French Creole, 'Structural outline of Caribbean Creole' *Word*, vol. 7, no. 1 (April 1951), p. 43-59. Here he recognizes the existence of several dialects of French Creole and English on the island, and discusses the impact of the latter on the former.

274 **Languages of the West Indies.**
Douglas Taylor, foreword by Sidney W. Mintz and Dell Hymes. Baltimore, Maryland; London: Johns Hopkins University Press, 1977. xix, 278p. bibliog.
This volume provides the summation of nearly fifty years' work on Amerindian and Creole languages by the author, 'one of the world's most distinguished authorities in the fields of his specialization' (Foreword, xvii). Part one discusses both dead and living Amerindian languages with detailed chapters on the phonology, grammar and vocabulary of Island Carib, with texts in Arawak, Central American Island Carib and Karina, and wordlists. In Part two, the author analyses Caribbean Creoles, focusing in particular on Saramaccan and Dominican Creole with texts in Sranan and Dominican Creole, and wordlists in nine Creoles. This book is a valuable resource for the generalist seeking a solid understanding of languages on Dominica (or thoughout the region), as well as for the specialist.

Names

275 **Names on Dominica.**
Douglas Taylor. *Names*, vol. 2, no. 1 (March 1954), p. 31-37.
A discussion of the impact of Amerindian, French Creole and English cultures on the names of places, flora, fauna, mountains, plantations and people of Dominica. The author believes the island 'offers an exceptional opportunity to the onomatologist at the present time' (p. 37). A second article with the same title in *West-Indische Gids*, vol. 36 (1955-56), p. 121-24, describes further the assortment of names on Dominica, or *uái-túkubuli* 'tall her-body', as the Island Caribs called it.

276 **Place names as a reflection of cultural change: an example from the Lesser Antilles.**
Marjorie Bingham Wesche. *Caribbean Studies*, vol. 12, no. 2 (July 1973), p. 74-98. maps. bibliog.
A study of the process by which place-names are given, maintained intact, modified, or replaced on Tobago, Grenada, St. Vincent and Dominica, between 1763 and the 1960s. For Dominica, which has by far the largest number of place-names, the author compares the Byres map of 1776 with the DOS (Directorate of

Overseas Surveys) map of 1960, showing changes in the number of French, English, Amerindian and other names. The author was then a PhD candidate at the University of Toronto.

Society and Social Conditions

277 Adolescent perception of parental power in three Caribbean islands.
Roy L. Austin, Elaine Porter. *Social and Economic Studies*,
vol. 29, no. 2-3 (June-Sept. 1980), p. 247-63. bibliog.
By analysis of questionnaires administered in 1975 and 1976 to 397 fifth- and
sixth-form students in Dominica, 'Antillia', and St. Vincent, the authors tested
four hypotheses regarding male dominance, socio-economic status, education,
and changes in dominance patterns between the 1950s and the 1970s. Males were
found to be three times as likely as females to dominate family decisions in
Antillia and St. Vincent, and five times as likely in Dominica. Social status, but
not economic status, and father's education are indicators of dominance, and
male dominance seems to have declined since M. G. Smith collected data on the
topic in 1955 (*West Indian family structure*, Seattle, University of Washington
Press, 1962). On Dominica, ninety-seven students, more than forty per cent of
those eligible, completed the questionnaires. 'Antillia' is a 'fictitious name used to
keep a promise to an individual that his cooperation would not be made public'
(p. 261).

**278 Social differentiation in Roseau: politico-economic change and the
realignment of class, status group and party among elites in a
Caribbean capital.**
Patrick L. Baker. PhD thesis, University College, Swansea,
Wales, 1982. 607 leaves. bibliog.
This anthropological study, based on fieldwork in 1972 and 1973, uses Weberian
concepts to analyse élites in Roseau in the light of political and economic changes
of the 1950s and 1960s. Particularly important changes among the élites resulted
from the rise of the banana industry, internal self-government and universal adult
suffrage. The author is Chairman of the Sociology and Anthropology Department, Mount Allison University, Sackville, New Brunswick, Canada.

279 The bubble trade.

Horace Beck. *Natural History*, vol. 85, no. 10 (Dec. 1976), p. 38-47. map. bibliog.

The author discusses smuggling in the Lesser Antilles. He estimates that 'up to 80 percent of the male population have taken part in the trade at one time or another; 5 or 10 percent pursue it full time. Of all the imported goods sold on the islands, perhaps 30 percent are contraband' (p. 41). Values emphasizing courage, cleverness, sexual prowess and beliefs in the supernatural help sustain the 'bubble trade', so named because contraband sometimes includes sparkling wine. Dominica is one of several islands described. Excellent colour photographs form part of the article.

280 The cave of Coulibistrie.

William Bunge. *Political Geography Quarterly*, vol. 2, no. 1 (Jan. 1983), p. 57-70.

A creative, dialectically-oriented account of life in a small coastal village on the leeward side of Dominica describing the rhythms of the daily life of its people, their reactions to their poverty, and their survival strategies. The author, who is at the Société pour l'Exploration Humaine in Quebec, Canada, discusses political movements from Dreadism to socialism, as well as the position of women and children. The metaphor of the cave is used because the village is located in a canyon between 'two sharp headlands' and 'the overall impression is that of being in the bottom of a cave whose roof has collapsed' (p. 57).

281 Mating patterns as environmental adaptations in Dominica, British West Indies.

Jo Ann Cannon. DrPH thesis, University of California, Los Angeles, 1970. 189 leaves. 5 maps. bibliog. (Available from University Microfilms, Ann Arbor, Michigan, 1970. Order no. 71-9216).

A study, based on the author's fieldwork in 1968-69, of women's mating patterns in a village on the northern leeward side of Dominica. The author analyses the influences of early childhood experiences and selected socio-economic and psychological factors on the three prevalent forms of mating (extra-residential, consensual cohabitation and legal marriage) among seventy women, aged between 18 and 60, in 239 households. She relates the findings to the need for appropriate community health education, her speciality. The appendixes include copies of the survey instruments used: household demography, age, sex and mating census, the interview schedule, internal-external control scale, and measure of delayed gratification.

282 **The Castle Bruce Farmers Co-operative: Dominca.**
Gordon M. Draper. In: *Contemporary Caribbean. A sociological reader.* Edited by Susan Craig. Maracas, Trinidad: College Press, 1982, vol. 2, p. 97-110. bibliog.

An historical overview of Castle Bruce Estate, the formation and organizational structure of a farmers' co-operative and a positive analysis of the co-operative's performance three years after its creation.

283 **Relative wealth and adaptive strategy among peasants in a small village community of Dominica, West Indies.**
Nobukiyo Eguchi. PhD thesis, University of North Carolina, Chapel Hill, North Carolina, 1984. 232 leaves. (Available from University Microfilms, Ann Arbor, Michigan, 1984. Order no. DA8415801).

In this community study based on fieldwork in 1982 and 1983, the author examines 'mechanisms of change in the peasant society, heterogeneous aspects of peasants' socio-economic statuses and behaviors, and peasants' involvement in national- and international-level socioeconomic affairs' (author's abstract). In a comprehensive examination of the village, he discusses family systems, landholding and inheritance, agricultural practices and the impacts of migration, emphasizing that peasants use adaptive strategies according to their relative wealth in order to survive.

284 **Inequality and ranking system among peasants: a case study of the Dominican peasants.**
Nobukiyo Eguchi. *Minzokugaku-kenkyu, Japanese Journal of Ethnology*, vol. 49, no. 4 (1985), p. 320-42. map. bibliog.

The author describes how the socio-economic status and behaviour of Dominican peasants are based on four factors: landholding; livestock, labour force; and occupation. With data collected between June 1982 and July 1983, the author analyses the effects of recent increases in monetization and emphasis on cash crop production on systems of social ranking. Although the main body of this article is in Japanese, a substantive synopsis summarizing the findings is in English. The author is Associate Professor of Anthropology in the Faculty of Literature at Ritsumeikan University in Kyoto and has published extensively on Dominica in Japanese journals since 1984.

285 **The allocation of scarce goods and values: a comparative analysis of mating patterns in Dominica, West Indies.**
Richard Eugene Gardner. PhD thesis, University of California, Los Angeles, California, 1974. 197 leaves. 5 maps. bibliog. (Available from University Microfilms, Ann Arbor, Michigan, 1975. Order no. 75-1974).

This anthropology thesis is a product of the author's fieldwork in Dominica in June-August 1968. Interviews with 299 household heads in four communities were analysed and compared with the studies of R. T. Smith, M. G. Smith and M.

Horowitz. The author found no evidence supporting a different set of values for peasant and proletariat groups with respect to mating (p. x). 'This study concludes that although conjugal status and the status of the conjugal union are independent of neither relative age or maternal well-being, the relative importance of these predictor variables itself varies with the life cycle.' (p. xi).

286 Some normative aspects of friendship in Dominica, West Indies: a preliminary analysis.
Richard E. Gardner, Jane E. Tinkler. *Anthropology*, vol. 1, no. 2 (Dec. 1977), p. 147-57. maps. bibliog.

Eighty-six interviews with a cross-section of adult Dominican males were conducted during 1975 and 1976 and analysed for this article. The authors describe mutual trust, sharing of confidences and mutual openness as essential aspects of Dominican friendship, and emphasize the interrelatedness of instrumental and emotional dimensions of friendship. At the time, the authors were at the University of California at San Diego and the State University of New York at Stony Brook, respectively.

287 Some further considerations on West Indian conjugal patterns.
Richard E. Gardner, Aaron M. Podolefsky. *Ethnology*, vol. 16, no. 3 (July 1977), p. 299-308. bibliog.

A random sample of 337 male and 210 female household heads in Dominica in 1968 was made to test M. G. Smith's thesis that marriage for peasant cultivators followed an age-specific pattern, whereas for more proletarianized West Indians, it did not. The study failed to replicate Smith's observation, concluding that both peasants and proletarians of Dominica's lower economic stratum delay marriage until the middle-to-later years of life. Both authors were at the State University of New York at Stony Brook.

288 Sociological analysis of Grand Bay.
P. I. Gomes. In: *Proceedings of the Eleventh West Indian Agricultural Economics Conference*. Edited by John Cropper. St. Augustine, Trinidad: University of the West Indies for the Caribbean Agro-Economic Society, 1977, p. 62-70.

An analysis of the main village of Berricoa (population 3,152), Grand Bay, Dominica, 'a typical area of rural underdevelopment' (p. 62). The author discusses the Grand Bay area, social amenities, the village economy and modes of subsistence, social status, village institutions, social organization and youth and their problems.

289 The hucksters of Dominica.
John Homiak. *Grassroots Development*, vol. 10, no. 1 (1986), p. 30-37.

The author, a post-doctoral fellow at the Smithsonian Institution, Washington, DC, vividly describes the difficulties confronting the 'hucksters' of Dominica as they sell surplus agricultural produce on the neighbouring islands. Since 1981, 500 hucksters, eighty per cent of whom are women, have joined the Dominica

Hucksters' Association, the first independent voluntary organization of its kind in the Caribbean. The organization trains these 'microentrepreneurs' to cope with market practices, government regulations, and packaging and handling requirements. Numerous photographs by Philip Decker illustrate the article.

290 Contemporary class structure in Dominica.
Bill 'Para' Riviere. In: *Contemporary Caribbean. A sociological reader.* Edited by Susan Craig. Maracas, Trinidad: College Press, 1982, vol. 1, p. 265-82.

Set in historical and economic contexts, this survey of social groups includes a discussion of planters, plantation workers, sharecroppers, tenant small cultivators, squatters, 'middle peasants', farmers, non-agricultural wage workers, salaried workers, small producers, small distributors, merchants, the unemployed (estimated by the author to be fifty per cent of the population) and students. Taken from an unpublished monograph 'The movement for socialism in the Caribbean: a case study of Dominica' (1975).

291 Contemporary class struggles and the revolutionary potential of social classes in Dominica.
Bill 'Para' Riviere. In: *Contemporary Caribbean. A sociological reader.* Edited by Susan Craig. Maracas, Trinidad: College Press, 1982, vol. 2, p. 365-83.

A selection from the author's unpublished 1975 monograph, 'The movement for socialism in the Caribbean: a case study of Dominica', in which he reviews the revolutionary potential of the Civil Service strike of 1973, the role of trade unions, student protest, the unemployed and the Black Power movement.

292 A comparative study of two rural farming communities: the social dimension.
R. E. Riviere, J. B. Yankey. In: *Proceedings of the Fifth West Indian Agricultural Economics Conference.* Edited by Dayanand Maharaj, John Strauss. St. Augustine, Trinidad: University of the West Indies, Department of Agricultural Economics and Farm Management, 1970, p. 53-64.

The authors test their hypothesis that 'given similar agro-economic conditions in agriculture, social characteristics can alter the levels of productivity' (p. 53) in two similar agricultural communities in south-western and south-central Dominica. Surveys of Giraudel, with sixty-eight homes for 325 residents, and Laudat, with sixty-six homes for 308 residents, tentatively suggest that 'farm tenancy is more conducive to higher productivity than outright ownership' and 'it is possible that dissatisfaction with farming income activates the farmer to strive for higher production levels' (p. 55). Numerous supporting data are offered in twenty-seven tables.

293 Incipient development and vocational evolution in Dominica.
William B. Rodgers. *Human Organization*, vol. 30, no. 3 (fall
1971), p. 239-54. bibliog.

A study of vocational diversity in sixty-five communities, demonstrating that
larger communities have a greater variety of specialized jobs and the sequence in
which they appear. The author is in the Department of Anthropology of the
University of California, Los Angeles.

294 **Environmental modification and system response: developmental
change in Dominica.**
William B. Rodgers, Miriam Morris. *Human Organization*,
vol. 30, no. 1 (spring 1971), p. 65-72. bibliog.

Using survey data collected on sixty-one communities in the summer of 1968, the
authors test and find supportable the hypothesis that 'communities with richer and
more exploitable environmental resources will be more internally developed or
economically differentiated' (p. 65). This research is part of a larger study to
define 'the correlates of modernization in Dominica', in terms of both the
determinants and the effects of community development and 'individual
modernization' (p. 70). The authors are, respectively, in the Department of
Anthropology and the School of Public Health at the University of California at
Los Angeles.

295 **Social structural changes in Dominica.**
Social Development Unit. Economic Commission for Latin
America and the Caribbean. Roseau: United Nations, Caribbean
Development and Co-operation Committee, Economic
Commission for Latin America and the Caribbean, 1 Nov. 1984.
230p. bibliog.

A substantial history of the island, with emphasis on the social structure. The
anonymous author (or authors) integrates data from a wide range of published
sources, describing changes in the island population from Amerindian times to the
1970s. This study was presented at the 'Meeting on Social Structural Changes in
Dominica' held in Roseau from 10-12 December 1984 and has a United Nations
publication number AHG/SEM/SSC/84/1.

296 **The economic integration of a Caribbean peasantry: the case of
Dominica.**
Michel-Rolph Trouillot.   PhD thesis, Johns Hopkins University,
Baltimore, Maryland, 1984. 408 leaves. bibliog. (Available from
University Microfilms, Ann Arbor, Michigan. Order no.
DA8501686).

This anthropological study, based on fieldwork in 1979, 1980 and 1981, 'argues
that a "peasant" type of work organization emerged in Dominica during slavery
and became, after emancipation, the central object of a long struggle between
cultivators and non-producers' (author's abstract). The present labour process for

banana production has been integrated into the capitalist world order. The author also examines emerging rural categories and the ongoing relevance of individual decisions among rural labourers.

297 **Caribbean peasantries and world capitalism: an approach to micro-level analysis.**
Michel-Rolph Trouillot. *Nieuwe West-Indische Gids/New West Indian Guide*, vol. 58, no. 1 & 2 (1984), p. 37-59. bibliog.

A theoretical and critical examination of the concept of 'peasant' for the Caribbean, combined with an examination of a variety of 'peasant' types from Dominica and their varying degrees of integration into the larger economic field. The author is Assistant Professor of Anthropology at Duke University, Durham, North Carolina, and based the article on fieldwork done in Dominica in 1979, 1980 and 1981.

298 **Peasants and capital: Dominica in the world economy.**
Michel-Rolph Trouillot. Baltimore, Maryland: Johns Hopkins University Press, 1987. bibliog.

The first scholarly book on Dominica. The author argues that a peasant type of work organization, or labour process, emerged in the island during slavery and became, after emancipation, the central object of a century-long struggle between cultivators and non-producers. Trouillot, Assistant Professor of Anthropology at Duke University, Durham, North Carolina, skilfully integrates research and perspectives from history, economics, and anthropology to describe the development of the nation from 1838 to 1949, the linkages of the banana production system to the world economy and the micro-level effects of that linkage in one village, Wesley Ville La Soye, emphasizing the vitality of local initiative and local response. The study is based on data from the Public Record Office in England and fieldwork conducted in 1979, 1980 and 1981.

Caribbean island with a problem.
See item no. 5.

Dominica.
See item no. 6.

The West Indians: how they live and work.
See item no. 7.

Our island culture.
See item no. 18.

West Indian societies.
See item no. 20.

The sense of time, the social construction of reality, and the foundations of nationhood in Dominica and the Faroe Islands.
See item no. 41.

Report on squatter problem and land use . . .
See item no. 60.

The Carib Reserve: identity and security in the West Indies.
See item no. 149.

The Caribs of Dominica: prospects for structural assimilation of a territorial minority.
See item no. 150.

Land, politics, and ethnicity in a Carib Indian community.
See item no. 156.

Conflict and ethnic boundaries: a study of Carib-Black relations.
See item no. 157.

Conquerors of the Caribbean.
See item no. 173.

The Dominica story: a history of the island.
See item no. 216.

'I love my home bad, but . . .': the historical and contemporary contexts of migration on Dominica, West Indies.
See item no. 251.

How Dominicans view political independence: no nation is an island.
See item no. 339.

God's work: perception of the environment in Dominica.
See item no. 398.

The utmost for the highest: a study of adolescent aspirations in Dominica.
See item no. 406.

A resource guide to Dominica, 1493-1986.
See item no. 489.

Religion

299 Witchcraft in the West Indies: the anthropologist as victim.
Nancy H. Owen. *Anthropology and Humanism*, vol. 6, no. 2-3
(June-Sept. 1981), p. 15-22. bibliog.
The author, who undertook anthropological fieldwork among the Carib Indians in
1970-71, relates her experiences when she became ill and learned her landlady
was a witch or *sukwia*. The author explains how she had internalized the Carib
belief system and was cured by a bush doctor.

300 Black religions in the New World.
George Eaton Simpson. New York: Columbia University, 1978.
415p. 2 maps. bibliog.
A sociological examination of the variety of black religious groups in the
Caribbean, South and North America and Britain, grouped as neo-African,
ancestral, revivalist, spiritualist and religio-political cults. In the last category, the
author, Emeritus Professor of Sociology and Anthropology at Oberlin College,
Oberlin, Ohio, considers Jamaican Ras Tafarians and Dominican Dreads (p. 128-
30).

301 Studying a society's secrets.
Jonathan Wouk. *Practical Anthropology*, vol. 14, no. 5 (Sept.-
Oct. 1967), p. 214-21. bibliog.
An account of witchcraft beliefs and sorcery in Dominica, and the author's study
of these during fieldwork, June-August 1964, for his senior honours thesis in
anthropology at Harvard University.

A history of the West Indies, containing the natural, civil, and ecclesiastical history of each island: with an account of the missions instituted in those islands, from the commencement of their civilizations; but more especially of the missions which have been established in that archipelago by the society late in connexion with the Rev. John Wesley.
See item no. 206.

The Dominica story: a history of the island.
See item no. 216.

A resource guide to Dominica, 1493-1986.
See item no. 489.

Health and Nutrition

Health

302 Two centuries of health care in Dominica.

David F. Clyde. New Delhi: Sushima Gopal, 1980. 198p. bibliog.
2 maps.

An exceptionally fine account of the evolution of health care from about 1771 to 1979. Through researches in London, Edinburgh and Dominica, the author has skilfully reconstructed a portrait of the health conditions, medical practices and significant individuals involved in the gradual improvement of health care on the island. The result is a history of Dominica, containing ten illustrations, with health as its central theme. The author holds the MD, PhD, and DTM&H degrees, and is a World Health Organization specialist in tropical medicine and malaria. He has written on health care in Tanzania and his recent book, *Health in Grenada: a social and historical account* (London: Vade-Mecum Press, 1985) contains numerous references to Dominica and to the work of Dr. Henry Nicholls.

303 Investigation of a typhoid outbreak on Dominica.

Roderick Anthony Joseph Fortune. *Bulletin of the Pan American Health Organization*, vol. 15, no. 4 (1981), p. 311-17.

This article analyses an outbreak of twenty-nine typhoid cases in Coulibistri, a small village on the west coast of Dominica, in October 1977-February 1978. The analysis points to transmission by food-handlers and identifies a number of carriers of the *Salmonella typhi* infection in the community. The author was Laboratory Superintendent, Princess Margaret Hospital, in Goodwill (Roseau), Dominica. His important public health recommendations for preventing future outbreaks include the screening of all food-handlers and the registration and treatment of identified carriers.

304 Paraquat poisoning in two Caribbean countries.
William E. V. Green. *CSR CAREC Surveillance Report*, vol. 12,
nos. 1 & 2 (Jan.-Feb. 1986), p. 1-9. bibliog.

Epidemiological analyses from Dominica and Surinam alert health practitioners to
the dangers of accidental or intentional pesticide poisonings. The Dominica data
reported by Dr. Green, Medical Officer of Health, National Epidemiologist,
Ministry of Health, show that twenty-eight people died from Paraquat and
Furadan in the period 1980-84 (p. 1-2). This happened as a consequence of the
unrestricted use of chemical pesticides following the upsurge of pests after
Hurricane David in 1979.

305 The management of diabetes in Dominica.
Gerald A. C. Grell. *Caribbean Medical Journal*, vol. 35, no. 3-4
(1974), p. 37-46. bibliog.

Dr. Grell, a Dominican physician specialist, discusses the incidence and treatment
of diabetes in the island's central hospital and diabetes clinics in 1971 and 1972.
From his preliminary survey, the incidence of diabetes in Dominica's population
appears to be higher than that found in Jamaica and the US; it is the leading
cause of admission to the hospital's female medical wards.

**306 Medical disorders in a small Caribbean island: an analysis of the
diseases of adults in Dominica in 1972 and 1973.**
G. A. C. Grell. *Annals of Tropical Medicine and Parasitology*,
vol. 70, no. 1 (March 1976), p. 1-10. map. bibliog.

The first analysis 'of the total picture of the medical disorders of adults' in
Dominica (p. 9). The author views the health situation of Dominica as a
transitional stage from underdevelopment to industrialization. Diabetes, hyper-
tension and parasitic infections are of major importance. The findings in
Dominica are compared with those from other Caribbean islands. This paper
presents the clinical picture during the author's first two years' experience as
Adult Physician at Princess Margaret Hospital, Goodwill, Roseau.

**307 Typhoid fever in Dominica, W.I. – report on the clinical features of
78 cases.**
G. A. C. Grell. *West Indian Medical Journal*, vol. 28, no. 2
(June 1979), p. 94-99. bibliog.

Although declining in most areas, 'in Dominica, typhoid fever is still endemic and
is of major importance in hospital practice' (p. 94). The author reports on the
analysis of case histories of seventy-eight patients with typhoid fever under his
care from 1972 to 1976, when he was Consultant Physician at Princess Margaret
Hospital, Goodwill, Roseau. He is now in the Department of Medicine at the
University of the West Indies, Mona, Jamaica.

308 Amoebic liver abscess: a clinical and pathological study.
G. A. C. Grell, E. I. Watty. *West Indian Medical Journal*,
vol. 27, no. 1 (March 1978), p. 40-48. bibliog.

An analysis of the epidemiology, clinical pictures and biopsies of twenty-seven patients with liver abscesses, the most serious complication of amoebiasis, seen by the authors in 1972-75 at Princess Margaret Hospital, Goodwill, Roseau.

309 An analysis of infections and infestations in Dominica, West Indies.
Gerald Grell, Edward Watty. *West Indian Medical Journal*,
vol. 25, no. 3 (Sept. 1976), p. 166-76. bibliog.

An analysis of infections and infestations using data primarily from 1972 and 1973 showing that gastroenteritis, typhoid fever, amoebiasis and helminthiasis were major health problems. The description includes data on infections seen in 1,173 paediatric admissions, the ten principal causes of death, reported communicable disease cases, parasitic infections, and bacteriological investigations at Princess Margaret Hospital, Goodwill, Roseau.

310 Observations on the characters of endemic fever in the island of Dominica; preceded by an account of the physical peculiarities of the island so far as they influence the formation and intensity of disease.
John Imray. *Edinburgh Medical and Surgical Journal*, vol. 70,
no. 177 (1 Oct. 1848). p. 253-87.

The author's fullest published account of the island's geography and climate and their relation to health. Writes physician David Clyde in *Two centuries of health care in Dominica* (New Delhi, 1980), this paper is 'a descriptive masterpiece which embraces not only the epidemiology, pathology and clinical management of malaria as he saw it but also a rhapsodic account of the physical features of the island' (p. 53). John Imray (Jan. 1811-Aug. 1880) contributed immeasurably both in medical care and in agricultural development, especially limes, during the forty-eight years he resided in Dominica.

311 Observations illustrating the characters of a febrile epidemic which prevailed in Dominica in 1838.
John Imray. *Edinburgh Medical and Surgical Journal*, vol. 53,
no. 142 (1840), p. 78-95.

The first of several distinctive medical articles on Dominica published by the author. The epidemic 'confining itself almost exclusively to the white and coloured natives of the island, and passing over, with scarcely any exception, the European residents' (p. 78), occurred between late 1837 and April 1838. The author describes the symptoms and his treatment in detail.

312 Observations on the mal d'estomac or Cachexia Africana, as it takes place among the Negroes of Dominica.
John Imray. *Edinburgh Medical and Surgical Journal*, vol. 59, no. 155 (1843), p. 304-21.
The author describes dirt-eating, a custom frequently found and once 'extremely destructive' (p. 305) among West Indian blacks, but which was declining in Dominica. He mentions the role of obeah men in predisposing people to geophagy, reviews symptoms, morbid anatomy and treatment, and presents ten case histories, the last of which focuses on the custom and consequences of snuff-taking by women on the island.

313 Observations on the nature, causes and treatment of yellow fever.
John Imray. *Edinburgh Medical and Surgical Journal*, vol. 64, no. 165 (1845), p. 318-40.
An attempt to elucidate the causes of yellow fever with an account of its high mortality, about twenty-five per cent, during the 1841 outbreak in Dominica through several case-studies of individuals. The author compares the epidemiology of the disease in Dominica to that in other islands, and favours climate and altitude as important explanations for the differences.

314 Tubal ligations in Dominica.
Evan Kildare-Donaldson, Errol A. Daley, B. A. Sorhaindo.
West Indian Medical Journal, vol. 21, no. 4 (Dec. 1972), p. 236-39.
bibliog.
An analysis of case notes on 404 of the 454 tubal ligations performed in Dominica between 1 September 1967 and 1 September 1970, with respect to laparatomy technique, patient age, pregnancy and contraceptive history, indications, length of hospital stay and post-operation follow-up.

315 Report on leprosy and yaws in the West Indies, addressed to Her Majesty's Secretary of State for the Colonies.
Gavin Milroy. London: William Clowes & Sons, for HM Stationery Office, 1873. 104p. (Great Britain. Parliament. March 1873, C. 729).
The result of an official investigation into the prevalence of leprosy and yaws in British Guiana, Barbados, Antigua, Trinidad, Jamaica and Dominica. The author visited Dominica from 28 February to 29 March 1872, and he observed that, unlike yaws, leprosy was not common (p. 27). One of the appendixes is Dr. John Imray's 'Memoir on yaws in Dominica' (p. 72-83), dated 22 March 1872.

316 Environmental modification and differential health practices.
Miriam Morris. *Social Science & Medicine*, vol. 4 (1970), p. 335-
42.

Colihaut, a leeward-side community in Dominica, is contrasted with Marigot, a
windward-side community, to test the hypothesis that culturally similar communities in different environmental settings show differences in health and health-
related practices and beliefs. Differences in illness reports, food preferences and
health concerns support the hypothesis. The author, on the faculty of the School
of Public Health, University of California, Los Angeles, conducted this field study
in the summer of 1968.

317 The fourth report of the medical superintendent of yaws hospitals.
H[enry] A[lfred] Alford Nicholls. London: Waterlow & Sons,
1880. 32p. bibliog.

The fourth and most extensive report by Dr. Nicholls on the rapidly spreading
disease that had 'created so much alarm in the public mind' (p. 2). A valuable
study with statistics, case histories, diet and correspondence for the history of
health care in the island and on the challenges of the disease to 19th-century
practitioners.

**318 The Leeward Islands Medical Journal, being the proceedings of the
Leeward Islands branch of the British Medical Association, 1891.**
Edited by H[enry] A[lfred] Alford Nicholls. London: J. & A.
Churchill, 1891. 188p.

The inaugural and only volume of papers of the Leeward Islands Medical
Association, edited by the esteemed senior Dominican physician. Included with
the minutes of the first annual meeting among the eleven papers are three
pertaining to Dominica: 'The treatment of dysentery', by H. A. Alford Nicholls
(p. 59-84); 'A few remarks on the existence of scrofula amongst the inhabitants of
one district of the island of Dominica', by John Armstrong (p. 85-93); and 'The
endemic fevers of Dominica', by H. A. Alford Nicholls (p. 94-120). With the
exception of the several papers on yaws, these articles provide the most varied
accounts of health conditions in Dominica published during this period.

319 Yaws.
Henry Alfred Alford Nicholls. In: *Twentieth century practice. An
international encyclopedia of modern medical science by leading
authorities of Europe and America.* Edited by Thomas L. Stedman.
New York: William Wood, 1899. vol. 16, p. 305-51. bibliog.

Dr. Nicholls of Dominica was perhaps the world authority on yaws when this
medical encyclopaedia was published. His comprehensive discussion of the
disease includes its history and geographic distribution, aetiology, symptomatol-
ogy, diagnosis, prognosis, histology, pathology, treatment and prophylaxis,
emphasizing isolation and improved sanitation. A bibliography and eighteen
drawings and photographs increase the article's usefulness.

320 Annual report of the Chief Medical Officer for the year 1972.
D[orian] C. Shillingford.   Roseau: Ministry of Education and
Health, 5 Dec. 1974. 50 leaves. map.

This descriptive and statistical report by the island's Chief Medical Officer is the
first published report since 1962 and provides in its twenty-four tables, seven
figures and four appendixes the most detailed data on the period available. The
material is presented in six sections: introduction; health situation (population
and vital statistics, mortality, morbidity); health services (individuals, nutrition,
environmental health services and supporting services); health infrastructure
(management, resources); voluntary agencies; and implementations of resolutions
of the Caribbean Health Ministers' Conference.

**321 Yaws: its nature and treatment. An introduction to the
study of the disease.**
J. Numa Rat.   London: Waterlow & Sons, 1891. 60p.
bibliog.

A medical treatise on the most prevalent medical problem in late 19th-century
Dominica, where the author was a medical officer from 1890 to 1902. The
comprehensive study includes a discussion of aetiology, epidemiology and
treatments, with a medical history of yaws and comparisons to syphilis and other
diseases. Dr. Rat provides an extensive chronological bibliography of yaws from
1535 to 1887 (p. 4-6), and argues for its pre-European New World existence.
Statistical tables and description of 'A yaws district' (p. 54-60) are based on his
experience in Dominica. The study is introduced with prefatory remarks by
Jonathan Hutchinson, late President of the Royal College of Surgeons (p. iii-ix).

**322 Black Britain's dilemma: a medico-social transcultural study of
West Indians.**
John Royer.   Roseau: Tropical Printers, 1977. vol. 1. 399p.
bibliog.

A wide-ranging study of the problems associated with West Indian migration to
Britain, particularly relating to mental health. The chapter '50 years of mental
health in Dominica' covers the years 1919 to 1972. The Dominica-born author is a
psychiatrist, resident in the UK for several years, and now living in Jamaica.

323 Tuberculosis in Dominica.
E. I. Watty, D. C. Shillingford.   *Caribbean Medical Journal*,
vol. 22, no. 1-4 (1960), p. 112-13.

A description of the known incidence, drug therapy and future plans for
tuberculosis patients in Dominica. The authors estimate that in the total
population of about 60,000 'there are about 600 known cases in the island, and
that less than half the adult cases are being hospitalized' (p. 112). E. I. Watty was
then the Acting Senior Medical Officer.

**Caribbean wild plants and their uses: an illustrated guide to some
medicinal and wild ornamental plants of the West Indies.**
See item no. 104.

Cabrits plants and their uses.
See item no. 108.

A treatise on the yellow fever as it appeared in the island of Dominica in the years 1793-4-5-6: to which are added, observations on the bilious remittent fever, on intermittents, dysentery, and some other West Indian diseases; also the chemical analysis and medical properties of the hot mineral waters in the same island.
See item no. 205.

Doctors and slaves: a medical and demographic history of slavery in the British West Indies, 1680-1834.
See item no. 238.

Witchcraft in the West Indies: the anthropologist as victim.
See item no. 299.

A resource guide to Dominica, 1493-1986.
See item no. 489.

Nutrition

324 A nutritional study of young children attending a day nursery in Dominica.
C. Close, R. Scragg, D. Defoe. *Cajanus*, vol. 17, no. 3 (1984), p. 172-75. bibliog.

This study of forty-eight children between the ages of three months and three years was conducted at the private, church-supported Social Centre in Roseau in September 1983. The results of the study show that those children who have spent less than six months at the nursery, while not clinically malnourished, have a low height-for-weight ratio compared with those children at the nursery longer. The authors are, respectively, paediatrician at Princess Margaret Hospital, medical student at the University of Manchester, and Co-ordinator of the Day Nursery, Social Centre, Roseau.

325 Childhood malnutrition in the Caribbean.
Miguel Gueri. *Bulletin of the Pan American Health Organization*, vol. 15, no. 2 (1981), p. 160-67. bibliog.

A comparative review of nutrition data for children under five in islands of the English-speaking Caribbean. Dominica has one of the worst records with 50.4 per cent of the 397 children studied showing some type of malnutrition. The author also discusses causes, costs and solutions for the problem.

326 **Pattern of weaning in Dominica.**
Frances A. Larkin. *West Indian Medical Journal*, vol. 20, no. 3
(Sept. 1971), p. 229-36. bibliog.
An analysis of interviews with 108 women with infants aged nine to fourteen
months in Roseau during July and August 1969. The author presents data and
discussion on maternal and infant diets, breast- and bottle-feeding patterns,
beliefs about breast-feeding, nutritional knowledge and housing conditions.

327 **Daily food for Dominican families.**
Deen Low. *Cajanus*, no. 8 (April 1969), p. 135-45.
The author, Pan American Health Organization/World Health Organization
Public Health Nutritionist for Dominica, describes the activities of a nutrition
booth at a four-day agricultural fair in Roseau in October 1968. Included are a
menu and several recipes for economical local meals as well as photographs of the
exhibition.

328 **The ecology of malnutrition in the Caribbean: the Bahamas, Cuba,**
Jamaica, Hispaniola (Haiti and the Dominican Republic), Puerto
Rico, the Lesser Antilles and Trinidad and Tobago.
Jacques M. May, Donna L. McLellan. New York: Hafner Press,
1973. 490p. maps. bibliog. (Studies in Medical Geography,
vol. 12).
A comprehensive survey of malnutrition and its causes in the region, with
summaries of background information, food resources and diets for each
territory. The authors describe the Dominica situation in which gastroenteritis
and deficiency diseases were the most prevalent health problems in 1970 (p. 387-
91).

329 **Cultural differences in the feeding of young children in the**
Caribbean.
Miriam Morris. *West Indian Medical Journal*, vol. 20 (1971),
p. 135-38. bibliog.
Based on her study of mothers' views of illness and well-being in four Dominican
communities in 1968 and 1969, the author reports variation in feeding practices
among different socio-economic stata. She stresses the need to move middle-class
women away from powdered milk toward breast-feeding, and the importance of
sensitivity to the ways the culture of the client may differ from the culture of the
practitioner.

330 **Nutritional status of hospitalised pre-school children in Dominica,**
before and after Hurricane David.
J. M. Wit, P. Gooder. *Disasters*, vol. 5, no. 2 (1981), p. 93-97.
This article discusses the nutritional consequences of a major natural disaster and
compares the nutritional status of ninety-three hospitalized pre-school children
after Hurricane David struck with a similar group of one hundred children
hospitalized prior to the hurricane. The expected decline in nutritional health due

to the hurricane did not occur and the authors suggest this was due to the well-organized distribution of food aid for the six months after 1 September 1979. The authors stress the importance of a well-coordinated international relief effort.

Periodicals

331   CSR CAREC Surveillance Report.
Port of Spain: Caribbean Epidemiology Centre (CAREC), Pan American Health Organization, Pan American Sanitary Bureau, Regional Office of the World Health Organization, (vol. 1, no. 1) March 1975- . bi-monthly and monthly.

Until November-December 1985 known as the *CAREC Surveillance Report*, this report provides the most current information on health issues for the entire region. Each issue features one or more articles on specific health issues and systematically updates cases of reportable diseases with cumulative totals for the present and previous year for each member country or island. It also alerts health officials to specific health problems such as dengue fever, environmental hazards or sexually transmitted diseases.

Politics

Pre-independence

332 Glimpses of a governor's life from diaries, letters and memoranda.
Hesketh Bell. London: Sampson Low, Marston, 1946. 212p.
The author, later Governor of Northern Nigeria (1909-12), of the Leeward
Islands (1912-16) and of Mauritius (1916-24), here describes his career as
Governor of Uganda (1905-09) and as Administrator of Dominica (1899-1905). A
dynamic and well-liked individual, his vigorous administration on Dominica
marked a period of rejuvenation and important local developments. He
remembers the time as 'one of the happiest of my life' (p. xi).

333 Broken atoms.
E[dward] C[arlyon] Eliot. London: Bles, 1938. 254p.
The author describes his civil service career which included various positions in
the Argentine and Uruguay (1888-92), British Guiana (1893-1900), Gold Coast
Colony (1900-10), Tobago (1911-13), Gilbert and Ellice Islands Protectorate
(1913-20), Uganda (1921-23), and concluded as Administrator of Dominica (1923-
31). The relatively brief chapter (p. 221-37) on Dominica includes accounts of the
'Carib War' of 1930, a visit to the Boiling Lake, and natural disasters.

334 **Eastern Caribbean elections, 1950-1982: Antigua, Dominica, Grenada, St. Kitts-Nevis, St. Lucia, and St. Vincent.**
Douglas Midgett. Iowa City, Iowa: Center for Development Studies, Institute of Urban and Regional Research, University of Iowa, 1983. 214p. 20 maps. bibliog. (Development Series no. 13).
This history and analysis of the elections on each island provides detailed data on voting patterns in each polling district. The Dominica elections of 1951, 1954, 1955, 1957, 1958, 1961, 1966, 1970, 1973, 1975, 1978 and 1980 are described (p. 39-71).

335 **Sleeping Beauty awakes.**
Graham Norton. *West Indies Chronicle*, vol. 90, no. 1525 (Feb.-March 1975), p. 72-73, 75.
The only press interview granted by Patrick John, Premier of Dominica, on his first official visit to Britain. The Premier discusses convicted murderer Desmond Trotter, the Racial Offences Act and several projects planned in Dominica.

336 **From a colonial governor's notebook.**
Reginald St. Johnston. London: Hutchinson, 1936. Reprinted, Westport, Connecticut: Negro Universities Press, 1970. 285p.
The author recounts his experiences as Acting-Governor of the Falkland Islands, Administrator of St. Kitts-Nevis, and Governor of the Leeward Islands. Chapter IV, 'Administration of Dominica' (p. 89-113) describes the Caribs, visiting naturalists, health conditions, and financial problems during his brief tenure in 1925. Other chapters describe later events on the island, regional problems and political developments. The volume includes eleven photographs.

337 **From Crown Colony to Associate Statehood: political change in Dominica, the Commonwealth West Indies.**
Cuthbert J. Thomas. PhD thesis, University of Massachusetts, Amherst, Massachusetts, 1973. 378 leaves. bibliog. (Available from University Microfilms, Ann Arbor, Michigan, 1973. Order no. 73-32,177).
This study provides a political history of Dominica, an analysis of its various constitutions and the political parties, including the Black Power Movement, active during the period of Associated Statehood. The author also discusses political and economic problems facing Dominica and their possible solutions.

338 **Revolutionary activity in the Caribbean: some notes on the Dreads of Dominica.**
Bert J. Thomas. *Guyana Journal of Sociology*, vol. 1, no. 2 (April 1976), p. 75-92. bibliog.
A generally sympathetic and extensive treatment of the Dreads of Dominica, a violent revolutionary group of about 200 lower- and middle-class largely unemployed young people. Ideologically the Dreads advocate a return to the

land, a more equitable distribution of resources, use of local goods rather than imported ones, and a rejection of current government and religions. The Dread Act and press treatment of the Dreads are also discussed. The Dominica-born author is in the Africana Department of Brooklyn College, Brooklyn, New York. Additional accounts on the Dreads by anthropologist Anthony Layng appear in the *Caribbean Monthly Bulletin*, vol. 9, no. 1 (Jan. 1975), p. 15, and no. 5-6 (May-June 1975), p. 44-49.

How Crown Colony government came to Dominica by 1898.
See item no. 200.

The Dominica story: a history of the island.
See item no. 216.

Social differentiation in Roseau: politico-economic change and the realignment of class, status group and party among elites in a Caribbean capital.
See item no. 278.

The Star.
See item no. 470.

Post-independence

339 How Dominicans view political independence: no nation is an island.
Deborah Louise Harvey. PhD thesis, Rice University, Houston, Texas, 1981. 207 leaves. bibliog. (Available from University Microfilms, Ann Arbor, Michigan, 1982. Order no. DA8216321).
The author, an anthropologist, spent six months living in the Carib Reserve in 1976-77 intending to write a phenomenological study of Carib ethnicity but then moved to Roseau for six months and enlarged her study to write 'a history of Dominica in the context of the larger West Indian experience and show how this history influenced, if not formed, Dominican independence' (p. 29). The result is an interesting study of how Dominicans 'created their social world by their accounts of their world' (p. 16).

340 The politics of independence in Dominica.
N. J. O. Liverpool. *Bulletin of Eastern Caribbean Affairs*, vol. 4, no. 2 (May-June 1978), p. 20-23.
An examination of the major obstacles which have blocked the road to independence since the declaration of this goal by the Dominica Labour Party in 1976. The author is on the Law Faculty of the University of the West Indies, Cave Hill, Barbados.

341 The Eugenia Charles victory: Dominicans swear they have found freedom at last!
Ric Mentus. *People*, vol. 6, no. 1 (Aug. 1980), p. 41-46, 51-56.
An excellent description of the 21 July 1980 elections in which the Dominica Freedom Party won 17 of 19 seats it contested for the House of Assembly. The author covered the elections, supplying numerous photographs for the article and is managing editor of *People Magazine*.

342 Leading the way.
Peter Richards. *Américas*, vol. 37, no. 5 (Sept.-Oct. 1985), p. 28-30.
The author, a St. Lucian and Caribbean News Agency (CANA) correspondent for Dominica, interviews Dominica Prime Minister Eugenia Charles, focusing on issues of women's roles in the politics and culture of the region.

343 Patrick John, Dominica and the signs of the time – a comment.
Lindel Smith. *Bulletin of Eastern Caribbean Affairs*, vol. 5, no. 2 (May-June 1979), p. 23-29.
In an article written during the first few days of the 1979 political crisis in Dominica, the author shows that the political roots of current events reach back at least four or five years. Dominican events are given regional context in comparison to the situation in Grenada where people also rejected authoritarian rule.

344 The political situation in Dominica.
Lindel Smith. *Bulletin of Eastern Caribbean Affairs*, vol. 5, no. 3 (July-Aug. 1979), p. 20-31. bibliog.
This article analyses the island's political parties and the political situation of 1979 which led to the setting up of a Committee for National Salvation (CNS) and an interim government. It suggests that the CNS came about to wrest the government from Patrick John because no single political group was strong enough to capture power from John's Labour Party. The author attempts a forecast of the next elections.

345 Dominica: the post-Hurricane 'David' period.
Lindel Smith. *Bulletin of Eastern Caribbean Affairs*, vol. 5, no. 4 (Sept.-Oct. 1979), p. 32-35.
An account and analysis of events in Dominica during September and October 1979, when Interim Government leader Oliver Seraphin dismissed two top members of his administration for alleged 'communist ideas'. This was reportedly done to satisfy the US government and other international donors. The author is a Research Assistant at the University of the West Indies, Institute for Social and Economic Research (Eastern Caribbean), Cave Hill, Barbados.

Background notes: Dominica.
See item no. 34.

The Dominica story: a history of the island.
See item no. 216.

Dominica admitted as 151st United Nations member state.
See item no. 356.

The Grenada Declaration, 1971.
See item no. 357.

Memorandum of understanding between the Government of Antigua and Barbuda, the Government of Barbados, the Government of the Commonwealth of Dominica, the Government of St. Lucia and the Government of St. Vincent and the Grenadines relating to security and military co-operation (1982) (Part 1).
See item no. 358.

Caribbean Insight.
See item no. 464.

Caribbean Monthly Bulletin.
See item no. 465.

The Star.
See item no. 470.

C/CAA's 1986 Caribbean and Central America Databook.
See item no. 473.

Countries of the World and Their Leaders Yearbook 1985.
See item no. 475.

Encylopedia of the third world.
See item no. 477.

A resource guide to Dominica, 1493-1986.
See item no. 489.

Constitution, Legal and Judicial Systems

346 Subsidiary law-making process: Antigua, Dominica and St. Kitts, 1960-1968 (a critique).
Urias Forbes. *International and Comparative Law Quarterly*, vol. 18, no. 3 (1969), p. 533-57. bibliog.

The author examines the procedures and practices followed in enacting subsidiary legislation in three territories whose constitutions of 1960 and 1967, when they became Associated States, were similar. He traces slight variations among the territories in the procedures, in allocation of subsidiary legislative powers, in the character and scope of legislative powers, legislation on principle and taxation, amendments of legislative laws, and explicit exclusion of judicial controls. Overall, he concludes that subsidiary legislation plays an important role, but that normal determinants of the process, such as time pressures and effective political strategies are not important factors. The third usual determinant, prevailing political values, comes not from popular pressures but from the party bosses and has remained largely unchanged over the years considered. In the three areas, 'the new political directorate has sought to accommodate itself within an established system of privilege and exclusive power rather than to create new dimensions of popular leadership' (p. 557).

347 Aspects of administrative law in the West Indies: a study of recent developments in Antigua, Dominica and St. Kitts.
Urias Forbes. *International and Comparative Law Quarterly*, vol. 21, no. 1 (1972), p. 95-118. bibliog.

This article offers a functional analysis of the decision-making powers conferred by several statutes, and of the structure of the decision-making agency and its operational conditions in three constitutionally similar island units. For Dominica, the author examines the Public Service Board of Review, the Income Tax Ordinance 1966 and the Transport Board and the Marketing Board Ordinance 1965. He is disturbed that 'what emerges quite clearly from this study is the high degree of involvement of the political executive in the adjudicative processes which take place within the administrative framework' (p. 116) and recommends changes. At the time of publication, the author was a Tutor in Public Administration, University of the West Indies, Mona, Jamaica.

348   The constitutional history of the Windwards.
Francis Otho Coleridge Harris.   *Caribbean Quarterly*, vol. 6, no. 2-3 (May 1960), p. 160-76.
The author discusses the political and constitutional history of Grenada, St. Vincent, St. Lucia and Tobago, and the 'whole of Dominica's constitutional history' despite that island having been one of the Leeward Islands until 1940. The Royal Commissions of 1884, 1895, 1897 and 1938 all proposed that Dominica should belong to the Windwards because of its closer geographic, cultural and historical similarity. The Dominica-born author, a lawyer, was for a time a member of the Legislative and Executive Councils of Dominica, and at the time of this article's publication was Legal Draftsman, Government of the West Indies.

349   West Indian constitutions: post-independence reform.
Sir Fred Phillips.   New York: Oceana, 1985. 370p. bibliog.
A critical evaluation by a distinguished barrister of judicial reforms in the island region. The author examines constitutional issues, issues concerned with the independence of the judiciary, and the occupational hazards encountered by heads of state. Grenada receives extensive attention. Chapter III 'Independence & mini-state political pressures' considers the cases of Dominica, St. Vincent and St. Lucia, including events in Dominica between 1976 and 31 March 1984 (p. 73-83).

350   British West Indian society and government in transition, 1920-60.
Jesse Harris Proctor, Jr.   *Social and Economic Studies*, vol. 2, no. 4 (Dec. 1962), p. 273-304. bibliog.
An account, focusing on the advances towards self-government and the achievement of federation, of changes in the British West Indies between 1920 and 1960. Most of the article is about the eastern Caribbean, with balanced attention to Dominica, among the other islands. The author is Professor of Political Science at Davidson College, Davidson, North Carolina.

351   Constitutional development of the West Indies: 1922-1968. A selection from the major documents.
Ann Spackman.   St. Lawrence, Barbados: Caribbean Universities Press in association with the Bowker Publishing Company, Essex, England, 1975. xxxxiv, 619p. bibliog.
The author, a member of the Department of Government, University of the West Indies, Mona, Jamaica, has compiled a varied selection of documents bearing on British West Indian constitutional development. Documents pertaining to Dominica range from the 1924 constitution, the 1939 Order in Council, federation

reports, and the 1966 Windward Islands Constitutional Conference. An extensive bibliography of constitutional documents of the West Indies for the period covered lists numerous items for Dominica (p. 560-63).

Commonweath of Dominica.
See item no. 15.

Report on Dominica for the Year . . .
See item no. 42.

Administration and Local Government

352 Historical notes on rural local government in Dominica.
L[oftus] A. Roberts. *Dominica Welfare Review*, vol. IV, no. 5
(Jan.-June 1968), p. 1-4.

The author, Social Welfare Officer, traces rural local government from its origins
in about 1934 to 1949 when the article was written. In Marigot Village the first
village board was formed as a voluntary association. Several boards were given
statutory status in 1939. After the Social Welfare Department was begun in 1945
it encouraged the formation of village boards. In 1949 'village boards' became
'village councils'. The author describes reasons for the opposition to or lack of
interest in village boards in the past. An editiorial note at the end summarizes and
updates the notes to 1968 when there were twenty village councils and four
District Associations of Village Councils.

Commonwealth of Dominica.
See item no. 15.

Report on Dominica for the Year . . .
See item no. 42.

Dominica Official Gazette.
See item no. 466.

Dominica Welfare Review.
See item no. 467.

Island Wide.
See item no. 468.

Labour and Welfare

353 Report to the Government of Dominica on the planning of social security.
M. H. Jenkins. Geneva: United Nations Development Programme Technical Assistance Sector, International Labour Office, 1973. 77p. (ILO/TAP/Dominica/R.1).

M. H. Jenkins, an International Labour Organization expert on workmen's compensation legislation, visited Dominica between 17 March and 31 August 1973 at the request of the Government of Dominica to examine and revise the existing Workmen's Compensation Law. The report reviews social security measures, compares them against a background of internationally agreed standards, and formulates detailed proposals for consideration by the government on the future shape of a social security scheme. Appendixes contain background information of demographic, socio-economic and general relevance.

354 Dominica: project findings and recommendations.
Robert W. Mitchell. Geneva: United Nations Development Programme, International Labour Organization, 1974. 104p. (Labour Legislation DMI/72/002).

International Labour Organization expert Robert W. Mitchell, then Director of the Legislative Research Branch, Ministry of Labour, Ottawa, Canada, lived in Dominica from 11 July 1973 to 17 May 1974 to assist the Dominica Government in updating, revising and consolidating its labour legislation. This report describes existing labour conditions in Dominica, examines in detail five proposed labour acts, and makes four major recommendations (p. 22-23). An extensive Appendix contains suggested drafts of relevant legislation.

355 Plantation to co-operative: managerial issues in the Castle Bruce transition, 1972-1978.
F. E. Nunes. Mona, Jamaica: Institute of Social and Economic Research, University of the West Indies, 1981. 110p. bibliog. (Working Paper no. 26).
History and analysis of the evolution of Castle Bruce Estate, written in 1978 when the Castle Bruce Farmers' Co-operative was about five years old. The author describes briefly the Co-operative's formation, appraises its accomplishments and analyses managerial processes, offering long- and short-term recommendations. In two appendixes, he critically reviews the literature on the Co-op and compares it with other Dominican co-operatives since the 1940s.

Foreign Relations

356 Dominica admitted as 151st United Nations member state.
UN Chronicle, vol. 16, no. 1 (Jan. 1979), p. 26-27.

On 18 December 1978, the General Assembly admitted Dominica as the 151st Member State of the United Nations. This article describes that event and the welcoming statements of numerous diplomats from the international community. Dominica became the 100th Member admitted since the founding of the United Nations, the seventh in the Caribbean region and the second Commonwealth member admitted in 1978. A photograph of A. J. Riviere, Permanent Secretary to the Prime Minister, accompanies the text.

357 The Grenada Declaration, 1971.
Edward Oliver LeBlanc.   Roseau: Public Relations Division, Premier's Office, [1971]. 20p.

The purpose of 'the Grenada Declaration, 1971 (July 25th 1971) as modified by the Meeting of Heads of Government of Signatory States on November 8th, 1971, at Georgetown, Guyana and declared by the representatives of the people of Dominica, Grenada, Guyana, St. Kitts/Nevis/Anguilla, St. Lucia and St. Vincent is "to seek to establish out of their Territories a new State in the Caribbean" ' (Introduction, p. i). This pamphlet contains the declaration and a detailed exposition by the island's Premier of the government's position on the issues surrounding the creation of a federation of states in the eastern Caribbean and Guyana. Premier LeBlanc vigorously supported the efforts towards federation. This effort ultimately failed but was the most important foreign relations initiative during the period of Associated Statehood (1967-78).

358 **Memorandum of understanding between the Government of Antigua and Barbuda, the Government of Barbados, the Government of the Commonwealth of Dominica, the Government of St. Lucia and the Government of St. Vincent and the Grenadines relating to security and military co-operation (1982) (Part 1).** *Caribbean Monthly Bulletin*, vol. 17, no. 11-12 (Nov.-Dec. 1983), p. 1-7.

An important and easily available statement of the areas of co-operation, the Council of Ministers, Central Liaison Office, Central Fund, jurisdiction, claims, training, maintenance, procurement, operation expenses, limited assistance, territorial waters, exclusive economic zone and visiting forces as agreed to by the signatories.

Economics and Trade

359 National income statistics, Dominica, 1961-1964.
Ernest Bartell. Cave Hill, Barbados: University of the West
Indies. Institute of Social and Economic Research (Eastern
Caribbean), [1965]. 19, 21 leaves. (Statistical Series, no. 2).
A useful report on the agricultural, industrial, tourist, finance and government
sectors with twenty-one detailed statistical tables for the years 1961-64 in the form
'A set of accounts on the format used by the United Nations'.

360 Dominica: where the magic of the marketplace is failing.
George Black. *Multinational Monitor*, vol. 5 (Oct.-Nov. 1984),
p. 16-19. map.
The author examines the influence of President Reagan's 1981 Caribbean Basin
Initiative (CBI) on Dominica and concludes, after interviews with Prime Minister
Charles and other leaders in the area, that the CBI has had minimal impact. A
chart details fifteen present and planned foreign investments in Dominica since
1981, ascribing only one to the CBI. The two American-owned companies on the
list have provided only fifty-five jobs, most for unskilled and semi-skilled female
workers. The author, editor of *Report on the Americas*, a bi-monthly magazine
published by the North American Congress on Latin America, visited the island
for this article.

361 Economic survey of Latin America and the Caribbean 1983.
Economic Commission for Latin America and the
Caribbean. Santiago de Chile: United Nations, March 1985.
2 vols.
Volume two (166p.) concerns the economies of twelve Caribbean countries,
including Dominica (p. 61-70). Part one, 'Evolution of the Caribbean economies',
analyses structural characteristics and main trends, output, the external sector and

120

inflation and unemployment in a general survey, using eleven tables to compare the countries. Part two covers 'Economic evolution of the individual countries'. Thirteen tables present 1981-83 data for important aspects of the Dominica economy. The volume has a UN publication sales no. E.85.II.G.2.

362 Commercial geography of Dominica.
Arlin D. Fentem. Bloomington, Indiana: Indiana University, Department of Geography, Dec. 1960. 18p. 4 maps. bibliog. (Office of Naval Research contract NONR-908 (13), Technical Report no. 5).

This is the fifth in a series of twelve reports on the commercial geography of British islands in the Lesser Antilles. It describes the island's physical setting, historical background, production and exports, imports, balance of payments and general economic status. Tables and graphs display relevant data.

363 Caribbean basin trade and investment guide.
Kevin P. Power, foreword by M. Eugenia Charles. Washington, DC: Washington International Press, 1984. 373p. maps.

This guide includes country profiles for the twenty-five nations and possessions in the Caribbean region, including Dominica (p. 67-75). Each profile includes information on history, political system, economic overview, labour and taxes, and sources for more information. The author is a business consultant in the region and is affiliated to the Caribbean Basin Investment Center, Aptos, California.

364 Report of the tripartite economic survey of the eastern Caribbean.
J. R. Sargent, G. V. Doxey, D. T. Edwards, W. D. Gainer, B. T. Moore, G. W. Wilson. London: HM Stationery Office, 1967. 279p.

The purpose of this study was to 'formulate plans for the achievement of economic viability and to suggest priorities for the next five years' (Preface, p. iii). The four parts of the study examine 'The growth problem', 'Some common restraints on economic growth in the islands', 'Priorities for growth in individual islands', 'An approach to a regional development policy', and statistical tables. Following the chapters on Antigua, St. Kitts, Montserrat, Barbados, Grenada, St. Lucia and St. Vincent is a chapter on Dominica (p. 221-38). All the islands are compared in the tables. The report was conducted during January-April 1966, and submitted 22 April 1966; it contains a wealth of carefully analysed economic data.

365 **Supplementary notes on foreign investment in the Commonwealth Caribbean.**

Beverly Watson. [Kingston]: University of the West Indies, Institute of Social and Economic Research, 1974. 92p. bibliog. (Working Paper no. 1).

An analysis of foreign investment in Barbados, Dominica and Guyana. The chapter on Dominica (p. 42-57) discusses the distribution of foreign enterprises in the economy, giving special attention to the question of land alienation, 'the central aspect of the problem in Dominica' (p. 42).

366 **Dominica, priorities and prospects for development.**

World Bank. Washington, DC: World Bank, Oct. 1985. 105p. map. (A World Bank Country Study).

Based on the work of an International Bank for Reconstruction and Development team which visited Dominica in October 1984, this analysis provides the most detailed, up-to-date compilation of statistical data easily available. The main text consists of a thirty-three page discussion of 'economic overview and development prospects', 'sector priorities and issues', and 'the level and allocation of investment'. Annex I is 'Government's project and technical assistance lists'; Annex II is an analysis of the 1981 population census. A fifty-eight page statistical appendix concludes this valuable resource.

Report of the Royal Commission (appointed in September, 1893) to inquire into the condition and affairs of the island of Dominica and correspondence relating thereto.

See item no. 214.

History of the colonies of the British Empire in the West Indies, South America, North America, Asia, Austral-Asia, Africa, and Europe; comprising the area, agriculture, commerce, manufactures, shipping custom duties, population, education, religion, crime, government, finances, laws, military defense, cultivated and waste lands, emigration, rates of wages, prices of provisions, banks, coins, staple products, stock, moveable and immoveable property, public companies, etc. of each colony; with the charters and the engraved seals.

See item no. 221.

The British Colonial library, comprising a popular and authentic description of all the colonies of the British Empire, their history – physical geography – geology – climate – animal, vegetable, and mineral kingdoms – government – finance – military defense – commerce – shipping – monetary system – religion – population, white and coloured – education and the press – emigration, social state, &.

See item no. 222.

Slave populations of the British Caribbean, 1807-1834.

See item no. 234.

The economic integration of a Caribbean peasantry: the case of Dominica.
See item no. 296.

Caribbean peasantries and world capitalism: an approach to micro-level analysis.
See item no. 297.

Peasants and capital: Dominica in the world economy.
See item no. 298.

The problems of marketing Dominica food crops in traditional and non-traditional markets.
See item no. 371.

The West India Committee Circular.
See item no. 471.

Latin America & Caribbean Review 1986.
See item no. 472.

C/CAA's 1986 Caribbean and Central America Databook.
See item no. 473.

Caribbean Business Directory and Yellow Pages 1986/7.
See item no. 474.

A resource guide to Dominica, 1493-1986.
See item no. 489.

Statistics

367 CARICOM statistics digest, 1970-1981.
Statistics Section, Caribbean Community Secretariat.
Georgetown, Guyana: Caribbean Community Secretariat,
Jan. 1984. 200p.
An invaluable source for recent comparative data on the thirteen units of the
Caribbean Economic community. 'This document is intended to provide
researchers, planners and policymakers with reliable series of basic socio-
economic data for the Community' (Preface, p. 2). Some sixty-eight tables cover
basic demographic and economic categories, as well as topics such as motor
vehicle types, tourism and medical facilities. This enlarged digest is the second in
a series; the first, *CARICOM statistics yearbook 1978*, was published in 1980.

368 Statistical digest no. 6.
Statistical Division, Ministry of Finance.   [Roseau]: Ministry of
Finance, 1985. 150p.
The first statistical digest published since 1980. Most tables cover the period 1975-
84. Sections covered include climate, travel and tourism, prices, labour and
economic activity, population and vital statistics, health, education, housing,
electorate, transport and communication, production, public finance, banking,
national accounts and external trade. The volume is available from the Statistical
Division, Ministry of Finance, 22 Bath Road, Roseau, Commonwealth of
Dominica. Other statistical digests were published in Roseau by the government
in 1965, 1966, 1969, 1972 and 1980.

Demographic survey of the British Colonial Empire.
See item no. 241.

Eastern Caribbean elections, 1950-1982: Antigua, Dominica, Grenada, St. Kitts-Nevis, St. Lucia, and St. Vincent.
See item no. 334.

National income statistics, Dominica, 1961-1964.
See item no. 359.

Economic survey of Latin America and the Caribbean 1983.
See item no. 361.

Dominica, priorities and prospects for development.
See item no. 366.

West Indian census 1946. Part B. Census of agriculture in Barbados, the Leeward Islands, the Windward Islands and Trinidad and Tobago.
See item no. 384.

A resource guide to Dominica, 1493-1986.
See item no. 489.

Industrial Development, Agriculture and Forestry

Industrial development

369 Industrial development of Dominica.
R. L. Williams. [Mona], Jamaica: Institute of Social and
Economic Research, University of the West Indies, Sept. 1971.
100p. bibliog.

The best published description of the principal agricultural and manufacturing
industries on the island. The author, a consultant to the Government of Dominica
in 1966, revised and expanded his 1967 report. About one-half of the report
concerns the marketing and processing of fresh citrus fruits and their by-products,
as well as discussions of cocoa, coffee, vegetable fats, cassava and essential bay,
citronella and vetiver oils. The author discusses industries based on traditional
skills (rum manufacture, basketry, straw weaving and dressmaking), as well as
those based on semi-skilled labour (tobacco and coir products and housing). The
final chapter describes governmental industrial incentives, training programmes
and the protection of domestic markets. Twenty-six tables provide useful data
from the 1960s.

Caribbean island with a problem.
See item no. 5.

Dominica.
See item no. 6.

The Imperial Road in Dominica.
See item no. 195.

Cinderella of the Antilles: Dominica's plight and remedy.
See item no. 208.

Report of the Royal Commission (appointed in September, 1893) to inquire into the condition and affairs of the island of Dominica and correspondence relating thereto.
See item no. 214.

The Dominica story: a history of the island.
See item no. 216.

Dominica, priorities and prospects for development.
See item no. 366.

A resource guide to Dominica, 1493-1986.
See item no. 489.

Agriculture

370 Bay oil distillation in Dominica.
G. R. Ames, Maureen Barrow, C. Borton, T. E. Casey, W. S. Matthews, J. Nabney, L. D. G. Coward. *Tropical Science*, vol. 13, no. 1 (1971), p. 13-26. bibliog.
The authors, members of the Tropical Products Institute, analyse current Dominican bay oil production methods, 'virtually unchanged in design and materials' (p. 13) from the beginning of production at the end of the 19th century, and suggest ways to improve the quantity and quality of the process. In the Caribbean, production of bay oil, used for perfumes and for bay rum, has ceased in St. Thomas, St. John and Puerto Rico, leaving Dominica as the only established source. Four photographs illustrate the equipment used in the process.

371 The problems of marketing Dominica food crops in traditional and non-traditional markets.
Collin Bully, Arthurton Martin. In: *Proceedings of the Tenth West Indian Agricultural Economics Conference.* Edited by S. C. Birla. St. Augustine, Trinidad: Caribbean Agro-Economic Society in association with the University of the West Indies, 1975, p. 102-10. bibliog.
This paper discusses marketing as the 'problem of underdevelopment at the micro level' (p. 102), focusing on targeting specific products for particular groups and countries, with examples. In addition, marketing and nutrition, farm problems, transport systems and marketing boards are briefly reviewed, with several recommendations offered to reduce the problems. The authors are, respectively, Chief Agricultural Officer, Dominica, and General Manager, Castle Bruce Farmers' Cooperative, Dominica.

372 Proceedings of the Eleventh West Indian Agricultural Economics Conference.

Edited by John Cropper. St. Augustine, Trinidad: University of the West Indies for the Caribbean Agro-Economic Society, 1977. 141p. map.

The Eleventh West Indian Agricultural Economics Conference was held in Roseau, Dominica, 20-24 April 1976, and was attended by seventy-four Dominicans and participants from eleven other islands. All of the papers and workshop reports of the proceedings pertain to Dominica. Of particular interest are M. G. White's 'The framework of analysis appropriate for deciding on approaches for rural sector development'; R. Russell's 'Survey of Melville Hall leasehold settlement scheme'; M. G. White's 'Survey of Castle Bruce Cooperative Project'; P.I. Gomes's 'Sociological analysis of Grand Bay'; C. Dunn and F. Nickles's 'Alternative strategies for the development of Geneva Estate'; workshops on rural community development'; and 'Proposals for the development of the Grand Bay area, Dominica' (p. 123-37).

373 Accessibility and the development of export agriculture in Dominica.

D. Aidan McQuillan. *Caribbean Geography*, vol. 1, no. 3 (May 1984), p. 149-63. 4 maps. bibliog.

Presents 'a superficial review of patterns of commercial agriculture in Dominica [which] seems to support the hypothesis that the variety and distribution of crop production are largely determined by accessibility. However, the basic assumptions of rational economic behaviour cannot be made. An explanation of the distinctive geographical patterns of estate agriculture lies in the historical development of agriculture in Dominica not in economic models of distance decay' (p. 149). Maps show the distribution of estates, the production of major crops, and road networks. The author is in the Department of Geography at the University of Toronto, Canada.

374 Dominica's ill-fated lime industry.

Robert E. Maguire. In: *Readings in Caribbean history and economics*. Edited by Robert Marx Delson. New York: Gordon & Breach, 1981, p. 197-200. bibliog.

A brief account of the rise and fall of Dominica's lime industry from 1900 to 1939. Production peaked at 400,000 barrels a year during the period 1915-21, but declined to 40,000 barrels a year in 1934-39 due to diseases, tariffs and a cheaper method of extracting citric acid from sugar.

375 **Proceedings of the Fifth West Indian Agricultural Economics Conference.**
Edited by Dayanand Maharaj, John Strauss. St. Augustine, Trinidad: University of the West Indies, Department of Agricultural Economics and Farm Management, 1970. 176p. map.

The proceedings of the conference at Roseau, Dominica, 5-11 April 1970, contains twenty papers, each accompanied by a discussion report. Those pertaining to Dominica are: C. Maximea, J. Robinson, 'Conversion of forest lands into agriculture' (p. 12-15); N. Prevost, B. Yankey, 'A preliminary investigation into the agricultural sector of Dominica' (p. 17-21); F. L. A. Charles, 'A programme for agricultural development: the case of Dominica' (p. 22-23); Michael G. White, 'The introduction and development of new crops in Dominica' (p. 24-26); S. McConaghy, 'The soils of Dominica' (p. 27-32); Frank Watty, 'Alien land ownership and agricultural development issues, problems and the policy framework' (p. 41-46); R. E. Riviere, J. Bernard Yankey, 'A comparative study of two rural farming communities: the social dimension' (p. 53-64); and a workshop report on 'Land and labour in the development of Dominican agriculture' (p. 172-73). Of the 130 participants at the conference, a large percentage were from Dominica.

376 **Agricultural diversification in a small economy – the case for Dominica.**
McCarthy John-Baptiste Marie. Cave Hill, Barbados: Institute of Social and Economic Research (Eastern Caribbean), University of the West Indies, 1979. 119p. 2 maps. bibliog. (Occasional Paper no. 10).

This study was originally submitted as an MSc thesis in the Department of Agricultural Economics and Farm Management of the University of the West Indies. The author examines the recent economic history of the island, focusing on the banana industry as a plantation system, land distribution and economic dependence. He argues for the benefits of a more diversified economy and proposes broad policy guidelines helpful in achieving agricultural diversity. At the time of publication, the author was a Temporary Lecturer in the Department of Economics, University of the West Indies, Cave Hill, Barbados.

377 **Report of C. O. Naftel, Esqr., (late inspector of plantations in Ceylon) on the forest lands and estates of Dominica, and on the agricultural capabilities of the island.**
C. O. Naftel. Roseau: Guardian Office, July 1897. 52p. map.
Also, London: HM Stationery Office; Darling & Son, 1898. 71p.
(Colonial Reports, misc. no. 9. C.8801).

A valuable report on the island at the close of the 19th century, made at the request of the legislature by an agricultural expert with twenty-two years' experience as planter and official in Ceylon, a highly successful agricultural colony. The author produced his 'Report on the agricultural capabilities of Dominica' after a nine weeks' inspection tour in April-June 1897. Though critical of the unsystematic efforts of many planters, he asserts that the island can be prosperous, especially in coffee production, with an influx of 'capital, cheap money, and experience' (Introduction, p. ii). Appendixes contain ample data on rainfall, temperature, and coffee, cocoa and lime-juice exports, as well as profiles of four large estates (Pointe Mulatre, Belvedere, Castle Bruce and Melville Hall).

378 Vanilla-growing in Dominica.
Leo H. Narodny. *Journal of the New York Botanical Garden*, vol. 48, no. 566 (1947), p. 33-37.

An interesting account of the production of the terrestrial orchid *Vanilla planifolia*, which must be pollinated by hand and the ripe beans picked about nine months later. In the early 1940s, Dominica became the world's leading exporter of this valuable crop for a short time, but eventually lost its market. The author, an American chemist, established a vanilla estate in Dominica and was President of the Dominica Vanilla Growers' Association. One of the four photographs illustrating the article shows the streets of Roseau lined with $40,000 worth of vanilla beans in February.

379 The cultivation of Liberian coffee.
Henry A[lfred] A[lford] Nicholls. *Timehri*, vol. 3 (Dec. 1884), p. 286-307.

Dr. Nicholls, a regional expert on tropical agriculture, recounts the history and proper cultivation of Liberian coffee (*Coffea liberica*) which it was hoped would survive better than had the blighted Arabian coffee. Liberian coffee 'was introduced into the West Indies from the Royal Gardens at Kew in the year 1874, when a few plants were sent by Sir Joseph Hooker to the Botanic Gardens at Jamaica and Trinidad, and to the late Dr. Imray of Dominica' (p. 286). Nicholls published this information in similar form earlier as *On the cultivation of Liberian coffee in the West Indies* (London: S. W. Silver, 1881, 31p.).

380 A text-book of tropical agriculture.
H[enry] A[lfred] Alford Nicholls. London, New York: Macmillan, 1892. 312p.

This clearly-written and information-filled volume is a revised version of Dr. Nicholls's prize-winning book on tropical agriculture selected by the Jamaican Government for use in colleges and higher schools. This edition went through eight printings and was translated into Spanish and French. After Nicholls's death, a new edition prepared by J. H. Holland (London: Macmillan, 1929. 639p.) was widely used. Written especially for the less-experienced planter, Part One, 'Elements of agriculture', contains chapters on: soils, plantlife; climate; manures; crop rotation; drainage, irrigation, tillage; pruning; budding and grafting. Part two, 'Agricultural products', gives instructions on a full range of tropical crops: coffee, cacao, tea, sugar-cane, fruits, spices, tobacco, drugs (cinchona, castor seeds, jalap, sarsaparilla), dyes, tropical cereals (maize, rice, guinea corn), and food plants (cassava, arrowroot, tous-les-mois, yams, sweet potatoes and tania). The book's sixteen figures are copied from the guide to the Kew Royal Gardens and from the author's drawings. The author's personal experience in Dominica is mentioned throughout the volume.

381 A survey of the institutions serving agriculture on the island of
Dominica, W.I.
John D. Shillingford. Ithaca, New York: Department of
Agricultural Economics, Cornell University, April 1972. 26p. map.
bibliog. (Cornell International Agricultural Development
Mimeograph 35).

The author examines the six most important institutions influencing and
supporting agricultural productivity on the island: the land tenure and the
plantation system; commodity associations, especially the Banana Growers'
Association and the Citrus Growers' Association; marketing; agricultural credit;
extension and research; and CARIFTA, the Caribbean Free Trade Association.
Ample supplementary data for this paper are drawn from the author's MSc thesis
at Cornell University.

382 The major agricultural land types in Dominica, West Indies, and
their potential for development.
John D. Shillingford. Ithaca, New York: Department of
Agricultural Economics, Cornell University, April 1972. 26p.
8 maps. bibliog. (Cornell International Agricultural Development
Mimeograph 36).

The author describes five major agricultural land types and discusses the
morphology, agricultural performance and agricultural potential of each. The
study is based on interviews with agricultural personnel, a detailed farm-
management survey of twenty-one farms throughout the island, and a study of the
morphological characteristics of the island. It represents a condensation of the
author's MSc thesis at Cornell University. The eight maps provide excellent detail
for the analysis.

383 A small agricultural economy in CARIFTA: a case study of
Dominica, West Indies.
W. R. F. Watty, J. Bernard Yankey. In: *Proceedings of the
Fourth West Indian Agricultural Economics Conference.* Edited by
D. T. Edwards. St. Augustine, Trinidad: University of the West
Indies, Department of Agricultural Economics and Farm
Management, 1969, p. 114-20.

The authors discuss the problems of Dominican agriculture in the Caribbean Free
Trade Area Agreement. Dominica and other small economies are at a
disadvantage compared to the larger territories due to a variety of internal and
external limitations. The authors were, respectively, an economist/planner in the
Department of Planning and Development, and an agricultural economist in the
Division of Agriculture, Dominica.

384 West Indian census 1946. Part B. Census of agriculture in Barbados, the Leeward Islands, the Windward Islands and Trinidad and Tobago.
Jamaica. Central Bureau of Statistics. Kingston: Government Printer, 1950. 74p. map.

Presentation of invaluable agricultural data gathered as part of the April 1946 population census in the eastern Caribbean. Tables give a full report on the size, number and ownership of farms, the crops and livestock raised, and data on fishing, fishing boats and gear for each of the islands. The findings are introduced briefly by L. G. Hopkins, Vital Statistics Officer.

385 The Dominica banana industry: an economic hazard.
Michael White. In: *Proceedings of the Second West Indian Agricultural Economics Conference.* Edited by Kenneth A. Leslie. St. Augustine, Trinidad: University of the West Indies, 1967, p. 56-70.

The author discusses the risks of Dominica's monocrop economy, stressing that with proper long- and short-range planning it is not necessarily a dangerous situation. His purpose is 'to show how far the Dominican banana industry falls short of what is required' (p. 56) of optimum planning and development, with statistical data to support his conclusions.

386 A study of the situation in agriculture and the problems of small scale farming in Dominica, West Indies.
Joseph Bernard Yankey. PhD thesis, University of Wisconsin, Madison, Wisconsin, 1969. 278 leaves. 1 map. bibliog. (Available from University Microfilms, Ann Arbor, Michigan, 1969. Order no. 69-4443).

The Dominica-born author analyses in detail the history and structure of small-scale farming in Dominica, including land tenure and land use, and special issues such as the proper balance between estate agriculture and small-scale farming. Part of the analysis is based on interview data collected on a field survey from a sample of ninety-six farmers, or three per cent of the farmer population.

Forestry

387   Relation of crown diameter to stem diameter in forests of Puerto Rico, Dominica, and Thailand.
José W. Perez.   In: *A tropical rain forest: a study of irradiation and ecology at El Verde, Puerto Rico.* Edited by Howard T. Odum, Robert F. Pigeon. Oak Ridge, Tennessee: Office of Information Services, US Atomic Energy Commission, 1970, book one, B105-B122. bibliog. 3 maps.

Detailed structural data, including measured values of crown diameter and stem diameter were collected for twenty-eight forest stands, six in the monsoon forests of Thailand, ten in montane and lower montane forests of Puerto Rico, six in xerophytic forests of Puerto Rico, three in rainforests of Puerto Rico, and three in Dominica rainforests. The results, displayed in numerous tables and discussed, permit aerial photographs to be used to estimate stem diameters, thus aiding in the analysis of forests. The author, a US Army Engineer at the Waterways Experiment Station, Vicksburg, Mississippi, collected the Dominica data in 1965.

388   A comparison of environments of rain forests in Dominica, British West Indies, and Puerto Rico.
Mario Soriano-Ressy, A. Paul Desmarais, José W. Perez.   In: *A tropical rain forest: a study of irradiation and ecology at El Verde, Puerto Rico.* Edited by Howard T. Odum, Robert F. Pigeon. Oak Ridge, Tennessee: Office of Information Services, US Atomic Energy Commission, 1970, book one, p. B329-B346. bibliog. 2 maps.

Comparative data on pedology, geology and vegetation were collected from three matured virgin forests in Dominica and from four Puerto Rican forests which had been selectively cut. In Dominica, stem diameters and heights of plants far exceeded those found in Puerto Rico, perhaps due to differences in rainfall and in soil fertility or soil structure. Extensive data are displayed in tables and figures, and thirteen photographs illustrate the text.

389   Dominica forest and park system plan.
David L. Shanks, Allen D. Putney.   Christiansted, St. Croix: Eastern Caribbean Natural Area Management Program, 1979. 155p. maps. bibliog.

This is the most detailed study available of the country's forest reserve and national park system plans, Chapters detail 'Land inventory and interpretations', 'Land use and designation of park and forest system units', 'Land use recommendations' and 'Unit descriptions'. The extensive list of references (p. 100-08) is valuable, as are the appendixes on native and exotic plant species, timber and wood imports, and four detailed maps on land ownership, agricultural limitations, rare or unique natural features and forest growth potential. Authors Shanks and Putney are a Peace Corps Volunteer assigned to the Dominica

Forestry Division and at the University of Michigan's School of Natural Resources, Ann Arbor, Michigan, respectively.

390   Is Dominica's forest doomed?
Bruce E. Weber.   *American Forests*, vol. 77, no. 7 (July 1971), p. 12-15.

An article decrying the Dominica Government's agreement allowing Dom-Can Timbers Ltd. to log the 'only large expanse of undisturbed flora remaining in the Lesser Antilles' (p. 13) and arguing for the creation of a national park.

Environment and Conservation

Conservation

391 Conservation and Caribbean regional progress.
Carl A. Carlozzi, Alice A. Carlozzi. Yellow Springs, Ohio:
Antioch, 1968. 151p. bibliog.

One of the earlier works on conservation in the region. The authors discuss the conservation opportunities for different types of island and offer several proposals for development, taking a farsighted regional view. There are numerous references to Dominica throughout the volume. The first author was Associate Professor of Research Planning in the Department of Forestry and Wildlife Management, University of Massachusetts, Amherst.

392 Survey of conservation priorities in the Lesser Antilles: Dominica.
Preliminary data atlas.
Eastern Caribbean Natural Area Management Program
(ECNAMP). [Christiansted, St. Croix]: Caribbean Conservation
Association, October 1980. [20]p. 18 maps. bibliog.

Separate reports on each of twenty-three islands or island groups were produced through a co-operative effort by the Caribbean Conservation Association and the School of Natural Resources of the University of Michigan to identify the natural resources of the eastern Caribbean and the problems threatening them. The booklet on Dominica maps out the locations of a wide range of variables, including population density, forest coverage, pollution and cultivation. The *Final report* by Allen D. Putney (Oct. 1982, 29p. maps. bibliog.) summarizes the conditions and priorities for each of the islands and island groups in the survey, and provides a list of endangered species for each. These publications are available from ECNAMP, c/o West Indies Laboratory, Teague Bay, Christiansted, St. Croix, United States Virgin Islands 00820.

393 **Dominica: a chance for a choice. Some considerations and recommendations on conservation of the island's natural resources.**
William Eddy, Robert Milne, Leonard Godfrey. Foreword by Sydney Howe. Washington, DC: Conservation Foundation, 1970. 48p. 6 maps. bibliog.

The report of a three-man planning team sent to Dominica in September 1969, by the Conservation Foundation. The team's mission was four-fold: to assess the Dominica Government's interest in establishing a national park; to designate lands for possible inclusion in a park; to ascertain the most suitable use for a park; and to prepare a report to help the government seek international support in creating a national park. This attractive booklet, with its colourful photographs and maps, argues for a programme of conservation and presents five specific recommendations for a national park. The authors are, respectively, a Conservation Foundation senior associate, a consultant in environmental education, and an ecologist on leave from the US National Park Service.

394 **Dominica multiple land use project.**
P[eter] G. H. Evans. *Ambio*, vol. 15, no. 2 (1986), p. 82-89. 4 maps. bibliog. (Royal Swedish Academy of Science).

An excellent survey article resulting from the author's long-term research project, begun in 1982 and aimed at finding ways to conserve Dominica's rainforest while encouraging development of the country's economy. The article examines the effects of different forms of land use on animals and plants, and reviews the economy of Dominica and its development, presenting the thesis that certain types of forest use are both more economic and more sparing of the animal community. The author is a research population geneticist with a particular interest in conservation biology, and is at the Edward Grey Institute of Field Ornithology, Department of Zoology, Oxford University.

395 **The dilemma of the *Amazona imperialis* and *Amazona arausiaca* parrots in Dominica following Hurricane David in 1979.**
Felix W. Gregoire. In: *Conservation of New World parrots. Proceedings of the ICBP parrot working group meeting.* Edited by R. F. Pasquier. Washington, DC: Smithsonian Institution for the International Council for Bird Preservation, 1981, p. 161-67. (Technical Publication no. 1).

The author, from the Forestry Division, Ministry of Agriculture, Lands and Marketing, discusses the effects of the island's major hurricane on these endangered parrot species, of which it is estimated only 150-250 and 250-400 individuals, respectively, existed before the storm. Their southern forest habitats were destroyed and the birds were forced into lower elevations making them vulnerable to hunters. Measures taken for their protection after the hurricane and recommendations are discussed. The Parrot Working Group concluded 'that conservation efforts on Dominica are of the highest priority in the Caribbean' (p. 5).

396   The Cabrits and Prince Rupert's Bay.
Lennox Honychurch.   Roseau: Dominica Institute, 1983. 39p.
map.

As part of the effort to conserve the 200-acre peninsula at Portsmouth, Dominica writer, historian and conservationist Honychurch wrote a history and nature guide. The booklet describes the natural setting and the fortification complex of Ft. Shirley 'one of the most impressive military sites in the West Indies' which was constructed between 1770 and 1795, and abandoned as a military post in 1854. The publication is available for a nominal charge from the Dominica Institute, PO Box 89, Roseau, Dominica.

397   Endangered parrots.
Rosemary Low.   Poole, Dorset, England: Blandford, 1984. 160p.
maps. bibliog.

This book is an exceptionally thorough survey of the world's endangered parrots, stressing repeatedly the role of aviculture in conservation in each country or island studied. 'The Dominican Amazons: zero point approaches' (p. 59-64) discusses the impacts of Hurricane David and expanding cultivation on shrinking populations of the island's two endangered parrots, the Imperial Parrot, *Amazona imperialis*, and the Red-necked Parrot, *Amazona arausiaca*. Colour photographs and distribution maps are included for each bird.

398   God's work: perception of the environment in Dominica.
Gail Ringel, Jonathan Wylie.   In: *Perceptions of the environment.
A selection of interpretative essays.* Edited by Yves Renard. St.
Michaels, Barbados: Caribbean Conservation Association, 1979,
p. 39-50. bibliog. (Caribbean Environmental Studies no. 1).

Based on fifteen months' anthropological fieldwork in Scotts Head, a village at the south-western tip of the island, the authors reflect on the Dominicans' attitudes towards God and their competitive and suspicious attitudes towards one another. Discussion of a wide range of values concludes that 'the outlook for conservationist programmes and ideals is bleak'. The idea that 'nature is beautiful and natural resources are something to be conserved is quite foreign to Dominican thought' (p. 47). The authors offer several positive suggestions to remedy these attitudes.

Flora and fauna of the Cabrits Peninsula.
See item no. 91.

Freshwater swamps and mangrove species in Dominica.
See item no. 107.

Cabrits plants and their uses.
See item no. 108.

The wildlife of Dominica.
See item no. 128.

The jungle crusade of 'Holly Parrot'.
See item no. 129.

Dominica forest and park system plan.
See item no. 389.

A resource guide to Dominica, 1493-1986.
See item no. 489.

Morne Trois Pitons National Park

399 Dominica's national park: concept and purposes; geology and soils; vegetation; water; wildlife.
P. Narodny Honychurch, assisted by Allen D. Putney.   Roseau: Dominica National Park Service, in collaboration with Caribbean Conservation Association and Rockefeller Brothers Fund, 1978. maps. bibliog.

These five separate booklets, each six to twelve pages long and amply illustrated by the author, are part of the National Park Service's education and conservation efforts. Each information-filled booklet explains its topic succinctly, and includes an island map and list of references. They are available at a nominal charge from the Dominica National Park Service, Botanic Gardens, Roseau, Dominica. The artist-conservationist author was assisted by Allen D. Putney of the University of Michigan.

400 National parks from the ground up: experience from Dominica, West Indies.
James W. Thorsell.   In: *National parks, conservation, and development. The role of protected areas in sustaining society.* Edited by Jeffrey A. McNeely, Kenton R. Miller. Washington, DC: Smithsonian Institution, 1984, p. 616-20. bibliog.

This paper describes the fourteen co-ordinated steps leading to the development of Dominica's Morne Trois Pitons National Park: developing local initiative; developing local public awareness; defining an area of priority interest; obtaining basic equipment; defining park boundaries; drafting protected area legislation; preparing interim management guidelines; undertaking a field demonstration project; establishing linkages with tourism and education; preparing the education and interpetative programmes; developing the management capacity; continuing the development of park facilities; establishing a research programme; and ensuring follow-up support. The paper suggests how the Dominica experience might be applied elsewhere. The author is from the College of African Management, Moshi, Tanzania. The volume presents proceedings of the World Congress on National Parks held in Bali, Indonesia, 11-12 October 1982.

401 Dominica's Morne Trois Pitons National Park.

J. W. Thorsell, George Wood. *Nature Canada*, vol. 5, no. 4 (Oct./Dec. 1976), p. 14-16, 33-34. 2 maps.

A brief, but informative, article on the formation of the park and the flora and fauna it preserves. Accompanying the article are six colour photographs of the park, including the best published picture of the Boiling Lake. The authors worked for the Canadian Nature Federation, one of the main agencies helping to make the national park a reality.

402 National park creation in a developing nation: a case study of Dominica. West Indies.

Bruce E. Weber. PhD thesis, Colorado State University, Fort Collins, Colorado, 1973. 269 leaves. bibliog. (Available from University Microfilms, Ann Arbor, Michigan, 1974. Order no. 74-17,553).

This study describes and analyses the resource potential, the proposal and the problems connected with the creation of a national park, formally proposed to the Dominica Government in 1970 after a decade of efforts by individuals and organizations. It discusses the major problems which needed to be overcome before the park could become a reality: issues of land use; finance; politics and legislation; and the lack of familiarity of the general populace with the national park idea.

403 After God the earth.

R. Michael Wright. Arlington, Virginia: Nature Conservancy News, spring 1975. 4p. map.

A brief description of Dominica's 'large expanse of undisturbed flora [that] is the last remaining in the Lesser Antilles', and the 950-acre tract donated to the Nature Conservancy by John D. Archbold of Virginia which became the core of the new national park.

404 Morne Trois Pitons National Park in Dominica: a case study in park establishment in the developing world.

R. Michael Wright. *Ecology Law Quarterly*, vol. 12, no. 4 (1985), p. 747-78. map. bibliog.

The author, Vice President and General Counsel of the World Wildlife Fund, and formerly Director of the International Program of the Nature Conservancy, describes in detail the creation of Morne Trois Pitons National Park. He explains the evolution of the park idea and passage of park legislation, the actions of the Dominica Government and private conservation organizations to transform the legal concept of the Park into a reality, and reasons for park creation in general and this Park in particular. 'The Article suggests that park creation in less developed countries most often takes place when the government is convinced that creating a national park is in its own best interests' (p. 748). A carefully documented article intended to serve as a model for park creation in other developing countries.

Education

405 A century of West Indian education.
Shirley C. Gordon. London: Longman, 1963. 312p.
A sourcebook of selections from key documents concerning education in the British West Indies from 1833-1933, especially taken from colonial reports. References to and items pertaining to Dominica and the Leeward Islands appear throughout the book.

406 The utmost for the highest: a study of adolescent aspirations in Dominica, West Indies.
Joyce Bennett Justus. PhD thesis, University of California, Los Angeles, 1971. 179 leaves. bibliog. (Available from University Microfilms, Ann Arbor, Michigan, 1971. Order no. 72-2837).
An analysis of questionnaire data collected from 245 primary- and secondary-school adolescents during the summers of 1968 and 1969. The analysis of the effects of expectations of significant others, such as parents and teachers, educational and occupational aspirations, and self-assessment and academic performance on educational aspirations, showed that parental influences were greater than any other. The author advances reasons for the finding that many expectations were unrealistically high. The Appendix includes the survey instrument.

407 The Commonwealth of Dominica. Education sector survey: an analysis of the education and training system and recommendations for its development.
W. L. Taylor, C. Carelli, T. Worku. Paris: UNESCO, April 1982. 124p. map. (UNESCO Doc. EFM/109).
This volume presents the findings of a sector study mission of UNESCO's Division of Educational Financing which visited Dominica between 18-22 May

1981. Its purpose is to 'identify areas of education and training which could be incorporated in the financing arrangements with external agencies, particularly the World Bank' (Foreword). In addition to numerous tables and statistics giving a profile of the educational system, the report contains a description and analysis of the general educational system, technical and vocational education, agricultural education and non-formal adult education, with recommendations for each.

408 An alternative to the current model of secondary education in the Commonwealth Caribbean: special reference to Dominica.
Bert J. Thomas. In: *Perspectives in West Indian education.* Edited by Norma A. Niles, Trevor Gardner. East Lancing, Michigan: West Indian Studies Association, Michigan State University, 1978, p. 176-86. bibliog.

The author describes the current limitations of the four secondary schools in Dominica and proposes an alternative model, derived from the José Marti School in Jamaica, in which the purposes of education would be to 'train people to develop fully the human potential and to train them to survive in their environment. This training will include a heavy emphasis on agriculture, industry, sports, political education and socialization, religion and ecology' (p. 180). He describes the organizational structure and 'the school in motion and action'. This was one of several papers presented at the Second Annual Conference of the West Indian Students Association of Michigan State University.

409 Planning the Waitikubuli Institute of Learning and Community Development.
Hilroy A. M. Q. Thomas. EdD thesis, Harvard University, Cambridge, Massachusetts, 1978. 240 leaves. bibliog.

The author, a member of Atkinson Village on the Carib Reserve, describes in this Harvard School of Education thesis-project his efforts to establish an institute that would provide opportunities for post-primary and non-formal education, a community-based learning experience and basic social services for the community. He reviews the background of education on the Reserve, the proposed model institute, and objectives and problems encountered during one year of implementation.

Literature

Major writers

410 The orchid house.
Phyllis Shand Allfrey.   London: Constable, 1953; New York:
E. P. Dutton, 1954. Reprinted, London: Virago, 1982. (Virago
Modern Classics); Washington, DC: Three Continents, 1985. 235p.

The only novel by the remarkable Dominica-born author. Phyllis Shand Allfrey
(1908-86) poet, writer and political activist edited with her husband Robert the
Dominica Herald (1961-65) and *The Star* (1965-82), both Roseau newspapers.
Mrs. Allfrey founded the Dominica Labour Party in 1955, and represented
Dominica as the only female minister in the West Indies Federation, 1958-62. She
published poetry and a children's book, but political interests and the rigours of
life on Dominica prevented the completion of her second novel *In the cabinet*,
which was in progress when she died in 1986. *The orchid house* is the story of the
return after a long absence of three young married sisters to their house,
L'Aromatique, on a small West Indian island. The story of the sisters, Stella,
Joan (who resembles Mrs. Allfrey) and Natalie, is told by Lally, the faithful
family nurse from Montserrat. The story takes place between the world wars and
traces the decline of the sisters' father and its impact on family members. The lush
setting, both beautiful and sinister, is unmistakably Dominica. *The orchid house*
was recently rescued from undeserved obscurity partially through the efforts of
Jean Rhys, a friend and correspondent of Mrs. Allfrey, whose own famous work,
Wide Sargasso Sea, was influenced by *The orchid house*.

411 Palm and oak II.
Phyllis Shand Allfrey.   Roseau: Star Printery, 1973. 21p.

Twenty-two poems, including 'Love for an island', some of which were published
in the author's three earlier collections of poetry: *In circles, poems* (Harrow
Weald, Middlesex: Raven Press, 1940); *Palm and oak* (London: privately printed,

142

1950); and *Contrasts* (Barbados: Advocate Press, 1955). 'While the young sleep' (p. 10) won second prize in an international poetry contest judged by V. Sackville-West in 1953. The theme of 'palm and oak' refers to Mrs. Allfrey's dual tropical and English heritage, and runs throughout much of her work.

412 Poesy: an anthology of Dominican verse. Book four.
Compiled by J[oseph] R[aphael] Ralph Casimir. Barbados: Advocate Company, 1948. 64p.

J. R. Ralph Casimir (1898- .), solicitor's clerk, bookseller, bookbinder, poet and elected member of the Roseau Town Council, encouraged the reading and writing of poetry by Dominicans, and produced the only anthologies of poetry by native Dominicans. Book four contains poems by Ianthe Lawton-Browne, Daniel Thaly, Roy H. S. Dublin, Daniel A. Nicholas, J. Albert Lawrence, Cynthia M. LeBlanc, Philip N. Griffin and Casimir. His other anthologies are *Poesy, book I* (Roseau: Joseph Press, 1943), *Poesy, book II* (Roseau: Chronicle Press, 1944), *Poesy, book III* (Roseau: Chronicle Press, 1946). Published collections of poetry by the author include: *Pater noster and other poems* (1967); *Africa arise and other poems* (1967); *A little kiss and other poems* (1968); *Farewell (and other poems)* (1971); *Dominica (and other poems)* (1968); and *The negro speaks* (1969) (all were published in Roseau by Chronicle Press).

413 Duet in discord.
Elizabeth Garner.   New York, London: Alfred A. Knopf, 1937. 230p. London: Arthur Barker, 1936. 279p.

A story of a brief, unhappy love affair told in the first person. The narrator, Carol, aged 43, survivor of two marriages and mother of a grown daughter and a younger son who spends his summers with her, lives on 'the most beautiful and the most primitive' island in the West Indies (p. 132), unmistakably Dominica. She falls in love with Tony Lancing, aged 26, a writer visiting the island, and for one month they have a tormented, on-again, off-again, relationship. Tony's impotence leads him to withdraw emotionally and to leave the island. Carol recounts their time together in the form of letters to Tony. Elizabeth Garner is the *nom de plume* of Elma Napier. The story takes place on the island's Windward side near Pointe Baptiste where she lived from 1932 to 1973 when she died. Several articles and short fictional pieces were published under this pseudonym as well as one other novel, *A flying fish whispered* (London: Arthur Barker, 1938).

414 No voyage for a little barque.
Elma Napier.   *BIM*, vol. 4, no. 14 (Jan. 1951), p. 85-87.

A brief fictional description of an encounter with a smuggler from Guadeloupe captures the flavour of the illegal trade between Dominica and the French islands, and the risk of sailing across open water at night. Mrs. Napier (1892-1973), who sometimes published under the pseudonym Elizabeth Garner, was from a distinguished Scottish family, travelled widely, and lived for years in Australia before settling in Dominica in 1932. She was the first woman elected to a West Indian legislature and is the grandmother of Dominican historian and writer, Lennox Honychurch. Sketches of her travels and two autobiographical volumes describing her life before settling in Dominica appeared as *Nothing so blue* (London: Jonathan Cape, 1928), *Youth is a blunder* (London: Jonathan Cape, 1948), and *Winter is in July* (London: Jonathan Cape, 1949).

415   Carnival in Martinique.
Elma Napier. *BIM*, vol. 4, no. 14 (Jan. 1951), p. 155-57.

This descriptive vignette of the mundane chores and hopeful longings of a servant woman in Fort-de-France at carnival time gives a feel for the colourful fête of the French islands as well as of Dominica.

416   Voyage in the dark.
Jean Rhys. London: Constable, 1934; New York: William Morrow, 1935. Reprinted, London: André Deutsch, 1967; New York: W. W. Norton, 1968. 159p.

The author's third novel, the story of Anna Morgan, a West Indian-born chorus girl of eighteen, searching for identity and companionship, and trying to survive in England. She frequently has flashbacks to her childhood and family on a lush, unnamed Caribbean island, contrasting it with her present cold, dark existence. This novel, as well as *After leaving Mr. Mackenzie* (London: Jonathan Cape, 1930), *Quartet* (New York: Simon & Schuster, 1929), *Good morning, midnight* (London: Constable, 1939) and *Wide Saragasso Sea* (London: André Deutsch, 1966) are published in *Jean Rhys, the complete novels* (New York: Norton, 1985) which includes photographs by Brassaï and an introduction by Diana Athill.

417   Wide Sargasso Sea.
Jean Rhys, introduction by Francis Wyndham. London: André Deutsch, 1966; New York: W. W. Norton, 1967; Harmondsworth, England: Penguin Books, 1968. 156p.

The author, who spent her childhood and adolescence in Dominica, published this remarkable novel when she was in her mid-seventies, twenty-seven years after her previous novel, *Good morning, midnight* (London: Constable, 1939). The story, set first in Jamaica and then on a lush Windward Island where French patois is spoken (Dominica is never named), creates the deeply alienated world of Creole heiress Antoinette Cosway in the 1830s. Cosway, driven mad and married to Edward Rochester, narrates the final part from her attic room in Thornfield Hall, England, which she sets on fire. This brilliant background to the characters of Charlotte Brontë's *Jane Eyre* won the 1967 W. H. Smith Annual Literary Award and the Royal Society of Literature Award. In a 1974 review in *The New York Times Book Review*, A. Alvarez called Rhys the 'best living English novelist' (17 March, p. 6).

418   Sleep it off, lady.
Jean Rhys. London: André Deutsch, 1976; New York: Harper & Row, 1976; Harmondsworth, England: Penguin Books, 1979; New York: Popular Library, 1976. 191p.

In this last collection during her lifetime, Jean Rhys published sixteen short stories, written in the 1970s, seven of which derive from her West Indian childhood. 'Pioneers, oh, pioneers', 'Goodbye Marcus, goodbye Rose', 'The Bishop's feast', 'Heat', 'Fishy waters' and 'The insect world' relate directly or indirectly to experiences Rhys had while growing up in Dominica or when she visited the island briefly in 1936. The haunting final story 'I used to live here once' is her return to the tropics as a ghost.

419 Tigers are better looking, with a selection from *The Left Bank*.
Jean Rhys. London: André Deutsch, 1968; New York: Harper & Row, 1974; Harmondsworth, England: Penguin, 1973. New York: Popular Library, 1976. 253p.

Eight short stories, three of them set in the West Indies, comprise *Tigers are better looking*. Among the nine stories included from *The Left Bank* (London: Jonathan Cape, 1927), Rhys's first book, are two set in Dominica: 'Mixing cocktails' and 'Again the Antilles'. *The Left Bank* was a collection of twenty-two stories, most of which she refused republication for this volume, introduced with a lengthy Preface by Ford Madox Ford, whose patronage facilitated her initial publications. Wrote Ford, 'Miss Rhys's work seems to me to be so very good, so vivid, so extraordinarily distinguished by the rendering of passion, and so true, that I wish to be connected with it' (Preface, p. 162).

420 Smile please: an unfinished autobiography.
Jean Rhys, foreword by Diana Athill. New York: Harper & Row, 1979. 151p. bibliog.

Jean Rhys, Dominica's most famous writer, was at work on her autobiography when she died in England on 14 May 1979 at the age of 89. Her editor at André Deutsch, Diana Athill, collected together the twenty-six brief pieces published here, described Rhys's perfectionist attitude toward style, and added thirteen photographs of Rhys and her environs. The first half of the volume, 'Smile please', containing vignettes and scenes from the author's childhood in Dominica (1890-1907), was finished before her death. The second part, 'It began to grow cold', was unfinished, and provides portraits of her life in England and Paris. A brief chronology of her life and bibliography of her books conclude the volume. Six of the photographs relate to Dominica.

421 Tales of the wide Caribbean.
Jean Rhys, selected and edited by Kenneth Ramchand. London, Kingston; Heinemann, [1986?]. 180p.

Twenty of Jean Rhys's short stories with West Indian settings or themes are drawn from her collections published between 1927 and 1979. These were selected, arranged and introduced by Kenneth Ramchand. Publication of this collection, emphasizing Rhys's Caribbean influences, is a significant acknowledgement of her acceptance as a West Indian writer.

422 L'île et le voyage: petite odyssée d'un poète lointain. (The island and the voyage. Minor odyssey of a distant poet.)
Daniel [Désiré Alain] Thaly. Paris: Le Divan, 1923. 237p.

Dr. Thaly's sixth volume of poetry, organized into twelve songs, relates the poet's romantic views as he journeys from an 'island rocky and wooded' through the

Lesser Antilles to the Mediterranean and eventually to Paris. Dominica is described lovingly in 'L'île bleue' (The blue island) (p. 234-35), as well as in the first song.

423 Héliotrope ou les amants inconnus. (Heliotrope, or the unknown lovers.)
Daniel [Désiré Alain] Thaly.   Paris: Le Divan, 1932. 98p.

Daniel Thaly, physician, ornithologist and Director of the Victoria Museum in Roseau, is the most neglected of Dominica's writers, because all of his work remains in French, and perhaps because of his personal modesty. Born in Dominica on 2 December 1879, he was educated at the Lycée St. Pierre in Martinique and studied medicine at Toulouse, France, until 1905 when he returned to the Antilles. For years he was an archivist at the Schoelcher Library in Fort-de-France, Martinique, before returning to Dominica where he died a bachelor on 1 October 1950. Between 1899 and 1932, he published ten volumes of poetry and contributed to Parisian magazines and, later, in English, to the *Canada-West Indies Magazine*. Ten poems, in French, appear in *Poesy: an anthology of Dominican verse. Book four*, edited by J. R. Ralph Casimir (q.v.). *Héliotrope* is a series of romantic poems written between two lovers reportedly found by Thaly after their ship sank. The poems are arranged in three sections: 'D'une plage des îles' (Of an island shore); 'L'île du bonheur' (The island of happiness); and 'Le regret d'Héliotrope' (Heliotrope's regret). Each is rich with images of the Antilles and in particular his native island.

424 The fatal gift.
Alec Waugh.   New York: Farrar, Straus & Giroux, 1973. 314p.

Waugh (1898-1981) visited Dominica several times and knew the island well. In *The fatal gift* he blends fact and fiction in an unusual novel. He himself narrates a story in the first person about Raymond Peronne, the second son of an affluent English peer, who meets and knows the people and places Waugh knew. In England, New York and Dominica between the wars, Peronne's complex life intertwines with Waugh's, his brother Evelyn's, and his cousin Claude Cockburn's; on Dominica the protagonist knows Elma Napier, John Archbold, and Stephen Haweis, island friends of Waugh. Ultimately, his love for a young girl, obeah, and the island's charm bind Peronne to Dominica. The title is from the Byronic phrase 'the fatal gift of beauty . . .'

425 Run masked.
Robb White.   New York, London: Knopf, 1938. 330p.

Robb White's novel set on the island of Caribia, a thinly-disguised Dominica, about tumultuous events during the three days of carnival when participants 'run masked'. The story revolves around erupting racial tensions and the struggles of American and British expatriates to succeed financially on Caribia. Reportedly, Elma Napier wrote *Duet in discord* (New York: Knopf, 1937) with White in mind and he responded with an unflattering portrayal of a character who resembled her in this novel.

Dies Dominica: a publication commemorating Dominica Day 1967.
See item no. 9.

Dies Dominica: a publication commemorating Dominica Day 1972.
See item no. 10.

Dies Dominica: a publication commemorating Dominica Day.
See item no. 31.

Hot countries.
See item no. 39.

O, call back yesterday.
See item no. 224.

The Star.
See item no. 470.

Literary history and criticism

426   West Indian literature: an index to criticism, 1930-1975.
Jeannette B. Allis.   Boston, Massachusetts: G. K. Hall, 1981.
353p. (A reference publication in Latin American Studies).
By indexing seventy-seven periodicals and newspapers from the Caribbean, North America, Europe and Africa, and five essay collections, the author provides a practical reference work for literature of the period. Indexes of authors, of critics and reviewers, of general articles by year and an appendix of books on West Indian literature enhance access to the materials. Forty-four references to reviews and articles on Dominican writers Phyllis Allfrey and Jean Rhys are included. The author is Documents Librarian at the Public Library in St. Thomas, United States Virgin Islands.

427   Jean Rhys's *Wide Sargasso Sea*: the other side/'both sides now'.
Paula Grace Anderson.   *Caribbean Quarterly*, vol. 28, no. 1-2
(March-June 1982), p. 57-65. bibliog.
A critical essay about the dualism permeating Rhys's acclaimed novel, *Wide Sargasso Sea*, which 'presents a vision of male/female roles which is intuitively perceptive, positively feminist, and essentially revolutionary' (p. 59). 'Both sides' refers to 'the male and the female, or alternatively the colonizer and the colonized' (p. 57). With detailed endnotes, the author connects the story to contemporary feminist and critical social analyses.

428   The social world of Phyllis Shand Allfrey's *The orchid house*.
Irving W. Andre.   *Caribbean Quarterly*, vol. 29, no. 2 (June
1983), p. 11-21. bibliog.

An astute analysis of Mrs. Allfrey's novel, grounded in the assumption that the
white family of *The orchid house* 'reflects the circumstances of a whole generation
of white settlers in Dominica' including 'financial adversity, physical/psychological
disease occasioned by adverse circumstances, and migration' (p. 11). The author's
discussion of symbolism, the role of the church and the use of the name 'Baptiste'
is based on a study of the novels and studies of the island and region by others.

429   Jean Rhys.
Carole Angier.   New York: Viking; Harmondsworth, England:
Penguin Books, 1985. 126p. bibliog. (Lives of Modern Women
Series).

An especially perceptive and poignant biographical study of the writer,
reconstructing her life from letters, interviews, and especially from the words of
female characters in her novels. The book traces Rhys's life chronologically in six
chapters from her arrival in England in August 1907 as Gwen Williams, aged 16,
through three marriages and nine books to her death in 1979, aged 88. A selection
of photographs of Jean Rhys and important people in her life is included.

430   A report from Dominica, W.I.
Elaine Campbell.   *World Literature Written in English*, vol. 17,
no. 1 (April 1978), p. 305-16. bibliog.

The author discusses the 'surprising similar flavors in spite of the great time
difference in the periods' (p. 309) of the West Indian novels of Jean Rhys and
Phyllis Shand Allfrey, the main focus of the article. Both are native-born
Dominicans and while the former's work has become well-known, Phyllis
Allfrey's work has been neglected. 'The current activity in Third World
Literature, particularly West Indian poetry and fiction, in conjunction with ongoing efforts on behalf of neglected women writers, pleads for recognition of
Phyllis Shand Allfrey as a poet and novelist' (p. 305). The author, then a member
of the faculty at Brandeis University, Waltham, Massachusetts, seeks to correct
this neglect with her literary analysis and includes information obtained in a 1977
interview with the late Mrs. Allfrey.

431   Fifty Caribbean writers: a bio-bibliographical critical sourcebook.
Daryl Cumber Dance, editor.   New York: Greenwood, 1986.
530p. bibliog.

An especially useful and up-to-date collection of description and critical
commentary. Among the fifty prominent writers discussed are two from
Dominica. Elaine Campbell, Assistant Professor of English at Regis College,
Weston, Massachusetts, was the author of 'Phyllis Shand Allfrey' (p. 9-18)
discussing the writer's biography, works, themes and critical reception. Jean
D'Conta provides an excellent survey of similar categories for 'Jean Rhys'
(p. 390-404).

432 Jean Rhys.

Cheryl M. L. Dash. In: *West Indian literature*. Edited by Bruce
King. Hampden, Connecticut: Archon Books, 1978, p. 196-209.
bibliog.

One of the better brief overviews of Rhys's work, with emphasis on *Wide
Sargasso Sea*. In this volume, the 'Introduction' by Bruce King (p. 108), and 'The
background' by Rhonda Cobham (p. 9-29), contribute a helpful context to the
individual articles.

433 Jean Rhys.

Arnold E. Davidson. New York: Frederick Ungar, 1985. 165p.
bibliog. (Literature and Life Series).

An excellent study of the Dominica-born writer. Chapters on the art and craft of
each of Rhys's novels are presented following an introduction 'From Dominica to
obscurity and fame' (p. 1-15) examining the relationship between biography and
literature. The concluding chapter 'The achievement of Jean Rhys' synthesizes
critical opinions and explains that, among other reasons, we read Rhys 'because
of the paradoxical hope promoted by her hopeless fiction' (p. 140). A chronology,
notes and bibliography make this a useful sourcebook for understanding Rhys's
life and art.

434 Neglected West Indian writers. No. 1: Phyllis Allfrey.

Barrie Davies. *World Literature Written in English*, vol. 11, no. 2
(Nov. 1972), p. 81-83.

Davies praises Allfrey's *The orchid house* (q.v.) as 'subtle and enduring, a
sustained and sensitive analysis of Dominican society' (p. 81). Following his
description and analysis of the novel, he writes, 'There is nothing hackneyed, no
comment, no moralising, no bitter flourish. Instead there is quiet pathos, for
people matched against an inscrutable and inexorable historical process' (p. 82-83).

435 A short account of the life and work of Phyllis Shand Allfrey, 1908-1986.

Ramabai Espinet. *Bulletin of Eastern Caribbean Affairs*, vol. 12,
no. 1 (March-April 1986), p. 33-35.

A biographical sketch based on interviews with the late Dominica novelist by a
PhD candidate in women's literature in the Department of English, University of
the West Indies, St. Augustine, Trinidad. Several personal observations make this
a valuable account. Mrs. Allfrey's second novel, *In the cabinet*, remained
unfinished at the time of her death.

436 Jean Rhys.

Louis James. London: Longman, 1978. 74p. bibliog. (Critical
Studies of Caribbean Writers).

A brief, but full-flavoured study of Jean Rhys and her works. Chapters include:
'The girl from the island'; 'The European'; 'The making of a writer'; 'The
Caribbean is a cold place'; '*Wide Sargasso Sea*'; and '*Wide Sargasso Sea* and the

Caribbean novel', as well as a select bibliography. The author, Reader in Victorian and modern literature at the University of Kent at Canterbury, dedicates the book to Phyllis Allfrey 'who has given so much to West Indian life and literature'.

437   Jean Rhys: woman in passage. A critical study of the novels of Jean Rhys.
Helen Nebeker.   Montreal: Eden Press Women's Publications, 1981. 223p. bibliog.

First book-length critical study of Rhys by a female scholar. The author, Professor of English at Arizona State University at Tempe, Arizona, analyses the themes and symbolism of Rhys's five novels and Brontë's *Jane Eyre*. Rhys's heroines are, with Jane Eyre, linked to archetypes of female consciousness in this interesting study.

438   The bottomless abyss: 'mad' women in some Caribbean novels.
Evelyn O'Callaghan.   *Bulletin of Eastern Caribbean Affairs*, vol. 11, no. 1 (March-April 1985), p. 45-58. bibliog.

Comparisons of Caribbean novels in which major female characters are 'mad'. Credible accounts of serious mental illness are found in Jean Rhys's *Wide Sargasso Sea*, Myriam Warner-Vieyra's *As the sorcerer said* (Longman, 1982) and Zee Edgell's *Beka lamb* (Heinemann, 1982). These fictional 'case histories' are compared with the experiences of Dr. Ermine Belle, psychiatrist at the Barbados Mental Hospital and found to be realistic portrayals of mental illness. The author is a Lecturer in the Department of English at the University of the West Indies, Cave Hill, Barbados.

439   Jean Rhys: a remembrance.
David Plante.   *Paris Review*, vol. 21, no. 76 (fall 1979), p. 238-84.

A very personal glimpse of the elderly Jean Rhys by an admiring younger writer who knew her well and worked with her on her unfinished autobiography. Includes details of her years in Europe and her marriages. The author is an American writer who has lived in London since 1968. His remembrance appears in more elaborate form in his fascinating and well-written study, *Difficult women: a memoir of three* (New York: Atheneum, 1983) which relates impressions of Jean Rhys (p. 7-61), Sonia Brownell Orwell, wife of George Orwell (p. 63-101), and feminist Germaine Greer (p. 103-50). 'The three' (p. 151-73) compares and contrasts the women in an alphabetical list of topics from 'abortion' to 'vocabulary'.

440   An introduction to the study of West Indian literature.
Kenneth Ramchand.   Kingston: Thomas Nelson, 1976. 183p. bibliog.

Eleven chapters, each on a major novel or novelist and each with a short list of critical readings, are based on a set of lectures delivered at the University of the West Indies, Mona Campus, Jamaica, where the author is Lecturer in English. The chapter '*Wide Sargasso Sea*' (p. 91-107) places the Rhys novel in its regional and literary contexts. A discussion of *Wide Sargasso Sea* revolves around the qualities making it a West Indian novel, and contrasts critical views by reviewers Wally Look Lai and Edward Brathwaite.

441 The West Indian novel and its background.
Kenneth Ramchand. Portsmouth, New Hampshire: Heinemann, 1983. 2nd ed. 320p. bibliog.
A version of the author's thesis presented at the University of Edinburgh. This is a scholarly study of prose fiction, mainly novels, written by people who were born or who grew up in the West Indies. In the chapter 'Terrified consciousness' (p. 223-36), originally published in *Journal of Commonwealth Literature*, no. 7 (July 1969), p. 8-19, the author offers an illuminating critical discussion of the works of four writers considered to be 'white West Indians': J. B. Emtage, *Brown Sugar* (1966); Geoffrey Draton, *Christoper* (1959); Phyllis Shand Allfrey, *The orchid house* (1953); and Jean Rhys, *Wide Sargasso Sea* (1966). Mrs. Allfrey was born and spent most of her life in Dominica; Jean Rhys lived in Dominica for her first sixteen years.

442 Jean Rhys: the art of fiction LXIV.
Jean Rhys, interviewed by Elizabeth Vreeland. *Paris Review*, vol. 21, no. 76 (fall 1979), p. 218-37.
A characteristically interesting and literate *Paris Review* article, introduced by the interviewer. Jean Rhys ranges over the influences on her life and her perspectives on literature. A photograph of Rhys and a manuscript page from *Smile please* are included. Jean Rhys, aged 84, died following an operation to insert a pin in her broken hip not long after the interview.

443 Jean Rhys is alive and well and living in Devon.
Colin Richards. *West Indies Chronicle*, vol. 84, no. 1457 (June 1969), p. 279-81.
An account of the rediscovery of Jean Rhys, with a brief biography and synopsis of her early novels.

444 The letters of Jean Rhys.
Selected and edited by Francis Wyndham, Diana Melly. New York: Viking, 1984. 315p. bibliog.
Originally published in London as *Jean Rhys letters 1931-1966* (André Deutsch, 1984), the collection provides valuable insights into the author's life and approach to literature. The volume is organized around letters to significant people and events in Rhys's life: 'Leslie (1931-1945)'; 'Max (1946-1950)'; 'Maryvonne (1951-1956)'; 'Selma (1956-1960)'; 'Cheriton Fitz Paine (1960-1963)'; and 'Wide Sargasso Sea (1964-1966)'. An 'Introduction by Francis Wyndham', 'Summary of main events in Jean Rhys's life before the letters start', 'A brief publishing history', 'General index' and 'Index of Correspondents' enhance the book's usefulness. References to Dominica appear throughout, and a letter from Rhys's only visit to the island as an adult, in 1936, is included.

Our island culture.
See item no. 18.

Caribbean writers: a bio-bibliographical-critical encyclopedia.
See item no. 476.

The complete Caribbeana 1900-1975: a bibliographic guide to the scholarly literature.
See item no. 482.

A resource guide to Dominica, 1493-1986.
See item no. 489.

The Arts

Visual arts

445 Agostino Brunias, Romano: Robert Adam's 'bred painter'.
Hans Huth. *Connoisseur*, vol. 151 (1962), p. 264-69. bibliog.
Brunias, also spelled Augustin Brunais, 1730-96, produced the only visual record
of social life in 18th-century Dominica in his oil-paintings. Here the author,
Curator of Decorative Arts at the Art Institute of Chicago, attempts to
reconstruct the artist's life based on the appearance of his works and minimal
biographical data. In *Our island culture* (Dominica Cultural Council, 1982),
Lennox Honychurch writes that Brunias lived mostly in Dominica from 1771 until
his death (p. 48).

Stephen Haweis of Dominica.
See item no. 2.

Mount Joy.
See item no. 17.

Our island culture.
See item no. 18.

A resource guide to Dominica, 1493-1986.
See item no. 489.

Folklore

446 Folk-lore of the Antilles, French and English.
Elsie Clews Parsons. New York: American Folk-Lore Society,
1933, 1936, 1943. 3 vols. bibliog. (Memoirs of the American Folk-
Lore Society, vol. 26, 3 pts.).
An exceptional compendium of island folklore. The author collected tales,
riddles, proverbs and verse during three trips to the Lesser Antilles and Haiti in
1924, 1925 and 1927. In Dominica, she spent two weeks anchored in Roseau
Roads before going to Portsmouth, which was 'richer in gossip of obeah. Some of
the obeah was described as Indian lore, dubiously I think, but I still regret that I
did not take the trail across the island to the Carib settlement' (pt. 1, Preface,
p. vi). During this brief period she recorded 118 tales, all but four in patois, from
twenty-three informants (pt. 1, p. 374-521). In Part three, edited by Gladys A.
Reichard due to Parsons's death, the tales are summarized in English, compared
by island source and theme and cross-referenced to an extensive bibliography
(p. 15-336). Also included are 121 riddles, only one of which is in English,
(p. 389-98) and eleven proverbs, one in English (p. 475).

Our island culture.
See item no. 18.

Island Carib folktales.
See item no. 138.

Carib folk-beliefs and customs from Dominica, B.W.I.
See item no. 165.

Notes on the star lore of the Caribbees.
See item no. 166.

Tales and legends of the Dominica Caribs.
See item no. 171.

The Dominica story: a history of the island.
See item no. 216.

A resource guide to Dominica, 1493-1986.
See item no. 489.

Costume

447 Step by step from livré to douillette.
Mabel A. 'Cissie' Caudeiron. In: *Dies Dominica. A publication commemorating Dominica Day 1972.* compiled by the Public Relations Division, Premier's Office. Roseau: Dominica Government, 1972, p. 25-27.

The late Mabel 'Cissie' Caudeiron, one of the island leaders in preserving folk traditions, describes the history and social meaning of the island's distinctive Creole dress from the 'uniform or livré of the estate' to the elaborate formal dress or douillette. This article is republished in *Our island culture* by Lennox Honychurch (Roseau: Dominica Cultural Council, 1982), p. 31-36, with illustrations of the styles and head ties mentioned by Mrs. Caudeiron.

Folk-songs and folk-music

448 Music and songs of Dominica.
Mabel A. 'Cissie' Caudeiron. In: *Dies Dominica. A publication commemorating Dominica Day 1972.* Compiled by the Public Relations Division, Premier's Office. Roseau: Dominica Government, 1972, p. 47-50.

The author describes island folk-songs and folk-music, and includes the French Creole lyrics of several songs, concluding with a plea for Dominicans to preserve their folk heritage. This article was reprinted in Lennox Honychurch's *Our island culture* (Roseau: Dominica Cultural Council, 1982), p. 26-31, and was accompanied by a description of folk-dances and illustrations of musical instruments (p. 36-38).

449 Chanté Domnitjen: folk songs of Dominica.
Alan Gamble, foreword by Alwin A. Bully. Roseau: Dominica Insititute, 1986. 64p. bibliog.

The author, a former Peace Corps worker in Dominica with an undergraduate degree in music, collected sixty-nine songs in French-based Creole, translated them into English, and provided their musical scores and descriptions of their contexts. The folk-songs are presented in seven groups: 'chanté-mas, or masquerade songs'; 'sa ki twavay, work songs'; 'hip hooray! children's songs and games'; 'mese kwik . . . kwak! songs in storytelling'; 'dansé, dansé, dansé, dance tunes'; 'ouvé pòt la, sewinals and parish fetes'; 'gade nou, recent songs of development'. The entire collection is introduced and indexed. It is available from the Dominica Institute, PO Box 89, Roseau, Dominica.

450 A survey of the folk music of Dominica.
Norris Stubbs, edited by Daniel Cauderion [sic].   Roseau:
Dominica Arts Council, n.d. 17p. bibliog.

The only paper on the subject, apart from M. A. Caudeiron's 'Music and songs of
Dominica' in *Dies Dominica* (q.v.). The author, a Bahamian, spent one week in
Dominica as part of his comparative study of folk-music of the Caribbean as a
Thomas J. Watson Fellow in 1972-73. Using recordings of folk-music provided by
Radio Dominica, materials at the Roseau Free Library and personal interviews,
his description divides local music into folk-songs, including the *chantemas* or
masquerade song, work songs, story-telling songs, songs associated with children's
games and lullabies, and dances, including the *bele* or *belaire*, and the quadrille. It
is available from the Dominica Arts Council in Roseau.

Our island culture.
See item no. 18.

Cookery

451 The art of Caribbean cooking.
Yolanda Cools-Lartigue.   Richmond, British Columbia: KoolArt
Publications, 1983. 235p.

An attractively organized and illustrated cookbook, full of Dominican specialities,
from calaloo soup and black pudding to lambie (conch) au gratin and crapaud
(frogs), as well as regional favourites. Well-indexed practical recipes cover
thirteen food groupings and include advice on seasoning, marinating and oven
roasting. The author is the daughter of Lady Eugene and Sir Louis Cools-
Lartigue, former Governor of Dominica (1967-78) and spent most of her early life
on the island, where she often catered for dinners and cocktail parties for visiting
dignitaries.

452 The complete book of Caribbean cooking.
Elisabeth Lambert Ortiz.   New York: Ballantine Books,
July 1986. 415p.

A comprehensive cookbook for the region with the island of origin noted for each
recipe. In addition to universal favourites such as fried ripe plantains, salt beef
and pork and planter's punch, the author lists hundreds of recipes for the major
categories of food and drink preparation. Recipes from Dominica include crapaud
(frogs), tannia soup, salt fish in chemise, cassava coo-coo, chicken calypso, hot
pepper sauce, baigner (fritters) and Hartley Auguste's rum punch. An introductory chapter 'Techniques of Caribbean cooking' (p. 1-14), a glossary (p. 380-92)
and an index (p. 397-415) make this an especially useful work. It was written in
1966-72.

453   The cooking of the Caribbean islands.
Linda Wolfe, editors of Time-Life Books, photographed by
Richard Meek.   New York: Time-Life Books, 1970. rev. ed. 1972.
208p. map. bibliog. (Foods of the World).

A colourful and lively account of foods and their settings throughout the region,
profusely illustrated with colour photographs by Richard Meek. In the chapter
'Legacy of the earliest islanders' (p. 33-47), the author describes her visit to
Dominica and the foods of the Carib Indians, and includes a sketch of a Carib
Indian house by John Frederick (p. 36). A glossary, an island eating-guide, a list
of mail order sources, and indexes complete the book. In addition to briefer
recipes in the main volume, a 143p. spiral booklet 'Recipes: the cooking of the
Caribbean Islands' gives full directions for the preparation of 143 Caribbean
foods.

Libraries and Archives

454 A guide to records in the Leeward Islands.
E[dward] C[ecil] Baker.   Oxford: Blackwell, for the University of
the West Indies, 1965. 102p. map.

A Rockefeller grant enabled the author to spend a year surveying the archives of
the Leeward Islands during 1962-63, and while surveying the Windwards in 1964
and 1965, he discovered more archival material listed here. Dominica was part of
the Leeward Islands from 1833 to 1939, when it was transferred to the Windward
Islands group. Among the Dominica records listed here are Methodist Church
records located in Antigua and St. Kitts, numerous Leeward Islands Federal
Records located in Antigua and microfilm records of fifteen damaged volumes of
minute books from the Legislative and Privy Councils and the House of
Assembly, now deposited in the library of the University of the West Indies,
Mona, Jamaica.

455 A guide to records in the Windward Islands.
E[dward] C[ecil] Baker.   Oxford: Blackwell, for the University of
the West Indies, 1968. 95p. map.

An invaluable source, compiled as a result of the author's survey of the Windward
Islands' records and archives in 1964-65, and published as a companion volume to
his *Guide to records in the Leeward Islands* (q.v.). The section on Dominica
(p. 64-89) remains the fullest account of records on the island. The introductory
'History of Windward Islands' archives' (p. vii-xii), recounts the efforts of earlier
researchers to improve the record keeping on the islands. He lists each volume
and bundle of records located in the Ministerial Building Archive Room, the
Registrar's Office, the Magistrate's Office, other official departments and offices,
the schools, hospital, library, and the records of the Anglican, Methodist and
Roman Catholic Churches, as well as briefly mentioning materials in the
possession of private companies and persons (p. 87) and Dominican newspapers
(p. 87-89).

456 Guide to British West Indian archive materials, in London and in the islands, for the history of the United States.
Herbert C. Bell, David W. Parker and others [sic]. Washington, DC: Carnegie Institution of Washington, 1926. 435p. (Publication no. 372).

The authors compiled an extensive listing of Colonial Office documents in London and of archival papers in the islands. For Dominica, the London documents consist of original correspondence of the Board of Trade (1770-78) and Secretary of State (1730-1815), Secretary of State entry books (1770-1807), acts (1768-85), sessional papers (1767-77) and shipping returns (1763-65). Many other materials on Dominica appear among the Grenada papers (p. 135-57) and general West Indian papers (p. 314-17). David W. Parker visited the islands' archives between September 1924 and January 1925. His listing of Dominica's records follows a critical account on the state of the official papers, some of which had been burned the previous year to make room for new ones (p. 348-55).

457 Origin and growth of the public libraries of Dominica.
Joseph A. Boromé. *Journal of Library History*, vol. 5, no. 3 (1972), p. 200-36. bibliog.

A detailed and meticulously documented account of the evolution of libraries from the Dominica Public Circulating Library in 1832 to the Free Public Library funded by Andrew Carnegie in 1905 to the contemporary library system introduced in 1967. The article is useful also for its descriptions of political factors and the growth of educational institutions in Dominica. The Dominica-born author was Professor of History at the City College of the City University of New York.

458 A guide to libraries and archives in Central America and the West Indies, Panama, Bermuda, and British Guiana, supplemented with information on private libraries, bookbinding, book selling and printing.
Arthur E. Gropp. New Orleans, Louisiana: Middle American Research Institute, Tulane University, Louisiana, 1941, 721p. map. bibliog. (Middle American Research Series. Publication 10).

An excellent description of Dominica's Free Public Library in Roseau, complete with a brief history and floor-plan, as well as the libraries of the Government Grammar School and the Supreme Court (p. 277-80). The author describes the contents of the archives according to a list made by the former Administrator in May, 1934, and other records observed in the Administrator's office, as well as the assorted records of the Registrar's Office (p. 299-304). This is the only published account of the archives prior to the listing of Government Records by E. C. Baker in *Caribbean Studies* (vol. 4, no. 1, supplement, April 1964). The author, librarian at the Middle American Research Institute at Tulane University, visited Dominica in 1938.

459 The development of library service in the West Indies through interlibrary cooperation.
Alma Theodora Jordan. Metuchen, New Jersey: Scarecrow Press, 1970, 433p. 6 maps. bibliog.

This book originally formed the author's 1960 PhD dissertation for the Columbia University School of Library Science, in which she surveyed the libraries in the region. Chapter VII, 'The Windward Islands', describes the organization and distribution of library services, library registration and literacy, usage, bookstock and circulation, staffing, resources, financing and special libraries in Dominica, Grenada, St. Lucia and St. Vincent.

460 Windward Islands records catalogue.
[E. C. Baker]. *Caribbean Studies*, vol. 4, no. 1 (April 1964), supplement, p. 1-13.

This detailed listing updates and amends a 1934 index of Dominica records including government documents, local government records and ecclesiastical records of the Anglican, Methodist and Roman Catholic churches. This is a preliminary accounting for E. C. Baker's *Guide to records in the Windward Islands* (q.v.).

Research guide to Central America and the Caribbean.
See item no. 483.

Sources for West Indian studies: a supplementary listing, with particular reference to manuscript sources.
See item no. 484.

A resource guide to Dominica, 1493-1986.
See item no. 489.

A guide for the study of British Caribbean history, 1763-1834, including the abolition and emancipation movements.
See item no. 491.

A guide to manuscript sources for the history of Latin America and the Caribbean in the British Isles.
See item no. 492.

Mass Media

461 Third World mass media and their search for modernity: the case of the Commonwealth Caribbean, 1717-1976.
John A. Lent. Lewisburg, Pennsylvania: Bucknell University Press; London: Associated University Presses, 1977. 405p. map. bibliog.

An impressively comprehensive volume for the Commonwealth Caribbean with extensive information on the media in the smaller islands. The author not only researched written materials, but interviewed publishers, editors and broadcasters, including Edward Scobie, Robert and Phyllis Allfrey, Stanley Boyd and Jeff Charles in Dominica. References to Dominican newspapers especially, and also to broadcasting appear throughout, and useful appendixes contain lists of known newspapers for most islands, a chronology of significant dates and 'The Allfrey story' (p. 350-53). Illustrations and a lengthy bibliography enhance the study. The author was Professor of Communications at Temple University, Philadelphia, in 1977.

462 The first printing in Dominica.
Douglas C. McMurtrie. London: Privately printed, 1932. 8p.

An account of the 167 years of newspaper printing from the first issues of the *Dominica Gazette*, established in July 1765 by William Smith, to the newspapers active in 1932. This brief account appeared originally in the *British and Colonial Printer and Stationer*, 19 May 1932, p. 460, and is the only published article devoted to this topic for Dominica.

Caribbean mass communications: a comprehensive bibliography.
See item no. 487.

General and Professional Periodicals

463 Bulletin of Eastern Caribbean Affairs.
Cave Hill, Barbados: Institute of Social and Economic Research
(Eastern Caribbean), (vol. 1, no. 1) March 1975- . monthly,
bimonthly.

An informative publication covering political and economic events in the eastern Caribbean in particular, but also notable social and cultural events. Issues contain longer articles often reported by staff researchers, as well as brief notes on the individual islands.

464 Caribbean Insight.
London: Publications Division of the West India Committee,
1978- . monthly.

A valuable source for timely, up-to-date information on current economic, political and social events in the Caribbean, with at least a brief synopsis provided for most island countries. Currently, *Caribbean Insight* incorporates the former *Caribbean and West Indies Chronicle*.

465 Caribbean Monthly Bulletin.
Río Piedras, Puerto Rico: Institute of Caribbean Studies,
University of Puerto Rico, (vol. 1, no. 1) Nov. 1963- . monthly,
bi-monthly, quarterly.

Although not a timely publication, the *Caribbean Monthly Bulletin* does provide extensive information on economic, political and social events in the region with feature reports and analyses on major issues, and brief notes on individual island nations in most issues.

466 Dominica Official Gazette.
Roseau: Government of Dominica, 5 April 1865- . weekly.
This chronicle of official activities and legislation provides the longest-running public account of governmental events available. It is valuable not only for contemporary information, but also for its record of historical events. A complete collection is available in the Roseau Public Library, and numerous older volumes are available at the Library of Congress, the New York Public Library and the British Library. Microfilmed volumes are available at the University of Florida, Gainesville, the University of the West Indies, Mona, Jamaica and the National Library of Jamaica.

467 Dominica Welfare Review.
Roseau: Social Welfare Division, Ministry of Home Affairs, (vol. I) 1964- . quarterly, irregular.
Once a quarterly publication, this review of news and articles pertaining to developments in the island's ten parishes succeeded the *Dominica Welfare News*, a monthly published from September 1947 to 1963 by the Social Welfare Department. The most recent volumes have featured the following reports: Volume VIII (1972-76), a history of the Social Development Division, 1945-1976, review of community development activities; Volume IX (1977-81), public assistance and the family; and Volume X (1982-84), juvenile delinquency, with data on juvenile cases in court in 1982.

468 Island Wide.
Roseau: Government Information Service, Prime Minister's Office, 1982- . bi-monthly.
A publication established by Prime Minister Eugenia Charles to inform citizens about events and developments in Dominica.

469 New Chronicle.
Roseau: Chronicle Printery, 1976- . weekly.
The *New Chronicle* continues the *Dominica Chronicle*, begun on 16 January 1909, as the longest-surviving Dominican newspaper. Owned by the Roman Catholic Church and unaffiliated politically, the *New Chronicle* provides reliable coverage of island events, thoughtful editorials, contributed articles and advertisements.

470 The Star.
Roseau: Robert and Phyllis Allfrey (vol. 1, no. 1) 31 July 1965-82. weekly, monthly.
During its years of publication by publisher Robert E. Allfrey and editor Phyllis Shand Allfrey, *The Star*'s (usually) six stencilled pages provided Dominicans with political commentary and brief current news items. As the voice of the Freedom Party, it often prodded the governments of E. O. LeBlanc and later Patrick John, as well as providing one of the few consistent outlets for news of cultural events and short creative literary efforts, notably a series by Cynthia Watt written in Creole, and occasional poetry by the distinguished editor. The paper ceased publication in early 1982, after appearing as a monthly since January 1980.

471   West India Committee Circular.
London: West India Committee, 1886-1958. bi-weekly.
A valuable source of reliable economic and often political and social information, the *West India Committee Circular* sought to inform planters, merchants and investors of the current state of islands in the British Caribbean. It provides a long-running source of information on trade and agricultural matters on Dominica. Its name and focus shifted as it sought to adapt to the changing region: *Chronicle of the West India Committee*, 1959-66; *West Indies Chronicle*, 1967-78; *Caribbean and West Indies Chronicle*, 1979- . It has now been superceded by *Caribbean Insight* (q.v.). Variable, often extensive, holdings of this serial exist in the University of the West Indies, the National Library of Jamaica, the Roseau Public Library, the British Library and the New York Public Library, as well as many other public libraries.

CSR CAREC Surveillance Report.
See item no. 331.

Encyclopaedias and Directories

472 Latin America & Caribbean Review 1986.
Anthony Ason, David Jamieson, publishers; Richard Green, managing editor. Essex, England: World of Information, 1985. 7th ed. 216p.

An up-to-date review of the larger region, especially oriented towards economic and business information. In the pages on Dominica (p. 173-74), political scientist Tony Thorndike succinctly surveys the July 1985 election, opposition politics, economics, military security, and presents a 'business guide' and 'key facts'.

473 C/CAA's 1986 Caribbean and Central American Databook.
Caribbean/Central American Action. Washington, DC: Caribbean/Central American Action, 1985. 416p. maps.

A useful data source for the thirty-four states of the Caribbean and Central America, and for information on regional organizations. For Dominica (p. 107-15), the compilation includes basic facts, plus lists of important government leaders, political parties, labour unions, shipping agents, newspapers, United States private organizations and business firms operating in Dominica, key economic indicators and an economic summary. A short Foreword is written by Dante B. Fascell, Chairman, House Committee on Foreign Affairs, United States House of Representatives and Trustee, Caribbean/Central American Action. C/CAA's address is 1333 New Hampshire Avenue NW, Suite 1010, Washington, DC 20036.

474 Caribbean Business Directory and Yellow Pages 1986/7.
Caribbean Publishing Company. Grand Cayman, Cayman Islands: Caribbean Publishing Company, [1986]. 804p. maps.

This directory, self-described as 'the region's most comprehensive business and destinations data base', combines a wealth of information on each island in its 222

165

white pages and 576 yellow pages. For each country or territory, including Dominica (p. 82-86), there is a section of useful descriptive information, supplied by the Caribbean Tourist Association, and an extensive listing of business phone numbers. In the yellow pages islands are listed separately under each topic. Copies of the directory are available from the official North American distributors: Caribbean Imprint Library Services, Box 350, 410 West Falmouth Highway, West Falmouth, Massachusetts 02574.

475 Countries of the World and Their Leaders Yearbook 1985.
Gale Research Company. Detroit, Michigan: Gale Research Company, 1984. 2 vols. maps.

An exceptionally useful resource, updated annually. The subtitle indicates its breadth: 'A compilation of US Department of State Reports on contemporary political and economic conditions, governmental personnel and policies, political parties, religions, history, education, press, radio and TV, climate, and other characteristics of selected countries of the world; together with travel alerts, passport and visa information, world health information for travelers, customs and duty tips for returning residents, and world climate highlights.' The section on Dominica includes the United States State Department 'Background notes', a list of leading government officers and other specific information, as well as two maps (Volume one, p. 24-25, 452-55).

476 Caribbean writers: a bio-bibliographical-critical encyclopedia.
[Edited by] Donald E. Herdeck, associate editors Maurice A. Lubin, John Figueroa, Dorothy Alexander Figueroa, José Alcántara Almánazar, general editor Margaret Laniak-Herdeck. Washington, DC: Three Continents Press, 1979. 943p. map. bibliog.

A remarkably comprehensive work with biographical information on some 2,000 writers of the region. Biographies, brief critical commentaries and bibliographies are included for twelve Dominican writers: Phyllis Allfrey, Alwin Bully, J. R. R. Casimir, Daniel Caudeiron, Royston Ellis, Stephen Haweis, Lennox Honychurch, Emmanuel Jean Baptiste, Elma Napier, Jean Rhys, Edward Scobie and Cynthia Watt. Dominica's Daniel Thaly, nearly all of whose poetry was published in French, is listed and discussed among the writers from the French West Indian islands (p. 512-13).

477 Encyclopedia of the Third World.
George Thomas Kurian. New York: Facts on File, 1982. rev. ed. 3 vols. maps. bibliog.

A practical compendium of data on developing nations. The information on Dominica is arranged in a broad range of standardized categories, including a 'Basic fact sheet', Cabinet list (1980), very brief chronology and a diagram of the government organization (Volume one, p. 488-95).

478 Personalities Caribbean: the international guide to who's who in the West Indies, Bahamas, Bermuda.

Founder editor-in-chief and managing director 1963-75 Owen Lancelot Levy, editor-in-chief and managing director 1975- . Anthony Lancelot Levy, senior contributing editor, Hedley Powell Jacobs. Kingston: Personalities, 1982-83. 7th ed. 1,027p.

Selected listings and biographical profiles of leaders in business and politics in the region. The guide began in 1963 and is revised every few years. Biographies of fifty-three Dominicans are included (p. 724-35).

479 The Caribbean – who, what, why.

Lloyd Sydney Smith. Amsterdam: Drukkerij Holland, 1965. 844p. 2nd ed. maps.

This volume, updated since the first edition in 1955, provides an especially useful set of information on the islands and their most important people. The section on Dominica (p. 722-46) contains numerous biographical sketches and business histories.

480 The Caribbean Handbook 1986.

Edited by Jeremy Taylor. St. John's, Antigua; London: FT Caribbean, 1986. 244p. maps. bibliog.

An excellent businessman's guide to the region, with sections on twenty-seven island territories, following and interspersed by brief articles covering banking, tourism, currency, rum and public holidays, to name only a few. The chapter on Dominica (p. 81-86) includes information on a variety of standard topics, plus telecommunications, press and television, diplomatic representation, banking, taxation, government, population and economy. This volume is the successor to sixty years of fact-filled publications beginning as *Yearbook of the West Indies and the Countries of the Caribbean*, 1926-27 to 1935, *The West Indies Year Book*, 1936 to 1948, *The West Indies and Caribbean Year Book*, 1953-54 to 1976/77, and *The Caribbean Yearbook*, 1977/78 to 1979/80 (Edited by Colin Rickards. Toronto: Caribook, 1980). For Dominica, a map and three photographs are included.

Bibliographies

481 Latin America and the Caribbean, a bibliographical guide to works in English.
S. A. Bayitch. Coral Gables, Florida: University of Miami; Dobbs Ferry, New York: Oceana Publications, 1967. 943p. (Interamerican Legal Studies, vol. 10).

Although the Caribbean (p. 803-926) forms only a small part of this total volume, there are useful lists for each island and island group. The author lists forty-seven references to Dominica, arranged by subject (p. 883-84), and more are found in the general British West Indies and Windward Islands sections. The author was Professor of Law at the University of Miami Law School, Florida.

482 The complete Caribbeana 1900-1975: a bibliographic guide to the scholarly literature.
Lambros Comitas. Millwood, New York: KTO Press, a US division of Kraus-Thomson Organization, 1977. 4 vols. maps.

With over 17,000 references to publications arranged in topical chapters, coded for geography, cross-referenced and indexed by author and geographic unit, this is easily the most comprehensive and usable bibliography for the post-1900 non-Hispanic and non-Haitian Caribbean. This is the first source any student of the region should consult. In the Index, vol. 4, there are 150 references to Dominica, 70 to the Windward Islands, and 69 to Douglas Taylor. In all there are approximately 400 references to the island, about twice the number found in the author's earlier *Caribbeana 1900-1965. A topical bibliography* (University of Washington, 1968).

483 Research guide to Central America and the Caribbean.
Kenneth J. Grieb, editor-in-chief; Ralph Lee Woodward, Jr.,
Graeme S. Mount, Thomas Mathews, associate editors.
Madison, Wisconsin; London: University of Wisconsin, 1985. 431p.

Appropriate experts wrote eighty-three topical essays on individual countries, and descriptions of archives and major resource depositories in the region, North America and Europe for this outstanding volume. Resources directly pertinent to Dominica are covered in essays by Joan E. Mount, 'The rest of the eastern Caribbean' (p. 375-81) and Wallace Brown 'Research on the Loyalist exodus primarily to the Bahamas, Jamaica, and Dominica' (p. 346-54). The brief description of document locations on Dominica is one of the most recently published accounts.

484 Sources for West Indian studies: a supplementary listing, with particular reference to manuscript sources.
K[enneth] E. Ingram. Zug, Switzerland: Inter Documentation
Company AG, 1983. 412p.

In 1,169 annotated entries the author describes source materials located in 135 British and Irish, two other European, seven West Indian and three Australian repositories. Intended as a supplement to the author's earlier *Sources of Jamaican history 1655-1838* (Zug, Switzerland, 1975), the work's detailed index provides access to material on most West Indian islands including fifty-five sources of Dominican historical material.

485 The catalogue of the West India Reference Library.
Institute of Jamaica, Kingston, West India Reference
Library. Millwood, New York: Kraus International Publications,
1980. 6 vols.

These six volumes consist of the photographic reproduction of the West India Reference Library's (now the National Library of Jamaica) card catalogue, with little introduction or explanatory material. Three volumes comprise the Catalogue of authors and titles, and three volumes the Catalogue of subjects. The National Library of Jamaica contains 'the world's outstanding collection of printed and manuscript materials relating to the history and culture of the West Indies'. (Introduction, p. [7]]. Under 'Caribs' and 'Dominica', a researcher will discover pages of important references (Catalogue of subjects, vol. 1, p. 2712-15, 2911-15).

486 The English-speaking Caribbean: a bibliography of bibliographies.
Alma Jordan, Barbara Comissiong. Boston, Massachusetts:
G. K. Hall, 1984. 411p. (A Reference Publication in Latin
American Studies).

An annotated listing of 1,406 references, including published and unpublished studies and journal articles, as well as bibliographies up to 1981, organized by island or island group and by numerous topics. The authors searched forty libraries in the region, the United States and Great Britain, and provide one location for each reference. Although only six references are specifically to

Dominica, numerous other listed sources contain useful information about the island. Alma Jordan is University Librarian and Barbara Comissiong is Deputy Librarian at the University of the West Indies, St. Augustine, Trinidad.

487 Caribbean mass communications: a comprehensive bibliography.
John A. Lent. Waltham, Massachusetts: Cross Roads Press, African Studies Association, 1981. 152p. (Archival and Bibliographic Series).

This listing of 2,653 items, organized by region and country, and author indexed, includes sources from the 18th century up to May 1980. For 'Dominica' and 'Windward Islands' (p. 65-66) there are fifteen references, including several brief references in regional newspapers.

488 Amerindians of the Lesser Antilles: a bibliography.
Compiled by Robert A. Myers. New Haven, Connecticut: Human Relations Area Files, 1981. 158 leaves. map.

An unannotated compilation of approximately 1,300 references by more than 480 authors, grouped according to 'Archaeology and prehistory'; 'Archives, history, travel and description, and social science research'; 'Languages'; 'Biology, nutrition and medicine'; and 'Literature'. The volume cites all papers from the first eight *Proceedings of the International Congresses for the Study of Pre-Columbian Cultures of the Lesser Antilles*. Geographical and name indexes provide access to the citations. More references are to Dominica than to any other island by far, and to Douglas Taylor than to any other author by far. A brief Preface (p. iii-vii) introduces the subject.

489 A resource guide to Dominica, 1493-1986.
Compiled by Robert A. Myers. New Haven, Connecticut: Human Relations Area Files, 1987. 649 leaves. 3 maps.

An attempt at a comprehensive compilation of all resources available for the study of the island and its people, listing approximately 5,700 items by more than 1,800 authors. Contents include: 'An outline history of Dominica'; 'Officers administering the Government of Dominica, 1763-1987'; 'Sources consulted'; 'Relevant works on the Caribbean'; twenty-five sections organized by topic; three sections of documents located in British, other European, United States, and West Indian archives and libraries, and one section listing chronological events pertaining to Dominica as they appeared in seven major international and Caribbean periodicals. All items are indexed in detailed name and subject indexes (p. 580-649). Authored and unauthored, scholarly and popular, as well as published and unpublished items are included, with a location identified for most. In addition to printed sources, the compilation includes films, recordings, paintings, photographs and aerial and satellite photography. A Preface discusses the complexities of bibliographic work for Dominica, surveys the most important publications, and gives an overview of the island and its natural history and peoples.

490 Dominica.
Compiled by N. W. Posnett, P. M. Reilly. Surbiton, Surrey, England: Land Resources Division, Ministry of Overseas Development, 1978. 71p. (Land Resource Bibliography, no. 12). The first published bibliography devoted exclusively to Dominica, this is an unannotated listing of 556 primarily United Kingdom sources organized into the following standardized sections: agriculture (45 sources); animal science (52); botany (36); climatology (2); crops (63); cultural studies (65); economics (69); forestry (34); geoscience (51); land tenure and reform (5); maps (15); miscellaneous (33); natural resources (21); population (35); soil science (22); and water resources (8). The compilation is particularly valuable for listing numerous studies and reports not easily found elsewhere, including 'formally and informally published documents and also unpublished documents which are not necessarily accessible to the public' (Foreword, p. v). The full address where this can be obtained is Land Resources Division, Ministry of Overseas Development, Tolworth Tower, Surbiton, Surrey, England KT6 7DY.

491 A guide for the study of British Caribbean history, 1763-1834, including the abolition and emancipation movements.
Compiled by Lowell Joseph Ragatz. Washington, DC: Government Printing Office, 1932. Reprinted, New York: Da Capo Press, 1970. 725p.
Scholarly annotations on material located in sixty-nine public and private repositories in the United States, Canada, Great Britain, Jamaica, France, Belgium and Switzerland make this the foremost compilation for the period covered. Sources on Dominica are concentrated in the sections on documents (p. 45-50) and historical writings (p. 184-86), but appear throughout the volume. A detailed index provides ready access to the documents, but information on document length and the particular location of each item is missing. This valuable work was prepared as a by-product of the author's study *Fall of the planter class in the British Caribbean, 1763-1833* (New York: Century Company, 1928. Reprinted, New York: Octagon, 1971), which provides a broad historical context useful also for the study of Dominica.

492 A guide to manuscript sources for the history of Latin America and the Caribbean in the British Isles.
Peter Walne, foreword by R. A. Humphreys. London: Oxford University Press, in collaboration with the Institute of Latin American Studies, University of London, 1973. 580p.
'This *Guide* represents the first comprehensive survey of the wealth of archival and manuscript materials relating to Lesser Antilles and the Caribbean preserved in public and private hands in the British Isles' (Intro. p. xix). Entries are arranged in alphabetical order by English counties, followed by Scotland, Wales, Northern Ireland and the Republic of Ireland. Invaluable collections of papers pertinent to Dominican history are found throughout the *Guide*.

Bibliographies

493   A bibliography of the Caribbean.
[Prepared by Audine Wilkinson].   Cave Hill, Barbados: Institute
of Social and Economic Research (Eastern Caribbean), University
of the West Indies, Sept. 1974. 167p. (Occasional Bibliography
Series, no. 1).
This provides a listing of books, articles, documents, papers and pamphlets
available in the Library of the Institute of Social and Economic Research (Eastern
Caribbean) in Barbados. The section for Dominica (p. 74-76), though brief,
contains a useful list of forty-one items, mainly articles and documents.

Fifty Caribbean writers: a bio-bibliographical critical sourcebook.
See item no. 431.

Index

The index is a single alphabetical sequence of authors (personal and corporate), titles of publications and subjects. Index entries refer both to the main items and to other works mentioned in the notes to each item. Title entries are in italics. Numeration refers to the items as numbered.

179

186

Map of Dominica

This map shows the more important towns and other features.

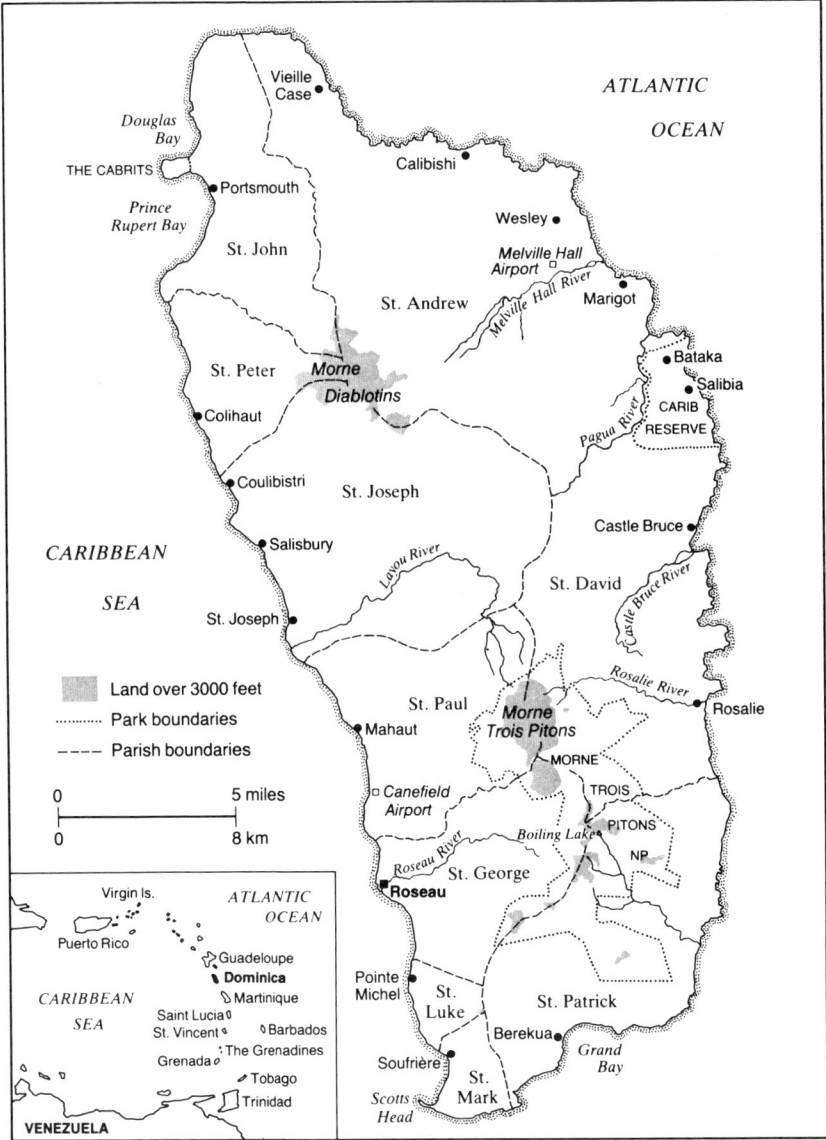

ATLANTIC OCEAN

Vieille Case •

Douglas Bay

THE CABRITS

• Portsmouth

Prince Rupert Bay

St. John

Calibishi •

Wesley •

Melville Hall Airport □

St. Andrew

Melville Hall River

Marigot •

St. Peter

Morne Diablotins

• Bataka
• Salibia

CARIB RESERVE

• Colihaut

• Coulibistri

St. Joseph

Pagua River

Castle Bruce •

CARIBBEAN

SEA

• Salisbury

Lavou River

St. David

Castle Bruce River

St. Joseph •

Land over 3000 feet
.... Park boundaries
- - - - Parish boundaries

St. Paul

Morne Trois Pitons

Rosalie River

Rosalie •

0   5 miles
0   8 km

• Mahaut

MORNE

□ *Canefield Airport*

TROIS

PITONS

Boiling Lake

NP

Roseau River

St. George

■ **Roseau**

Virgin Is.

ATLANTIC OCEAN

Puerto Rico

☆ Guadeloupe

Dominica

CARIBBEAN

Martinique

SEA

Saint Lucia ◊
St. Vincent ◊

◊ Barbados

Grenada ◊

The Grenadines

✐ Tobago

□ Trinidad

VENEZUELA

Pointe Michel •

St. Luke

St. Patrick

Berekua •

Grand Bay

Soufrière •

St. Mark

Scotts Head